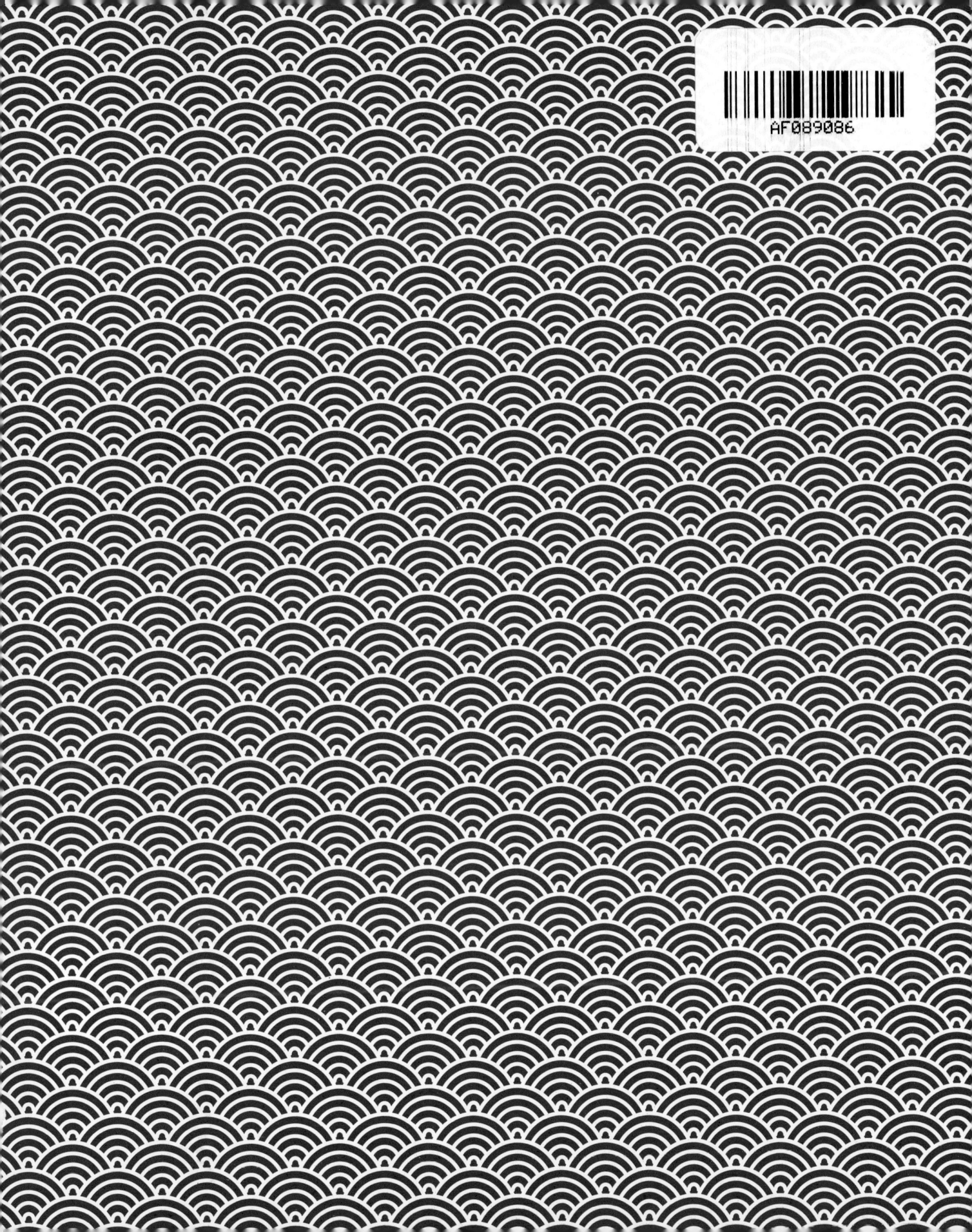

ULTIMATE
JAPAN

ULTIMATE
JAPAN

100 *must-do experiences for the trip of a lifetime*

CONTENTS

Welcome to Japan 6

Iconic Japan 20

Timeless Japan 52

Culinary Japan 84

CONTENTS

Outdoor Japan 112

Futuristic Japan 138

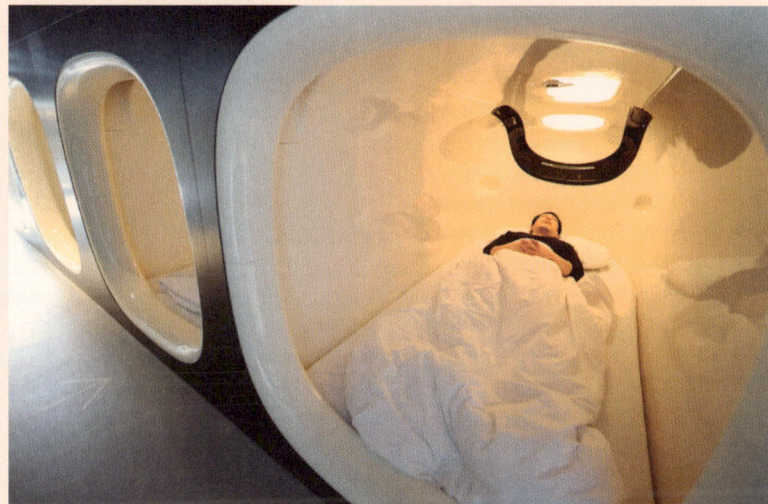

Journeys in Japan 166

Popular Japan 194

Seasonal Japan 222

Index 250

Acknowledgments 254

WELCOME

TO JAPAN

You'll never forget the first time you set foot in Japan, a land where ancient traditions and futuristic innovations thrive equally. Ready to make that trip of a lifetime a reality? Let's get started.

WELCOME TO JAPAN

Neon-lit Tokyo at night

Introducing Japan

Visiting Japan is to fulfill a lifelong dream, and for that, every moment deserves to be truly special. In *Ultimate Japan*, we've curated 100 experiences to ensure your Japanese adventure not only lives up to but surpasses expectation. Here you'll find those iconic experiences – gazing at Mount Fuji or enjoying a bowl of ramen – alongside overlooked adventures in every prefecture that reveal a new side to Japan. Each themed chapter also includes an itinerary, so if you want to hone in on Japan's pop culture, say, or explore its foodie hotspots, there'll be the perfect trip for you.

After all, Japan has captured the world's imagination. Its sprawling cities and centuries-old traditions place it at the top of our travel bucket lists – and for the many millions of visitors arriving on its shores each year, there are countless more yearning for that trip of a lifetime. We dream of tea ceremonies and kimono, sumo and sushi. And though we think we know Japan from stories, films and postcards, it remains as elusive as it is legendary – an enigma that only deepens its appeal.

But what draws so many of us to this incredible country? The archipelago is huge, for a start, with a tapestry of landscapes stretching across four main islands and thousands of smaller ones. Then there are the cities like Tokyo and Osaka – bastions of culture, with neon-lit skyscrapers and thriving fandoms that create an unrivalled urban energy. Across the country, Japan shows that celebrating tradition doesn't mean neglecting the future, as bullet trains speed past feudal fortresses and service robots take hospitality into the modern age. And just as you think you've seen it all, the seasons change and the country invents itself anew. Writing up that bucket list? You might need a bigger notepad.

ON THE MAP
WELCOME TO JAPAN

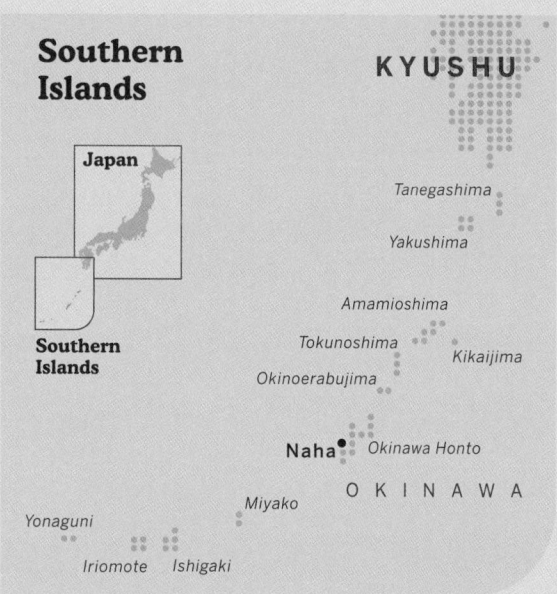

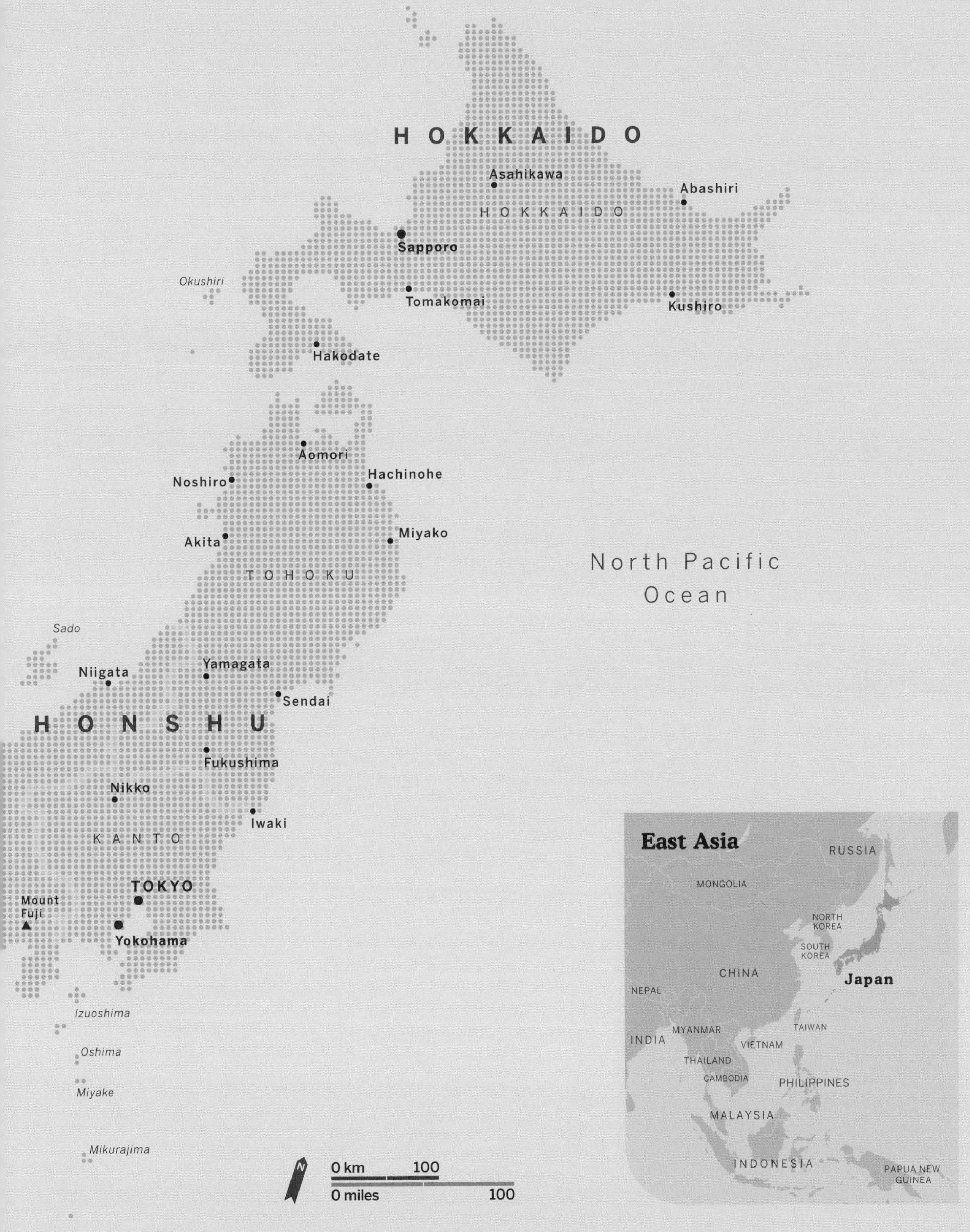

HOKKAIDO

- Asahikawa
- Abashiri
- HOKKAIDO
- Sapporo
- Okushiri
- Tomakomai
- Kushiro
- Hakodate

HONSHU

- Aomori
- Noshiro
- Hachinohe
- Akita
- Miyako
- TOHOKU
- Sado
- Niigata
- Yamagata
- Sendai
- Fukushima
- Nikko
- Iwaki
- KANTO
- TOKYO
- Mount Fuji ▲
- Yokohama
- Izuoshima
- Oshima
- Miyake
- Mikurajima

North Pacific Ocean

0 km 100
0 miles 100

East Asia

RUSSIA, MONGOLIA, NORTH KOREA, SOUTH KOREA, CHINA, NEPAL, **Japan**, INDIA, MYANMAR, TAIWAN, VIETNAM, THAILAND, CAMBODIA, PHILIPPINES, MALAYSIA, INDONESIA, PAPUA NEW GUINEA

Getting to know Japan

Japan may look small on the map, tucked up beside mainland Asia's eastern coast in the wide Pacific Ocean, but it actually stretches for over 1,900 km (3,000 miles) from north to south. That length means it enjoys a range of climates – the cherry blossoms bloom in the subtropical south even when the deep north remains covered in snow.

Japan's four main islands are Honshu (the largest), Hokkaido (to Honshu's north), Kyushu (off Honshu's southwestern tip) and Shikoku (south of Honshu). Curving away from the southern tip of Kyushu is a string of smaller islands, culminating in the archipelago of Okinawa. It's useful to think of Japan in terms of the regions outlined below.

KANTO

Most people's first stop in Japan is its capital – the sprawling, incomparable metropolis of Tokyo. Every image you have of hypermodern Japan is found here: white-gloved attendants squeezing commuters into trains; robot baristas pouring coffees; video billboards of idols and anime characters. Tokyo might seem to stretch on indefinitely, but the region of Kanto is home to plenty more beyond the capital, with a perfect synthesis of natural beauty and religious architecture. A selection of temples and shrines spread throughout Kamakura and Nikko; Hakone is home to luxurious hot springs with epic Mount Fuji views; and then there's international Yokohama, Japan's second-largest city.

TOHOKU

Taking up Honshu's northern third, Tohoku is defined by its dramatic landscapes. In its "Snow Country", cold Siberian winds meet a jagged line of mountains, producing impeccable powder snow that draws winter sports fans from around the world. In warmer months, you can enjoy some of Japan's best summer festivals, and savour the fresh sea breeze as you walk sections of the 1,025-km (637-mile) Michinoku Coastal Trail along the spectacular coastline. In every season, the region captivates with its living folk traditions and tales, wild national parks and welcoming, unpretentious cities.

HOKKAIDO

Head north for Japan's second-largest island: Hokkaido, home to the Indigenous Ainu people and their rich culture, and with a charming and laid-back capital in Sapporo. Outdoor enthusiasts will gravitate towards Hokkaido's six jaw-droppingly impressive national parks; Daisetsuzan and Shiretoko live up to their names, "Great Snow Mountain" and "Edge of the Earth" in Japanese and Ainu respectively. With the *shinkansen* only nudging into Hakodate (a friendly port city) in the very south, you'll need to settle into slower train travel to explore this beautiful prefecture.

REGIONAL TOURIST BOARDS

Here's a list of some of the key tourism organizations across the country.

Greater Tokyo
Covering Tokyo and surrounding prefectures (greatertokyo.jp).

Tokyo Convention & Visitors Bureau
Tourists guides and advice for the city (gotokyo.org).

Tohoku Tourism Promotion Organization
Information on what to see and do in Tohoku (tohokukanko.jp).

Hokkaido Tourism Organization
Sample itineraries and area guides (visit-hokkaido.jp).

Central Japan Tourism Association (Central Honshu)
Tips on visiting central Japan (shoryudo.

Kyoto City Tourism Association
Travel tips for travelling around the city of Kyoto (kyoto.travel).

Kyushu Tourism Organization
Planning tools for Kyushu (visit-kyushu.com).

CHUBU

Chubu spans the centre of Honshu, its rugged topography defined by spectacular mountains. All 20 of Japan's peaks over 3,000 m (9,800 ft) are here; naturally, the Japan Alps are the heart of Japan's alpine culture, attracting both hikers and skiers. Scattered through the plains nearby are charming villages such as Shirakawa-go and Gokayama, with their steeply thatched *gassho-zukuri* houses. Must-see cities include Matsumoto, with its large castle, elegant Kanazawa, and modern Nagoya.

KANSAI

Though it has some lively cities in Osaka and Kobe, Honshu's Kansai region is really known as a place of living history. It's here that you'll find temple-filled Nara, Japan's 7th-century capital, and Kyoto, famous for its shrines, temples and geisha, the cultural legacy of over 1,000 years as the Imperial capital. Other sites in the area include Ise-jingu, with its links to the Imperial family, and the UNESCO-registered Kumano Kodo network of pilgrimage trails.

CHUGOKU

Western Honshu's Chugoku is like a microcosm of Japan – think lakes and mountains, historic towns, modern cities and world-class hospitality – but all blissfully free of crowds. Its most famous destinations, Hiroshima and Itsukushima, are well worth visiting to learn important history and see Japan's most iconic torii (shrine gate). Head a little more off the beaten path and you explore art installations on the Seto Inland Sea islands and cycle the Shimanami Kaido.

SHIKOKU

Shikoku is a place to slow down and take a breath. The 88-temple Shikoku Henro pilgrimage route rings its coast, linking laid-back villages, forested mountains, and friendly coastal cities like Takamatsu and Matsuyama. The island's hot-spring towns include one of Japan's most famous – Dogo Onsen, the Imperial family's preferred resort. Further inland, Yusuhara showcases how to integrate modern architecture into traditional settings, and the mysterious Iya Valley focuses on maintaining its unique ways of life, developed over centuries of near isolation due to the forbidding peaks and vertigo-inducing gorges surrounding it.

KYUSHU

The land feels alive in Kyushu, where two of Japan's most active volcanoes (Mount Aso and Sakurajima) are found, along with steaming, sulphurous *onsen* resorts. With landscapes this powerful, it's no wonder Kyushu is brimming with myths and stories. You can explore local folklore at sacred spots like Takachiho, continue your spiritual explorations at the "Hidden Christian" sites of the Goto Islands and marvel at millennia-old trees in the Yakushima rainforests. Kyushu's strategic location between Japan's main islands and the rest of Asia means the region has a long history of trade. Explore its links with Okinawa in Kagoshima or take to foodie Fukuoka, which maintains an international, maritime atmosphere.

OKINAWA

Japan's most southerly prefecture is a dazzling string of subtropical islands, home to fascinating historical sights (many near its capital city, Naha). The archipelago is also famed for its record-breaking number of centenarians, and the longevity of the locals may have something to do with the plethora of active pursuits found here: go hiking in rainforests, kayaking through mangroves or scuba diving over coral reefs.

Planning the ultimate trip

Whether it's chancing upon an interesting shop or asking around for local recommendations, some of the best travel experiences in Japan happen when you're a bit spontaneous. But there's no denying that a certain level of planning makes things run more smoothly, and helps ensure you don't miss out on what you really want to do.

In a country as jam-packed with exciting experiences as Japan, you won't be able to do everything in one trip. But it's possible to fit a lot into the time you do have, whether it's a week or a month. Consider which experiences make your "must-do" list (the 100 entries and eight itineraries in this book should spark some ideas) and you're on your way to creating a trip that perfectly matches your own particular interests. Ready to make your trip a reality? It's time to get planning.

BUDGET

First things first, consider your budget. Flights aside, Japan is a less expensive destination than most people think – especially if you travel outside of peak times – so you can do a lot with a little.

If you're on a shoestring budget expect to pay around 10,000 yen (the equivalent of £50, $65 or €60) a day. On this budget, limit yourself to two or three main regions and plan to take highway buses between them; while Japan's bullet train network (p16) is efficient and reliable for long-distance travel, it's not cheap. Budget accommodation is plentiful; as well as hostels, look up capsule hotels, *minshuku* (guest-houses) and even love hotels (designed primarily for couples in need of some privacy). When it comes to food, don't overlook convenience stores and supermarkets, which usually have high-quality boxed meals at shockingly good prices. Otherwise, dine at cheap-and-cheerful chain restaurants like Marugame Seimen, Kura Sushi and Nakau; food stalls; and *tachinomiya* (standing bars that serve some food).

If you've got a little more money to play with, you'll likely spend around 20,000 yen per day (£100, $130 or €120). For this budget, a rail pass (p17) is a good investment; they pay off if you're taking more than a couple of bullet train journeys. For accommodation, consider business hotels (reliable chains include Dormy Inn and Toyoko Inn), glamping, temple stays and *ryokan* (traditional inns, p74). You'll also be able to add activities like skiing and even some geisha experiences to your trip with a mid-range budget.

With an expansive budget, expect to splurge at least 40,000 yen (£205, $260 or €245) a day. To make your trip a luxury experience, look into a "Green Car" railcard to ride in the first-class car – comfier and less crowded – of any JR train (providing they have a Green Car on that service). For more ways to travel in style, look into multi-day luxury train journeys like the Seven Stars, Shikishima and Twilight Express

TOUR OPERATORS

It's easy to plan your trip to Japan independently, but if you'd prefer to work with a tour operator, look for those local to the region you're exploring and who take sustainability into account. Here are a few suggestions.

Anytime, Ainutime!
Tours led by Indigenous Ainu guides around the Lake Akan area in Hokkaido (anytimeainutime.jp).

InsideJapan Tours
B Corp-certified company with guided, self-guided and bespoke itineraries (insidejapantours.com).

Oku Japan
Guided, self-guided and custom-made trips across Japan focusing on deep cultural experiences and responsible, community-led tourism (okujapan.com).

Walk Japan
Guided, self-guided and custom walking tours throughout Japan (walkjapan.com).

wondertrunk & co.
End-to-end luxury, bespoke trips utilizing insider knowledge and great local connections (wondertrunk.co).

Mizukaze services. Private transfers, guides and translators will open up less accessible and developed corners of the country, too, and you'll be able to try some of Japan's many Michelin-starred spots and venerable *kaiseki* restaurants (p105) and enjoy private dinners with geisha. Accommodation-wise, pick from interesting, independent boutique hotels and centuries-old luxury *ryokan*.

MONEY

For a country so attuned to the future, it's perhaps surprising that cashless isn't the norm. While contactless is accelerating in cities like Tokyo, it's wise to carry around some cash at all times. It can be tricky to find an ATM that accepts foreign cards (those that do are usually found in 7-Eleven convenience stores and post offices), so withdraw enough cash to get by for a while. As usual, check if your bank will charge you for using your card abroad.

TOUR OPERATORS

Budget aside, another key thing to consider is *how* you'd like to travel. Are you a keen independent traveller who wants to research and book everything yourself? Or would you prefer to leave that to a professional? Would you like to travel alone (or with friends and family), or does joining a tour group appeal? Or maybe you want a mix of all possibilities – easy enough to implement, since so many tour operators (see opposite page) specialize in specific regions or activities. For instance, you could plan a week in Kansai, Chugoku and Kyushu by yourself – shopping, cycling, soaking in hot springs, visiting museums and restaurants – then join a guided multi-day walk along the Shikoku Henro (p191) or Kumano Kodo (p170).

If you're booking things yourself, plan out key parts of your journey like internal flights, car hire or long-distance train and bus journeys (and pre-book them where possible). There are several transport passes that will save you money (and prevent you having to buy tickets for every journey), many of which are cheapest if you buy them from outside Japan. Allow plenty of time to map out major journeys.

WHEN TO GO

Once you've decided on what you want to see and do, figure out if you need to be in the country at a particular time. If your trip falls around a busy period, plan well in advance. Spring cherry blossoms and autumn leaves are popular, but the main times to bear in mind are the three busiest periods for domestic travel: Golden Week, a string of national holidays in late April and early May; Obon, a major festival in mid-August; and New Year, a big celebration for families at the end of December and start of January. These are all exciting times to be in Japan, but they bring huge crowds and spikes in hotel prices.

Then there's the question of weather. Japan is mostly temperate, and has four distinct seasons; if you're looking to travel in the summer, bear in mind *tsuyu*, the June to mid-July rainy season. Japan experiences typhoons too, generally between May and October; they're more likely further south, are especially common in August and September, and are well predicted so shouldn't hit you unaware. If you're travelling in peak seasons, expect hotels, activities and high-end restaurants to book up early. Generally, aim to book anything you really don't want to miss four to six months in advance, especially if you have particular hotels, trains or activities in mind. For other things, leave your schedule more open if you value flexibility over the assurance of having reservations in place.

THE BASICS

Currency Japanese yen (¥)

Time zone Japan Standard Time (JST), UTC+9

Population 124 million

Capital city Tokyo

Prefectures 47

Country calling code +81

Emergency number 119

Power sockets Type A and B

Tap water Safe to drink unless otherwise stated.

Government Japan is a constitutional monarchy with a parliamentary government.

Language Japanese is the official language, and learning some key phrases (p19) goes a long way. Ryukyuan languages are also spoken in Okinawa, Ainu in Hokkaido, and Hachijo in some Izu and Okinawan islands.

International airports Japan's largest airports include Narita (near Tokyo); Haneda (Tokyo); Kansai (Osaka); Chubu Centrair (Nagoya); New Chitose (Sapporo, Hokkaido); Fukuoka (Kyushu); and Naha (Okinawa).

Phones and Wi-Fi Foreign mobile phones may not work in Japan, so check with your operator before travelling. Some cafés, tourist attractions and trains offer free Wi-Fi, but it's worth buying pocket Wi-Fi or e-sims before travelling to Japan just in case.

Exploring and getting around Japan

You've done the planning, sorted your budget and have finally landed in Japan. Now it's time for a little local know-how.

CROSS-COUNTRY TRAVEL
Japan's public transport network is extensive and reliable. The three largest islands (Honshu, Hokkaido and Kyushu) are connected by *shinkansen* (or bullet trains), a network of high-speed railway lines. Gaps in the *shinkansen* network are filled in by trains, buses and coaches, and cable cars and funiculars in the mountains. As Japan is an archipelago, there are places where you'll rely on ferries and planes, too. For boat trips, tickets can often be bought at ferry terminals on the day of departure; for domestic flights, book ahead.

Multiple companies run the public transport infrastructure, which can be confusing. Japan Rail (JR) is the largest rail operator, covering about 70 per cent of the network, including all *shinkansen* lines. JR also operates the ferry from Hiroshima to Itsukushima. Other major rail companies include Kintetsu, Tobu, Seibu, Odakyu, Keisei and Tokyu.

The efficiency and extent of the rail network means that few visitors use long-distance coaches, but the bus network is comprehensive, and is a much cheaper option than the train.

With such an excellent transport network, there's really no need to drive in Japan. If you are heading out on a scenic road trip (p176), rent a car at major train stations or ports of entry, and show an international driver's licence. Car rental companies are generally not used to dealing face-to-face with customers in English, although many offer online booking in English. Note that while rented cars are usually equipped with sat-nav systems, these are in Japanese.

LOCAL TRANSPORT
Most cities have a good network of trains, subways, buses and trams. They all work a bit differently, but a quick look at the local tourist board website should demystify things. Basic fare tickets for short distances on trains and subways are normally bought from ticket machines at stations, which usually (but not always) have an English translation button, and accept both card and cash. Many stations also have maps in English.

Bus depots are often located outside of train stations in cities. The method of paying fares varies. Some buses are boarded at the front, and the fare – often a flat rate – is deposited into a slot beside the driver, but most also have card readers next to this slot. Exit from the door in the middle of the bus. A second system invites passengers to step aboard toward the centre or back of the bus, where a machine distributes numbered tickets. The number on this ticket appears on a screen at the front of the bus, which corresponds to the fare to be paid. Before you disembark, drop the indicated amount and your ticket into the box beside the driver.

WEBSITES AND APPS

Try these resources to get the most out of your trip.

accessible-japan.com
Information about accessible travel in Japan.

Japan Travel by Navitime
Route planner that calculates cost and distance.

japan.travel/en
The Japan National Tourism Organization.

japan-guide.com
Useful English-language site for checking opening times, entry fees, transport and information about key sights.

japangayguide.com
Information on LGBTQ+ culture and events in Japan.

JapanTaxi
Taxi booking app.

jma.go.jp
Weather forecasts, plus updates on natural events.

MyMizu
Lists water refill spots.

vjw.digital.go.jp
Carry out immigration, customs and tax-free shopping procedures.

YomiWa
Japanese dictionary app that translates photographed text.

TRANSPORT PASSES

The JR Pass, which comes in 7-, 14- and 21-day varieties, is great value if you're travelling extensively cross-country. It covers almost all bullet trains (a supplement is required for the fastest models, the Nozomi and Mizuho). There are many *jiyu-seki* (unreserved seats) carriages, but it's worth booking a seat if you're travelling a long way or with large bags; book yours at JR stations. If you're only travelling within certain regions, look into regional JR Passes instead. Japan Rail has East, Central, West, Kyushu, Shikoku and Hokkaido divisions, and most regional passes stick to one or two of those areas – for instance, the JR East Tohoku Area Pass covers Kanto and Tohoku for five days.

If you don't plan on using *shinkansen* much, or will be using other companies' networks, a JR Pass may not be the right choice. Many regions and cities have their own special passes, and local tourist information centers can provide information and advice. In Tokyo, there are a variety of options, including the "Free Kippu", which allows unlimited travel on most of the subway, bus and tram lines in the city centre for 24 hours. But, unless you are planning on making a lot of journeys in one day on many forms of transport, use a physical or app-based transit (IC) card. Physical cards can be purchased at tourist information centres and ticket counters. Alternatively, simply buy tickets for each journey individually – most machines will have an English button, and staff at counters can help you figure out your options.

TAXIS

Japan's taxis are clean, comfortable and easy to find in large towns and cities. In rural spots, ask your accommodation to pre-book one. To flag one down, look for the light in the window – red means available, green means booked.

EMERGENCIES

Japan is generally a safe country with low crime rates. If you do need to contact the police, call them on 110 or drop into a *koban* (police box). Note that you're required to carry your passport at all times when exploring the country.

For medical advice, visit a pharmacy for minor ailments or a specialized clinic for significant problems. There are also large hospitals offering high-quality care in every big city. Check the rules on bringing medicines to Japan, and take out comprehensive health insurance to avoid potentially high fees if you visit the hospital.

TRAVELLERS WITH SPECIFIC REQUIREMENTS

In part due to its ageing population, Japan has fairly good infrastructure for people with restricted mobility, sight or hearing – tactile paving was even invented here. *Tamokuteki toire* (multi-purpose toilets) are becoming more common in stations, department stores and on bullet trains, and are suitable for wheelchair users; they also have emergency call buttons.

New-build hotels need to adhere to accessibility regulations, and most older ones have at least one "barrier-free" room. Induction hearing loops and adjustable beds are uncommon, though.

LGBTQ+ SCENE

LGBTQ+ travellers are unlikely to have any problems in Japan. Public displays of affection between both mixed and same-gender couples are not the norm in Japanese culture.

There's little knowledge of non-binary or transgender identities, but the cultural approach is to leave people to go about their business. *Tamokuteki toire* (multi-purpose toilets) are a good option if you'd rather avoid using gendered bathrooms.

Customs and etiquette

Japanese culture is famously polite, with multiple levels of respect woven into the language. To outsiders, this can be both appealing and intimidating – it's lovely to see people treating each other so respectfully, but mortifying to think about unknowingly offending someone. At its root, though, it's not that complicated: most Japanese customs and rules of etiquette are based on pro-social behaviour and the idea that the needs of the collective come before those of the individual. So the two best things you can do are pay attention to what people around you are doing, and be considerate of their comfort. Your thoughtfulness will be met with the same; people go out of their way to help visitors, even if there's a language barrier.

RESPECTING OTHERS

While some people will happily initiate a handshake or even a hug, the default is to bow when greeting someone. There's no need to go overboard and bend 90° – about 30–45° should suffice. Pressing your hands together as though praying while you bow is a norm in other parts of Asia, but not Japan.

Try to apply a respect for personal space to as many situations as possible. If you see someone in traditional dress, especially geisha or *maiko*, remember that they're just people trying to do their job. Don't crowd them for photos, interrupt their day or point at them. In fact, don't point in general – it's more polite to gesture with an open hand.

TIPPING

Tipping is not part of the culture in Japan. Attempts to do so could lead to confusion and be taken as an offence, with servers doing their best to return money.

DINING OUT

There is, however, one extra charge in some restaurants, bars and *izakaya* (traditional pubs): the *otoshi* fee. This functions like a table charge, but you get an *otoshi*, a small appetizer like edamame or potato salad, for it. You'll probably also get an *oshibori* when you sit down, a wet towel (often hot in winter, cold in summer) for cleaning your hands, plus free water or tea.

Start your meal by saying *itadakimasu*, a phrase that expresses gratitude for what you're receiving. Follow through on that gratitude by clearing your plate whenever possible.

Chopsticks are the default, but don't worry if you struggle with them. You won't offend anyone if you take a while, or ask for a fork. If you are using chopsticks, make sure you don't point with them or stick them upright in food, which looks like a funeral rite. When you've finished eating in a restaurant, forget any ideas of being quiet in public: call *"sumimasen!"* ("excuse me!") and use the scribbling-in-the-air sign to ask for your bill. A couple of extra-credit table manners: use the other end of your chopsticks to serve yourself from communal plates, and slurp your

---

IF YOU ONLY REMEMBER FIVE THINGS...

People often feel overwhelmed by Japanese etiquette, worried that they'll make a mistake and offend someone. But as long as you're doing your best, you'll find most Japanese people are very forgiving of any faux pas. So, if you only remember a few things, make it these:

1
If in doubt, take off your shoes

2
Respect the queue – don't jump ahead

3
Don't tip

4
Treat sacred spaces respectfully

5
Above all else, be considerate of others

noodles; it cools them down as you eat and shows enjoyment.

SHOPPING CULTURE
You'll be greeted in most shops with a chorus of *"irassahimase!"* or "welcome!". Browse at your leisure, try on clothes if needed (many changing rooms are shoes-off areas, and they may have thin paper or fabric sheets or bags to put over your face to prevent make-up transfer), then pay at the till. Cash rarely changes hands directly; put it into the small tray on the counter instead.

SHOES OFF
Changing rooms aside, other shoes-off areas include private homes, temple and shrine buildings, and any tatami-matted floor. It's a frequent occurrence, so pack plenty of quick-to-remove shoes and nice socks. If you're wearing sandals, your feet might get dirty, so carry socks to change into when entering those spaces. Bathrooms tend to have slippers to change into – just don't wear them out of the bathroom.

VISITING TEMPLES AND SHRINES
In sacred spaces like shrines and temples, err on the side of quiet and respectful. You don't need to tiptoe around in hushed reverence, but you certainly shouldn't get in the way of people practising their religion. You're generally welcome to take photos, but keep an eye out for signs saying not to (usually by the main idol). When entering Shinto shrine grounds *(p36)*, you'll pass under a torii gate. To be extra respectful, bow at the threshold and walk on the left – the centre is reserved for the gods. At both temples and shrines, you're welcome to pray, buy amulets and fortune-telling slips, and enter the public buildings. Remember to remove your shoes when you enter sacred buildings.

VISITING *ONSEN*
Following a few simple guidelines will ensure you get the most out of your time in Japan's hot springs, and respect the country's bathing culture. Firstly, leave your shoes in lockers at the front of *onsen* or *sento* (public baths) before heading into the changing rooms. If you have tattoos, check the bath's policy on them before you arrive, or ask at the front desk; historically, tattoos have been associated with *yakuza* (mafia) and although things are changing, many *onsen* don't allow people with tattoos.

Before entering the baths, wash thoroughly in the showers and tie your hair up if it's long. Enter the baths naked (they're often gender-segregated), and rinse off between pools if there are several. Don't swim, splash or shout – people come here to wash and to socialize in a relaxing environment.

ON PUBLIC TRANSPORT
Remain fairly quiet on public transport. You're welcome to chat, but use headphones to listen to music, put your phone on quiet mode and leave the carriage if you have to take a call. Lots of people wear masks for myriad reasons; if you have a cold or are nervous about catching something, wear one too.

If you have a reserved seat, look for the lines on the platform that indicate each carriage and door, join the right one and don't queue jump. Many trains without reserved seats have priority seating areas, and during rush hour some carriages are women-only (indicated by a pink panel on the ground and carriage with "women only" written in multiple languages).

Eating on local trains is considered rude, but if you're travelling a long way – especially by *shinkansen* – it's fine. In fact, there's a thriving culture of *ekiben*, or boxed meals sold in train stations specifically to eat on board.

KEY PHRASES

You'll see a lot of English in Japan, especially on public transport and in large cities. However, most people aren't confident English speakers, and learning a few key phrases can go a long way towards showing respect and building connection.

Konnichiwa/konbanwa
Hello/good evening

Sayonara
Goodbye

Hajimemashite
Pleased to meet you

Onegai shimasu
Please

Arigatou (gozaimasu)
Thank you (very much)

Eigo ga hanasemasu ka?
Do you speak English?

Sumimasen
Sorry/excuse me

Wakarimasen
I don't understand

Hai/iie
Yes/no

[Kore] wa ikura/ doko desu ka?
How much/where is [this]?

[Kore] ga suki desu
I like [this]

[Kore] o kudasai
I would like [this] please

Itadakimasu
Bon appetit (a polite phrase said before eating)

Oishii!
Delicious!

Kanpai!
Cheers!

Nihon
Japan

Toire/otearai
Toilet

ICONIC

JAPAN

To get to know the very best of this country, there's no better place to start than with these iconic experiences. And they're famed for a reason, each one capturing something quintessential about Japan.

ON THE MAP
ICONIC JAPAN

1. Find inspiration in Mount Fuji's serene beauty
2. Experience geisha and *maiko* culture in Kyoto
3. Meditate with the Great Buddha of Kamakura
4. Slurp some of Japan's best ramen in Kitakata
5. Stroll around Tokyo's Imperial Palace grounds
6. Contemplate peace in Hiroshima's Peace Memorial Park
7. Witness the controlled chaos of Shibuya Crossing
8. Step back in time at Kyoto's temples and shrines
9. Speed through Japan on a blink-and-you'll-miss-it bullet train
10. Gaze up (and up) at Tokyo Skytree
11. Enter the Crow Castle in Matsumoto
12. Savour fresh sushi and sashimi
13. Wonder at Nikko Tosho-gu's ornate carvings
14. Marvel at the giants of sumo

ICONIC JAPAN

"If views of the peak are inspiring, then the view from it is nothing short of epic."

Mount Fuji

1

Find inspiration in Mount Fuji's serene beauty

Pilgrims and painters are continually drawn to this sacred mountain – and little wonder why

While some three-quarters of Japan is mountainous, there's one peak that rises above the rest. At 3,776 m (12,388 ft), Mount Fuji (or Fuji-san) towers over its nearest rival, Yamanashi's Mount Kita, by almost 600 m (2,000 ft). But Fuji-san's stature is far from the only reason for its national icon status.

The mountain's picturesque surroundings and pleasing symmetry – given a touch of *wabi-sabi* (a Japanese aesthetic that finds beauty in imperfection) by a small second peak – has made it the subject of countless works of art. And its location near Tokyo means it has caught the eye of plenty over the centuries. Tokyo, previously called Edo, has been the political heart of Japan since the great samurai Tokugawa Ieyasu established his government there in 1603. For the following 260 years, the country's daimyo (feudal lords) had to spend alternate years in Edo and Kyoto (traditionally the imperial capital), with many of them travelling between the two on the Tokaido, the "Great Eastern Sea Route". The journey took weeks, and involved crossing rivers and navigating treacherous mountain passes along the way. But once the daimyo glimpsed Mount Fuji, they knew they were nearing the final stretch. It's no surprise, then, that this vast landmark looms large in the many ukiyo-e (woodblock prints popular from the 17th to the 19th century) depictions of the route.

One of the most admired ukiyo-e artists was Hiroshige, whose series *The Fifty-Three Stations of the Tokaido* shows each different *shuku* (post town) along the Tokaido, with several prints featuring Mount Fuji. In his depiction of Maisaka-juku, it's just a small cone in the background. But by the time we reach Hara-juku, the peak is so close that it breaks out of the print's border. Hokusai's *Great Wave off Kanagawa* from his now iconic *Thirty-Six Views of Mount Fuji*, also features the peak; amid the chaos of the waves, Mount Fuji sits serene and unmoved.

If views of the peak are inspiring, then the view *from* it is nothing short of epic. Though Mount Fuji has importance in Buddhism and Shinto, it's the Shugendo (mountain worship) ascetics of centuries past who began climbing it, then leading others along the paths they'd forged. During the annual July to early September climbing season, hundreds of thousands of people now make the ascent, and there are still some white-clad Fuji-ko pilgrims in their ranks.

There are four routes up, each divided into ten stages (though buses go as far as stage five). Many climbers opt to hike to stage eight, stay the night at a lodge (which helps with altitude sickness), then finish before dawn. The reward? The chance to witness *goraiko*: sunrise from the summit, the clouds below you turning into a sea of gold as you watch. Now that's a picture to capture.

— MAKE IT HAPPEN —

Mount Fuji straddles the border of Shizuoka and Yamanashi prefectures, about 100 km (60 miles) west of Tokyo.

If you're planning to climb Mount Fuji, stick to the official climbing season and make sure you're well prepared. Though not a technical climb, it's still tiring and can be dangerous. Check the Ministry of the Environment's official website *(fujisan-climb.jp/en)* for up-to-date information on conditions and restrictions. The Yoshida Trail is the most popular route, and has the most facilities. The Fujinomiya Trail is faster but steeper. If you'd rather avoid the crowds (and don't mind minimal facilities) choose the lesser-walked Subashiri and Gotemba routes.

Kawaguchiko station and Fujisan station are linked to nearby destinations, including Tokyo, by bus and train. There are several bus routes around the Fuji Five Lakes area, at the base of Mount Fuji.

Experience geisha and maiko culture in Kyoto

Kyoto's "children of the arts" are an icon of Japan's ancient capital

Maiko makeovers are quite popular with visitors to Kyoto. Head to the historic Gion district, and you're almost certain to spot a tourist in an extravagant kimono, perhaps stumbling slightly on the cobbles as they get used to their *geta* (wooden sandals). At a glance, you might even think they're the real thing. But if you happen to see an actual *maiko* (geisha in training, literally "dancing girl"), you'll be left in no doubt. There's something different about the way they move – from the delicate, shuffling gait to the elegant tilt of the head. You can put on the clothes and the make-up, but you just can't fake the years of training.

Geisha, in many ways, represent a pinnacle of Japanese artistic expression. Kyoto is considered the birthplace of the art form, and contains five iconic *hanamachi* ("flower towns", likening the geisha to flowers), the districts in which the geisha live and work. The oldest *hanamachi* (Kamishichiken) is in the northwest of the city, with others clustered around the Kamo River: three in the Gion area, and one in Pontocho just across the water. All of the *hanamachi* have a slightly mysterious, even secretive atmosphere. The teahouses and traditional restaurants in which the geisha work – usually performing dances and songs, pouring drinks, and chatting and playing drinking games with customers – are so discreet that they often don't even have signs.

Technically, Kyoto doesn't have geisha ("people of the arts"); here the local word *geiko* ("children of the arts") is used instead. From the time young women – usually teenagers fresh out of junior high school – start training, they use the Kyoto dialect – no matter where they come from originally. Acquiring this new language is just one facet of their intensive training, which also includes studying traditional instruments, singing and dancing, and learning how to provide hospitality, from tea ceremonies to engaging conversation. As with any career in the arts, it's a risky undertaking, one that trainees generally feel called to by a deep love for tradition.

Of course, after all that hard work, the *maiko* and *geiko* are keen to showcase their mastery of the arts. Several times a year, Kyoto's *hanamachi* hold festivals called Odori, where the women perform; the Kamishichiken *maiko* and *geiko* also run a summer beer garden. Tea ceremonies and dinner performances (with an interpreter if needed) are another way of interacting with these highly skilled women.

Kyoto's children of the arts embody Japanese aesthetic principles. If you see a *maiko* or *geiko*, try to call one of those principles to mind: *mono no aware*, or the bittersweet beauty of transience. Rather than trying to corner her for photos (some *hanamachi* levy fines to combat this issue) just appreciate your incredible good luck.

MAKE IT HAPPEN

Gion's three *hanamachi* are just east of the Kamo River and west of Yasaka Shrine. Pontocho is directly across the river, while Kamishichiken is up in northwest Kyoto, by the shrine of Kitano Tenmangu.

To book a private tea ceremony or dinner, ask specialist tour operators or book online via *mai-ko.com*. Dress smartly and assume you'll be in a traditional setting, which means taking shoes off and sitting on the floor. Treat the *maiko* and *geiko* with respect, whatever the setting. Avoid physical contact and do not take photos without permission.

Gion and Pontocho are close to Kyoto's main shopping streets, around the Shijo-Kawaramachi intersection, where there are several metro stations and bus stops. For Kamishichiken, take the bus (get off at Kitano Tenmangu) or the Randen electric railway's Keifuku line, which connects with Ryoan-ji and Ninna-ji temples.

ICONIC JAPAN

"You can put on the clothes and the make-up, but you just can't fake the years of training."

Left Traditional *maiko* make-up
Above Strolling in a kimono
Below Perfectly coiffed hair

3

Meditate with the Great Buddha of Kamakura

This huge bronze statue has been peacefully meditating in this spot for centuries

Encircled by the sea on one side and hills on the other, Kamakura sits in Kanagawa prefecture, near Tokyo. Now a laid-back coastal town, it was once at the heart of an important and bloody era. The powerful shogun (samurai leader) Minamoto no Yoritomo established his seat of government here around 1192, marking the beginning of Japan's Kamakura period. By the end of the period, in 1333, the area had become a centre of Zen Buddhism, which fitted the ruling samurai class's emphasis on self-discipline and simplicity.

The shogunate may be long gone, but the Buddhist connection remains strong. Today, Kamakura is home to around 65 temples, including Kotoku-in and its crowning jewel: the Daibutsu, or Great Buddha. Completed in 1252, the bronze statue – Japan's second tallest, at over 13 m (44 ft) including the base – depicts Amida Nyorai (the Buddha of Infinite Light) in seated meditation, hands in a *mida-no-jouin* mudra position, eyes half closed. The statue has survived fires and earthquakes, typhoons and tsunamis, and the rise and fall of armies and empires. Visit on a quiet day, and you may be tempted to join it in its endless meditation, the wind rustling through the trees around you and only the sky for a roof.

MAKE IT HAPPEN

 Kamakura is on the coast in Kanagawa prefecture, just south of Tokyo. The Great Buddha is at Kotoku-in temple in the town's western Hase district.

 Pay a small fee to enter the temple and the Buddha itself, which is hollow. The temple is open daily but check website for hours (*kotoku-in.jp*).

 JR's Tokaido, Yokosuka and Shonan-Shinjuku lines serve Kamakura. Change to the Enoden line for Hase station, which is a short walk from the temple.

ICONIC JAPAN

Combine with SAGAMIHARA

If you're driving from Kamakura to Tokyo, make a detour to Sagamihara (p152). In the unexpected location of a used tyre shop, you'll find around 100 retro vending machines serving everything from ice creams to steaming bowls of noodles to fortune-telling papers.

Kamakura's Great Buddha at Kotoku-in

29

ICONIC JAPAN

4

Slurp some of Japan's best ramen in Kitakata

With the country's most ramen shops per capita, Kitakata is a must-visit for noodle fans

Ramen is a serious business in Japan. Regions have fierce rivalries over whose style is better, and ramen joints jostle with high-end restaurants for Michelin stars.

Kitakata takes it, if possible, even more seriously. This small city in northern Honshu is known for many things – high-quality sake breweries, historic converted *kura* (warehouses), local wood and lacquer crafts – but it's the 100-plus ramen restaurants that take the crown. Not that it's about quantity over quality. Most shops specialize in a specific style of ramen – miso ramen in one, perhaps, *shio* (salt) ramen in another – so you know it's done well. It's the eponymous Kitakata style that you can't miss, though. In this local take on ramen, the noodles are satisfyingly thick and chewy, the *shoyu* (soy sauce) broth is rich but not cloying. Toppings vary, but you're likely to see fatty *chashu* pork, spring onions and bamboo shoots.

To truly immerse yourself in Kitakata's noodle culture, make sure to stay overnight. That way, you can start your day the Kitakata way: with a piping hot bowl of *asa-ra*, or "morning ramen". And one last thing: be sure to slurp the noodles as you eat, to show the chef you appreciate their craft – and their early morning.

— MAKE IT HAPPEN —

Kitakata is in Fukushima, in northern Japan.

Most restaurants don't take bookings. You may find queues, but they move fairly quickly.

The scenic JR Ban'etsu train line links Kitakata with Aizu-Wakamatsu.

Combine with MORIOKA

Continue your northern Japan noodle odyssey in Morioka (p100), where you can try three completely different dishes: refreshing reimen, *hearty* jajamen *and the all-you-can-eat* wanko soba.

Roasted pork fillet noodles

Nijubashi, the most famous bridge in the Imperial Palace grounds

5

Stroll around Tokyo's Imperial Palace grounds

There's a lot to explore in the palace grounds, from manicured gardens to museums

— MAKE IT HAPPEN —

The Imperial Palace is located just west of Tokyo station.

The grounds are free but the museums are ticketed. The gardens directly around the palace are only accessible on pre-booked twice-daily tours.

There are subway stations near every entrance to the grounds.

Tokyo's Imperial Palace is one of the most visited sites in the metropolis. Or rather, its grounds are. The palace itself – a low-lying building dating to the 1960s – is the main residence of the Imperial Family, so off limits to the public, but the grounds are the perfect place to spend a relaxing few hours.

Start at the southeastern corner, where two bridges span the palace moat, itself overlooked by an elegant tower. This 17th-century structure looks like a mini castle, and indeed it's one of the only remaining parts of the original Edo Castle that stood here when Tokyo was the base of Japan's samurai government (at the time, the emperor was relegated to Kyoto).

Make your way north across the wide Imperial Plaza and you'll reach the manicured gardens of Higashi Gyoen. Here, there are painstakingly clipped trees, ponds dotted with lily pads and colourful blooms that change with the seasons.

Finally, you'll reach Kitanomaru-koen, a park that contains the National Museum of Modern Art. Best of all, the park is home to 90 *sakura* (flowering cherry) trees. In springtime, crowds gather to catch the cherry blossom at its best. If you're lucky enough to join them, rent a rowboat, paddle around the Chidori-ga-fuchi Boat Pier and watch the petals floating down around you.

Contemplate peace in Hiroshima's Peace Memorial Park

Reflect on the past and look to the future in Hiroshima's thought-provoking park and museum

At first glance, Hiroshima's Peace Memorial Park is simply a lovely green space in a bustling city. But look closer, and you'll understand its purpose: to end the use of nuclear weapons by remembering the horrors endured by Hiroshima on 6 August 1945, when it became the first city to be targeted with a nuclear bomb. In the closing days of World War II, the US demonstrated the terrible power of its new weapon by using it on Japan, the only Axis power yet to surrender. In Hiroshima and Nagasaki (where a second bomb was dropped on 9 August), around 125,000 people were killed in the space of four days.

In the Peace Memorial Park, fresh flowers lie before a simple granite-and-concrete arch, underneath which a stone coffin is inscribed: "Let all the souls here rest in peace, for we shall not repeat the evil." Framed through the arch is the Genbaku Dome, the sky peering through its exposed metal ribs. The image shimmers in a heat haze from the Flame of Peace; lit in 1964, it will not be extinguished until all nuclear weapons have been destroyed. The dome itself was one of few buildings left standing after the blast, which killed 80,000 people immediately. Some 60,000 more died in the next few months, and more still in the following years from the effects of radiation.

The poignant Children's Peace Monument, which remembers the youngest victims, stands nearby. It is always festooned with origami cranes. Sasaki Sadako, a young girl hospitalized with leukaemia in 1955, tried to fold 1,000 of the paper birds in the hope that it would cure her illness (cranes are linked to longevity). She died before she could finish, but her effort made the origami cranes into a symbol of peace. The Korean Victims and Survivors Memorial Monument remembers the 20,000 Koreans killed, most of them forced labourers brought over during Japan's colonization of Korea.

The Peace Memorial Museum gives context. Allow plenty of time to absorb the exhibits, from dispassionate assessments of the proliferation of nuclear weapons to deeply affecting personal accounts. A diorama shows Hiroshima at the moment of the blast, then photos and displays of everyday items retrieved from the ruined city give voice to individual human stories.

The museum's final message exhorts visitors to hope and to action. Beyond its walls is a peaceful, verdant park, planted on ground that no one thought would bloom again. And beyond that is the thriving, modern city of Hiroshima, rebuilt in the wake of devastation to become a testament to human hope and resilience.

─ MAKE IT HAPPEN ─

Hiroshima is located in the far western part of Honshu Island (the largest island in Japan), along the shores of the Seto Inland Sea. It's a city of some size, with over one million inhabitants.

Hiroshima's Peace Memorial Park is free but there is a small fee to enter the museum. Due to the museum's popularity, it's advisable to book tickets ahead of your visit, to avoid queuing. Opening hours vary throughout the year, so check the museum's website before visiting (*hpmmuseum.jp*).

Hiroshima is a stop on the San'yo Shinkansen line between Osaka and Hakata (in Fukuoka); it takes about 90 minutes from Osaka to Hiroshima. Some bullet trains provide through services to Kagoshima on the Kyushu line or Tokyo on the Tokaido line. Trams and buses connect Hiroshima station with the Peace Memorial Park.

ICONIC JAPAN

The Genbaku Dome at Hiroshima Peace Memorial Park

Combine with SHIMANAMI KAIDO

Onomichi, in the east of Hiroshima prefecture, marks the start of the Shimanami Kaido cycle route (p178), which links Honshu with Shikoku via several scenic islands in the Seto Inland Sea.

ICONIC JAPAN

"The crowds around you move in unison, stepping out onto the intersection's five zebra crossings."

7

Witness the controlled chaos of Shibuya Crossing

Immerse yourself in one of Tokyo's most iconic street scenes

If you've seen one image of Tokyo, it's probably this one: up to 2,500 people simultaneously pouring across multiple zebra crossings, the city's ad-laden highrises a riot of colour around them. This is Shibuya Scramble Crossing, and seeing it in action is one of the quintessential experiences to have while in Japan.

The air is thick with noise as soon as you arrive: vehicles navigating the network of roads; the clamour of conversations in several languages; announcements ringing out from Shibuya train station; the latest pop song playing from one of the huge video billboards overhead.

Then suddenly, a new sound – the distinctive chirp of the road-crossing signal. The crowds around you move in unison, stepping out onto the intersection's five zebra crossings. As you walk forward with them, the foot traffic smoothly flows around occasional obstructions (mostly tourists pausing for a selfie before the lights change). In a few seconds, the tide has carried you to the other side.

Now that you've experienced the perfect example of Tokyo's controlled chaos, you may wish to head to one of the viewpoints overlooking the crossing to marvel at it from above. Or maybe just stay on ground level and go with the flow – Tokyo style.

The busy Shibuya Crossing

MAKE IT HAPPEN

 As the name suggests, Shibuya Scramble Crossing is in central Tokyo's Shibuya district, close to the Hachiko exit of Shibuya station.

 For a bird's-eye view of the crossing, book a ticket for Shibuya Sky (shibuya-scramble-square.com) or head to a coffee shop such as L'Occitane Café.

 Shibuya station is the world's fourth busiest. It's served by several train lines, with the JR Yamanote line platforms closest to the Hachiko exit.

ICONIC JAPAN

Above The hilltop Kiyomizu-dera
Left A tunnel of torii at Fushimi Inari Taisha

Visiting a Shinto shrine

1
Entering the shrine
The torii (gates) that mark the entrance to shrine grounds aren't just used by humans, but by gods too. Stay slightly to one side, leaving the central path for the deities, and bow as you cross the threshold.

2
Ritual purification
You'll see a basin of water (usually made of stone and with several ladles) shortly after entering a shrine. This is for purification. Pour some water over your left hand, then your right. Finally, pour a little more into your left hand and use it to quickly rinse your mouth.

3
Praying
Throw a coin into the offering box – five yen is considered especially auspicious, as it's pronounced go-en, a homonym for "luck". Shake the rope in front of you to ring a bell, then, with the gods now paying attention, bow twice and clap twice before praying. Bow once more when you're finished.

8

Step back in time at Kyoto's temples and shrines

The ancient capital's religious sites are the jewel in its glittering crown

Cobbled streets lined with wooden houses. Painstakingly arranged gravel gardens. Immaculately dressed geisha and *maiko*. Think of Kyoto and these images likely spring to mind: the city is the heart of Japanese culture and the proud home of many of the country's most important shrines, temples and imperial sights. A tour of as many as possible, then, is a must.

And it doesn't take long to see your first. Mere minutes from Kyoto's modernist train station are two UNESCO-listed Buddhist temples. Nishi-Hongan-ji, established in 1591, is associated with the Jodo (Pure Land) Buddhist sect, and its imposing buildings and huge stone terraces make a strong impression. To-ji, further south, has lush, green grounds overlooked by a spectacular five-storey pagoda, which was built in 826.

To see more of Kyoto's UNESCO-listed sites (there are 17 in and around the city, collectively known as the Historic Monuments of Ancient Kyoto), head for the edges of the city. To one side is the district of Higashiyama, or "Eastern Mountain", where Kyoto's rigid grid plan dissolves into winding paths that follow the contours of the land. Here lies the city's most famous temple: Kiyomizu-dera, which dates to the 8th century. There's a phrase, "to jump from the stage of Kiyomizu", which means "to take a leap of faith". Standing atop the precipitous 13-m (40-ft) terrace, it's easy to see why it became the stuff of proverbs. Be sure to explore Kiyomizu's other buildings too, including the Jishu-jinja (the shrine is Shinto, Japan's native animistic religion, rather than Buddhist), where people pray for luck in love. At Higashiyama's northern end is Ginkaku-ji, a 15th-century Zen temple known for its manicured gardens.

While restrained Ginkaku-ji was the centre of Higashiyama culture, lavish Kinkaku-ji spearheaded the preceding Kitayama ("Northern Mountain") culture. Covered in gold leaf and reflected in a still pond, it's one of Kyoto's most iconic sights. Nearby Ryoan-ji is best known for its *karesansui* (dry sand garden) with 15 rocks – only 14 of which you can see at any one time, no matter where you stand.

It'd be a shame to limit yourself to the UNESCO list, however. Some of the city's most famous religious sites aren't featured, including key Shinto shrines like the hugely popular Fushimi Inari Taisha in the southeast, with its hundreds of red torii (shrine gates). With so many sites to visit, one thing's for sure – you'll need to adopt a Zen mind-set, and accept that you simply can't see everything in one visit.

— MAKE IT HAPPEN —

The temples and shrines are dotted throughout the city, but some of the most famous are clustered in the far west (Arashiyama) and east (Higashiyama).

You'll need to buy a ticket to enter most of the shrines and temples – note that there are extra fees to enter some areas, including Kiyomizu's *tainai-meguri* (underground chamber). Remember that these are active religious sites, so be mindful of how you're behaving and be respectful to staff and worshippers.

Kyoto is on the Tokaido *shinkansen* line between Tokyo and Osaka, and several local train lines. Once in the city, it's easy to get around by train, bus and subway. The grid pattern and lack of hills also makes it easy to explore the centre and tick off the temples on foot or by bike.

Kinkaku-ji (Golden Pavilion) temple in Kyoto

Speed through Japan on a blink-and-you'll-miss-it bullet train

Enjoy a high-tech, high-speed journey through spectacular landscapes on the Tokaido *shinkansen*

The bullet train isn't just a convenient way to travel between cities. It's also a distillation of many key aspects of modern Japanese society – most obviously, technological innovation. When the Osaka–Tokyo Tokaido *shinkansen* line opened in 1964, it became the world's first high-speed rail line, cutting the journey time between the two cities from six and a half hours to four hours. Since then, things have only got faster, with the network expanding and engineers working hard to shave off more and more minutes from the journey time. And while speed is of the essence – the fastest Tokaido bullet trains whizz by at up to 285 kph (177 mph) – safety is also paramount. By 2021, the *shinkansen* network had carried over 6.4 billion passengers – and not one life had been lost in a collision or derailment.

But what's it like to ride one? Despite the breakneck speed, travelling by bullet train is surprisingly peaceful, largely due to the care and attention to detail of the Japanese hospitality onboard. Staff bow as they enter and leave carriages, and are always impeccably dressed in pressed uniforms and spotless white gloves. The train is thoroughly cleaned by a small army of people at each end of the line, who again bow at the passengers politely queuing on the platform once they're finished. And the interior design puts passengers' comfort and convenience first – on most of them, rows of seats can be turned 180 degrees, allowing groups to sit together and luggage to fit snugly behind them.

All is lovely onboard, but you're also here for the views of Japan's spectacular landscapes. There are a plenty of scenic routes to choose from, with the network zipping all the way from Hokkaido island in the north to Kyushu island in the south. The original line, however, remains the most iconic. Named for the ancient road linking Kyoto and Tokyo, the Tokaido route has long been the most-used *shinkansen* line. Following this route on foot would take weeks, but the fastest bullet train can do it in a blistering two and a quarter hours. Today's travellers and those from centuries ago do have one thing in common however: the hope of glimpsing Mount Fuji along the way. Maximize your chances by asking for a Fuji-*gawa* (Fuji-side) seat when booking your tickets and be sure to have your camera ready. It's more than worth the effort: the view of the mountain (all snow-tipped and symmetrical) will surely take your breath away … if the bullet train hasn't already.

— MAKE IT HAPPEN —

The Tokaido *shinkansen* runs between Tokyo and Osaka, with major stops along the way including Yokohama, Nagoya and Kyoto.

There are several models of *shinkansen*, rolled out as technology improved and maximum speeds increased. The JR Pass covers travel on most of them, but for the very fastest (Nozomi and Mizuho) you'll need to pay a supplement. All trains have sections for *jiyuuseki* (unreserved seats) and *shiteiseki* (reserved seats). Seat reservations cost a little extra, but JR Pass holders can make them for free.

There are two Tokaido *shinkansen* stations in Tokyo. The most central is Tokyo station; Shinagawa is further south, convenient for Haneda airport. The terminus of the Tokaido line is Shin-Osaka, a dedicated *shinkansen* station.

ICONIC JAPAN

A bullet train speeding past Mount Fuji

Tokyo Skytree rising above Tokyo's cityscape

Combine with TOKYO TOWER

The only problem with the view from Skytree is that, well, it doesn't include Skytree. Fix this by heading to the city's other iconic tower: Tokyo Tower (p154), from which you can get a great view of Skytree to the north.

10

Gaze up (and up) at Tokyo Skytree

The world's tallest tower, Skytree is an iconic feature of the Tokyo skyline

--- MAKE IT HAPPEN ---

Located in Sumida ward, in northeastern Tokyo.

Pre-book a timed-entry ticket online *(tokyo-skytree.jp)*.

Take the Tobu Isesaki line to Tokyo Skytree station or one of three lines to Oshiage station.

Even in a city of skyscrapers, Tokyo Skytree is jaw-dropping. At 634 m (2,080 ft), it's the tallest tower, and the third-tallest structure, in the world.

Yes, Skytree is sleek and futuristic, a marvel of modern engineering, but traditional Japanese principles are also woven into its design. It uses a hanging central pillar as part of its earthquake-proofing, a feature inspired by surprisingly sturdy traditional wooden pagodas. The colour of its airy latticework is based on *aijiro*, the palest shade of blue used by indigo dyers. Even the height of the tower has cultural significance – 634 can be read as "Musashi", an ancient province of Japan that encompassed much of present-day Tokyo.

Impressive though it is, the design ultimately comes second to something else at Skytree: the breathtaking view. There are two observation decks, Japan's first- and second-highest at 350 and 450 m (1,150 and 1,480 ft), from where you can enjoy a 360-degree view of the city, stretching away to the haze of the horizon. And on that horizon? Something taller than Skytree itself: Mount Fuji.

11

Enter the Crow Castle in Matsumoto

Step into samurai history at one of Japan's few original castles

The provincial city of Matsumoto in central Honshu has a plethora of attractions to its name. Its picturesque historic core centres on a canal, and restored white *kura* (warehouses) line the surrounding streets. The bright, polka-dotted works of the artist Yayoi Kusama (who was born here) spill joyfully out of the city's art museum and into its grounds. But top billing surely goes to the iconic Matsumoto-jo, one of Japan's few original castles. Most of the other castles in Japan are (very impressive) replicas, but Matsumoto-jo dates back to 1594, when it was built by the powerful Ishikawa samurai clan during the civil unrest of the "Warring States" period that spanned the 15th and 16th centuries.

The castle is simultaneously elegant and austere, scenic and imposing. Its black walls have earned it the nickname "Crow Castle", and when you see it set against the snow-capped Japan Alps, the delicately curved roofs seeming to spread out like wings, you could almost believe it's about to take off.

You're not limited to admiring it from the grounds, either. Step inside to see the vast beams that support the structure, plus fascinating displays of samurai armour, swords and guns from past centuries. Right at the top, you'll spot a tiny Shinto shrine tucked into the eaves – the warriors were confident, but a little extra divine protection never hurts.

— MAKE IT HAPPEN —

Matsumoto is in central Honshu, near Nagano.

Check hours and fees online (*matsumoto-castle.jp*). Note that the stairs in the castle are extremely steep and narrow.

Take a direct Limited Express train from Tokyo to Matsumoto or the Shinkansen to Nagoya or Nagano, and then a local train.

Cherry blossom framing Matsumoto-jo

ICONIC JAPAN

Top tips for enjoying sushi

1
Learn basic manners
You can use chopsticks or your hands. Eat each piece in one bite after dipping the fish side (the rice may break) in soy sauce.

2
Pick the right place
First timer? Try a kaiten-zushi (conveyer belt sushi) restaurant, where you can try small servings of lots of types for a low price.

3
Know your options
If you're nervous about raw fish, look for alternatives like tamago-yaki *(omelette)*, cucumber maki, seared beef, inari *(seasoned tofu)* and tempura.

12

Savour fresh sushi and sashimi

Japan's most famous culinary export is still best enjoyed in the country where it was invented – and perfected

"Shiogama is famous for having more sushi restaurants per person than anywhere else in the country."

At the turn of the century, sushi was a rarity outside Japan. But fast forward to today, and you can get your fix of seasoned rice and (usually) raw fish all around the globe. Still, sushi's home country remains the best place in the world to enjoy it. You could make a reservation at one of Tokyo's Michelin-starred *omakase* (chef's choice) restaurants, or just pop into a *kaiten* (conveyer belt) spot for a quick bite. But for a deeper experience, skip Tokyo entirely and make straight for the "sushi capital of Japan".

The seaside town of Shiogama in northern Honshu is famous for having more sushi restaurants per person than anywhere else in Japan, and the locals are deservedly proud of its quality. Not only can you expect super-fresh fish (Shiogama is best known for its tuna) but beautifully fragrant rice, grown locally in Miyagi, the prefecture in which Shiogama is located. Any of the town's sushi restaurants is sure to impress, but naturally it's at the fish market that you'll find the very freshest fish. Head to one of the market's on-site sushi counters, or pick out the most appealing wares as you explore and make up your own *kaisen-don* (sashimi on a bowl of rice). While you're here, try Matsushima Bay oysters, too. The scenic Matsushima itself is just a short train ride from Shiogama – for some of the highest-quality oysters in the country, why not?

Skilfully sliced fresh sashimi

MAKE IT HAPPEN

 Shiogama is located in Miyagi prefecture on the northeastern coast of Honshu island, not far from Sendai and Matsushima.

 The fish market is only open until early afternoon (check *nakaoroshi.or.jp*), but there are plenty of sushi restaurants to visit afterwards.

 From Tokyo, take the Tohoku *shinkansen* to Sendai, capital of Miyagi, from where Shiogama is just a short trip on the JR Senseki line.

13

Wonder at Nikko Tosho-gu's ornate carvings

The final resting place of the samurai who helped unite Japan is one of the country's most impressive shrines

Tokugawa Ieyasu was a man of simple tastes. As the samurai who ended the fragmented "Warring States" period (a time of great civil unrest and almost constant fighting in the 15th and 16th centuries) and began the more stable Tokugawa era, he's one of the most important figures in Japanese history. But when facing his own death, he noted that he didn't want anything fussy for his memorial – just a "small shrine" from which his spirit could protect the nation.

His grandson, Iemitsu, had a different opinion. Ignoring his grandfather's wishes, he decided to commission the most lavish mausoleum Japan had ever seen, a monument befitting Ieyasu's legendary status. We'll never know what Ieyasu thought of the end result, but in the centuries since his passing in 1616, Nikko Tosho-gu – his mausoleum and the spectacular shrine complex surrounding it – has become one of the country's most beloved and artistically important sights.

Tosho-gu showcases the pinnacle of 17th-century Japanese craftsmanship, with each of its buildings a work of art in its own right. While the glittering Tomei-mon (Sun Blaze Gate) and lofty, five-story pagoda are highlights, the wood carvings seen throughout the site are perhaps the most captivating (and arguably most unique) elements of the shrine. Near the entrance, one in particular catches the eye: three brightly painted monkeys, seated in the "see no evil, speak no evil, hear no evil" poses. This playful touch carries through to many other carvings, like the "imagined elephants" nearby (the artist had never seen one, and decided to give them claws) and the surprisingly sweet, domestic-looking "sleeping cat", found at the entrance to the long flight of stone steps that lead to the mausoleum.

It's at the mausoleum that Ieyasu's more restrained tastes finally win the day. Small and sombre, the tomb is shaded by mature trees and finished in a minimalist style. After the elaborate design of the shrine, this simplicity is quite moving, and provides the space to pause and contemplate Ieyasu's incredible achievements.

Once you've descended from the mausoleum and left the shrine complex, make your way to Nikko's many other shrines and temples. Together, they make up a UNESCO World Heritage site (the Shrines and Temples of Nikko), recognized for their deep cultural importance and artistic merit. Perhaps it's little wonder Iemitsu decided to go big: Ieyasu's shrine had other monuments to compete with.

— MAKE IT HAPPEN —

Nikko is located north of Tokyo. It's close enough to go on a day trip (a two-hour drive or so), but it's worth staying the night and exploring the rest of the city and the rich landscapes of the wider Oku-Nikko region.

The shrine is open every day (but best visited in the morning to avoid the crowds). Nikko Toshogu Museum, just outside the shrine complex, is also worth visiting for more context about Tokugawa Ieyasu's life and times; you can buy individual or combined tickets for the shrine and museum.

JR and Tobu trains connect Nikko and Tokyo, with trains leaving from Tobu-Asakusa, Tokyo, Ueno and Shinjuku stations in the capital. The shrine is located a 30–40 minute walk or ten-minute bus ride from Nikko's stations.

ICONIC JAPAN

Left Nikko's famous three painted monkeys
Below The intricately decorated Nikko Tosho-gu Shrine

Combine with KYOTO

Just like Nikko, Kyoto (p37) has an embarrassment of riches when it comes to UNESCO-registered shrines and temples. Both cities are easily accessible from Tokyo, with regular shinkansen and limited express train connections, so it's possible to visit both on the same trip to Japan.

ICONIC JAPAN

14

Marvel at the giants of sumo

Seeing Japan's national sport in person is a thrilling experience

Sumo is all about anticipation. Tournament days start with the lower-ranked *rikishi* (wrestlers), the crowd growing as the high-profile bouts draw closer. By mid-afternoon, camera lenses are glinting in the crowd, the air thick with excitement.

This is when the true giants of the sport make their entrance: the *makuuchi*. These top-ranked *rikishi* enter the ring in a formal procession – bare-chested, hair slicked back in a topknot, brightly coloured aprons around their waists. Details like this, which highlight sumo's centuries-long history and close ties with Japan's indigenous Shinto religion, are part of what elevates the sport from "fun to watch" to iconic. Last are the *yokozuna*, the top tier of the top tier, with their traditional ring-entering ceremony.

Finally, the matches between the *makuuchi* can start. Two wrestlers face off across the ring, intimidating each other with glances, deep squats and thunderous stamps. Occasionally, one will turn away, grab purifying salt and fling it onto the ground. Then, in a split second, they begin, charging towards each other in a violent clash of skin and muscle.

It's usually all over in seconds. One wrestler need only touch the ground with a body part other than his feet – or, more dramatically, be thrown out of the ring. The referee whips a fan to one side to indicate the victor, calling out the name of his winning move. And the crowd goes wild!

Two wrestlers competing in a sumo tournament

Combine with AKIHABARA

Tokyo's Ryogoku district is just a couple of stops from Akihabara (p198). Experience Japan's famous mix of the traditional and the hyper-modern by spending your afternoon watching the Shinto-inflected rituals of sumo, and your evening in the arcades and late-night gaming cafés of Akiba (as the locals call it).

MAKE IT HAPPEN

 There are three annual tournaments in Tokyo, at Ryogoku Kokugikan (Ryogoku district); three more alternate between Osaka, Nagoya and Fukuoka.

 Check sumo.or.jp/En for schedules and tickets. Pre-booking is advisable. The website buysumotickets.com also lists associated special events.

 Ryogoku Kokugikan, where most of the sumo tournaments take place, is close to Ryogoku station, which is reached on the JR Sobu line.

A classic tour of Japan

SUGGESTED DURATION 14 days **START** Tokyo; fly into one of the city's international airports, Narita or Haneda **GETTING AROUND** Both regular and bullet trains; ferry to and from Itsukushima **END** Hiroshima; bullet trains run from the city to Tokyo in 4–5 hours

Area of map

Taking in some of the country's best-known sights and experiences, this itinerary is perfect for first-time visitors to Japan. It travels along the length and breadth of the country's biggest island, Honshu, stopping at historic towns, modern cities and coastal ports along the way. Many visitors to Japan arrive in the capital city of Tokyo, which also happens to be the best place to start a grand tour; spend a couple of days here getting to grips with the country's rhythms before setting off. Over the course of a couple of weeks, you'll then experience all those things that make Japan iconic: strolling around atmospheric temples, sampling the freshest sushi and the tastiest ramen, gazing up at futuristic skyscrapers, not to mention the country's incredibly efficient train network. By journey's end you'll have made memories to last a lifetime.

9. HIROSHIMA
The *shinkansen* from Shin-Osaka station will whisk you to Hiroshima, a city reborn after the devastating 1945 atomic bomb *(p32)*.

8. OSAKA
A 15-minute *shinkansen* ride from Kyoto is the infectiously energetic Osaka, Japan's third-largest city. Spend the night here soaking up its neon-drenched districts and world-class food scene.

END

10. ITSUKUSHIMA
To see Japan's most iconic torii (shrine gate) take a day trip from Hiroshima to Itsukushima. It's a 25-minute JR train to Miyajimaguchi, then a 10-minute ferry to Itsukushima. Return to Hiroshima to see out your trip, perhaps with a traditional dinner of okonomiyaki.

7. KYOTO
Topping most visitors' Japan to do lists is Kyoto, once the capital and seat of the imperial family for over 1,000 years. It's reachable from Toyama in 2.5 hours (use a *shinkansen* then a JR train) and has plenty of sights to occupy at least 2–3 days *(p37)*.

2. NIKKO
It's time to leave the capital. Take a two-hour Tobu train from Asakusa to Nikko (*p46*), and spend some time (1–2 days should suffice) exploring its UNESCO-listed temples and shrines and soaking up the scenery.

6. TOYAMA
From Matsumoto, it's two hours to Toyama by JR train. Use the city as a base to explore stunning alpine landscapes, charming villages and an incredible artisan crafts scene.

3. KITAKATA
The four-hour journey (combining regular and bullet trains) from Nikko to Kitakata might be long but it's more than worth it: Kitakata has more shops serving ramen than any other city (*p30*).

4. SHIOGAMA
Hungry for more iconic food? Rise early and head to Japan's sushi capital, taking the train to Koriyama, then the *shinkansen* to Sendai and JR Tohoku main line to Shiogama. Four hours later, enjoy a late lunch at a sushi restaurant (*p45*).

5. MATSUMOTO
Seeing Matsumoto's iconic castle (*p43*) is a must, so prepare for a long journey from Shiogama. It's worth breaking the trip in Tokyo – Matsumoto is just 2.5 hours from the capital by JR train.

1. TOKYO
Japan's capital is the perfect place to start your trip. Stay here for a couple of days, exploring both the city's traditional side (like the Imperial Palace; *p31*) and its dynamic core (the Roppongi Art Triangle is recommended).

START

TIMELESS

JAPAN

As Japan speeds ahead into the future, it seems all the more remarkable just how rooted in tradition it remains. Wherever you go, you'll feel the threads binding past to present.

ON THE MAP
TIMELESS JAPAN

- **15** Take part in a tea ceremony
- **16** Immerse yourself in Ainu culture at Upopoy
- **17** Dip into Japan's indigo dyeing tradition
- **18** Discover the hidden Christian history of Nagasaki
- **19** Watch a colourful kabuki performance
- **20** Dig into Jomon life at Sannai-Maruyama
- **21** Celebrate Ryukyuan culture in Okinawa
- **22** Soak in Kinosaki Onsen's welcoming springs
- **23** Appreciate the beauty of Motonosumi Inari Taisha
- **24** Admire intricate Arita porcelain
- **25** Feed your spirit with a temple stay
- **26** Relax and recharge at a *ryokan*
- **27** Commune with the haiku master in Iga-Ueno
- **28** Get to grips with the art of woodblock prints

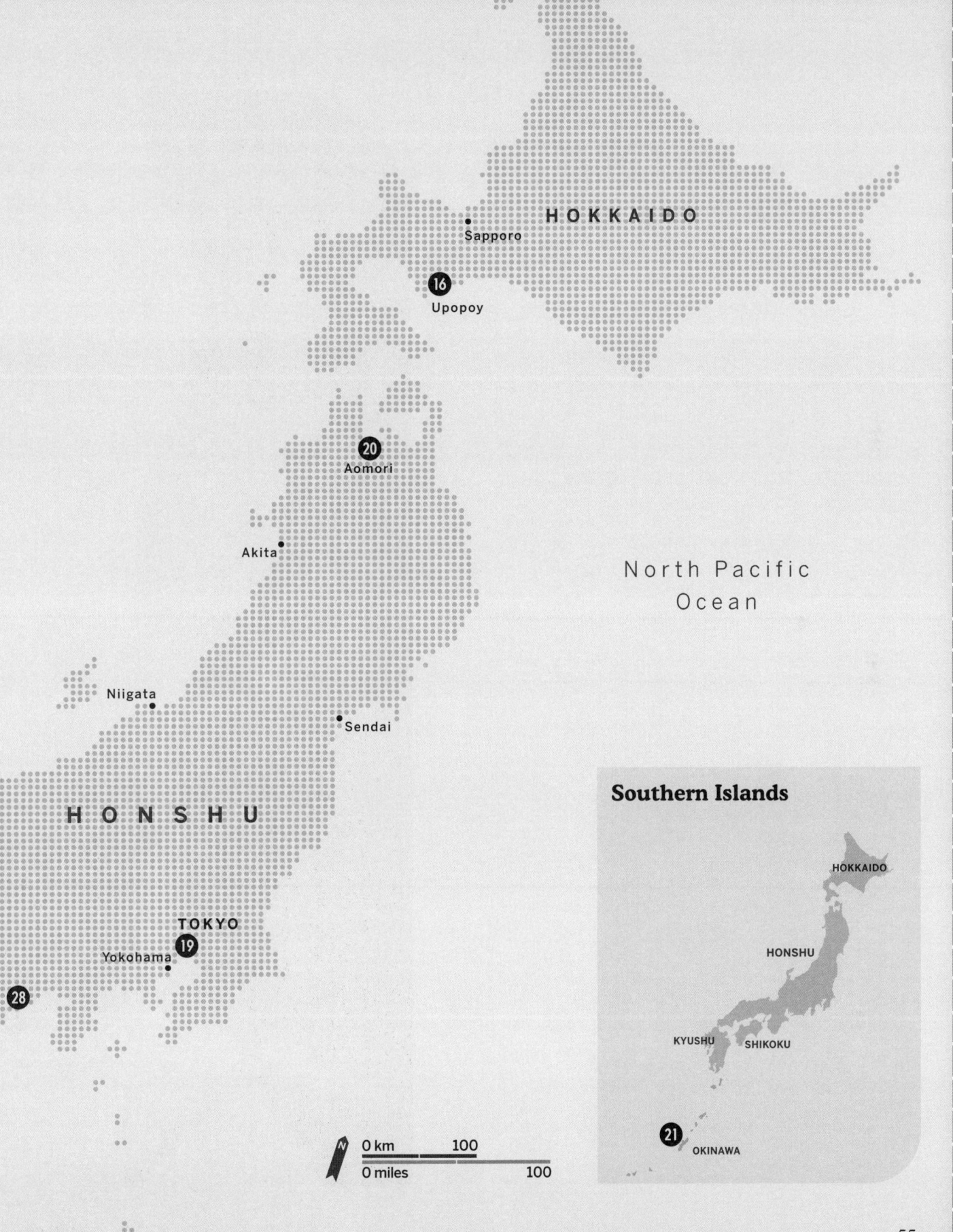

15

Take part in a tea ceremony

Chado is a celebration of Japan's refined tea culture

Japan is known for taking the everyday and elevating it to something extraordinary, and that's exactly what *chado*, or "the way of tea", does. Tea first came to Japan from China in the 9th century, and in the following centuries nobles hired tea masters to conduct private ceremonies. The principles that guide modern *chado* – simplicity and mindfulness – came to the fore in the 16th century, when the tea master Sen no Rikyu promoted a kind of ceremony rooted in the tenets of Zen Buddhism. Rikyu set the stage for the democratization of the tea ceremony, and over the centuries, it became something that everyone could enjoy.

Whether it's a four-hour or 20-minute ceremony, *chado* is a highly choreographed ritual that centres around Rikyu's teachings. There are many rules during the ceremony, but in short, it starts with a walk through the grounds (often a garden) to reach the teahouse. Once inside, the host usually serves *wagashi* (traditional Japanese sweets), then whisks powdered green tea (matcha) and hot water. The ceremony ends when every cup has been drunk.

Japan offers tea ceremonies in abundance, many taking place at traditional gardens. But to taste some of Japan's best tea while enjoying the art of *chado*, head to the city of Uji. Enjoy a ceremony at the Chazuna museum or the elegant Taiho-an teahouse, and simply let your mind clear.

MAKE IT HAPPEN

Uji is in Kyoto prefecture, south of Kyoto city. The Chazuna museum is near Uji's Keihan-line station, and Taiho-an teahouse is near the JR-line station.

Chazuna (uji-chazuna.kyoto) and Taiho-an (kyoto-uji-kankou.or.jp/taihoan-en.html) are open daily, but pre-booking is required to experience a tea ceremony.

The JR Nara line links Kyoto and Uji. Uji's Keihan-line station is connected to Chushojima station, from where you can take the train to the eastern part of Kyoto.

A host preparing tea at a tea ceremony

TIMELESS JAPAN

Chado etiquette

1

Respect the room
If your tea ceremony is in a traditional setting, you'll enjoy it sitting on tatami mats. Bring clean white socks to change into, so you don't dirty the floor, and look at the decorations (usually a scroll and flower arrangement in the alcove) before sitting down.

2

Admire the cup
When you're handed the cup, its best side will be facing you. Take a moment to admire it, then turn the cup around to drink from the other side.

3

Drink up
Eat the whole of the wagashi you're served before the tea and drink all the matcha. It's been prepared with great care, so it's considered rude to leave any.

Immerse yourself in Ainu culture at Upopoy

This fascinating national museum is dedicated to northern Japan's Indigenous people

Northerly Hokkaido, Japan's second-largest island, is famous for many things: rich dairy products, pristine powder snow and rolling farmland, to name a few. In recent years, there's been a new addition to that list: Upopoy National Ainu Museum and Park, where the region's Indigenous Ainu culture is recorded and celebrated. Of course, the culture itself is far from new. From at least the 13th century, the Ainu were the dominant cultural group in Hokkaido. They lived harmoniously with the land, drawing on the rich bounty of the island's soil and seas to make it through the icy winters. They also developed their own animistic religion with a rich pantheon of gods (*kamuy*), who traverse the border between the spirit (*kamuy mosir*) and human realms (*ainu mosir*).

From around 1600, Ainu produce like kelp and salmon, plus quality silks they'd obtained through trade with China, formed the basis of a thriving trade relationship with the Japanese, who lived on the islands to the south. Yet over the centuries, this relationship shifted. In 1869, Japan annexed Hokkaido and later pursued policies of forced assimilation. Because of this – and because many hid their ancestry to avoid discrimination – it's hard to know how many people of Ainu descent are alive today (estimates range from 15,000 to 200,000).

It wasn't until 2019 that the Japanese government officially recognized the Ainu as an Indigenous people of Japan, following decades of Ainu activism. A year later, Upopoy (named after the Ainu word for singing in a group) was opened to document Ainu culture and educate visitors to the island. Set on the wooded shores of Lake Poroto, it's now Japan's most northerly national museum. The site celebrates Ainu culture even before you step inside, with its arresting modern architecture drawing inspiration from Ainu imagery. Its top-heavy structure recalls stilted *pu* storehouses, while the geometric design around the entrance is based on the woven reed mats you'd see in any traditional Ainu home.

Inside the museum, signage is written in multiple languages – including in Ainu-itak, which UNESCO has classified as critically endangered. The engaging exhibits explore subjects including traditional clothing and everyday objects, which balance practicality (for example, treated salmon-skin snow shoes) and beauty (such as swirling wood carvings). But you're not limited to just looking at objects. Try a hands-on craft activity or watch a performance of rhythmic Ainu dance and music – a powerful way to experience this living, breathing culture for yourself.

— MAKE IT HAPPEN —

Set on the shores of Lake Poroto, Upopoy is located in the town of Shiraoi, near Noboribetsu in southern Hokkaido.

The museum is usually closed on Mondays; check the website for detailed hours and information about events and activities (*ainu-upopoy.jp/en*). Some activities and special exhibitions aren't included in the price of admission; register your interest at the venue first then purchase your extra tickets from the ticket vending machines.

Trains on the JR Hokkaido line between Hakodate and Sapporo stop at Shiraoi station, from where the museum is a few minutes' walk. If you're coming from Honshu, take the Tohoku *shinkansen* to Aomori then the Hokkaido *shinkansen* to Hakodate, before changing onto local trains. Alternatively, fly to Sapporo's New Chitose airport, then take the train.

TIMELESS JAPAN

Traditional Ainu clothing

Combine with HAKODATE

On the southern tip of Hokkaido, Hakodate is a port city that serves as the hub for rail links to Honshu via the world's deepest undersea railway tunnel (p175). Historically, the city was the trading post between the Ainu and the Japanese, with kitamaebune ("northern-bound ships") from as far afield as Osaka docking here.

TIMELESS JAPAN

17

Dip into Japan's indigo dyeing tradition

Make your own indigo-dyed fabric at a shop founded in 1580

Indigo has been a prized plant dye in Japan for centuries, but it reached its peak in the Edo period when the cultivation of cotton, easy to dye with indigo, increased. The art of *aizome* (indigo-dyeing), which combines the dried leaves of the indigo plant and clear water with other natural ingredients, flourished; soon, people from all walks of life were wearing clothing of a deep blue hue.

With the advent of chemical dyes, the craft has become less common, and only a handful of towns keep the practice going today. One such town is Gujo-Hachiman, home to its last remaining *aizome* shop, Watanabe Somemono-ten. Under the direction of a 15th-generation owner, artisans continue the shop's over four-century legacy of creating fabrics with natural indigo, which are made into beautiful blue clothes, accessories and decorative hangings. Join an *aizome* experience to learn about the skill and care that go into the craft, submerging your own cloth into dye, then binding, pressing and wrapping it to create a unique souvenir.

— MAKE IT HAPPEN —

Gujo-Hachiman is in Gifu prefecture, in central Honshu.

Book the *aizome* experience ahead (*visitgifu.com*).

Take a 90-minute bus from Nagoya to Gujo-Hachiman.

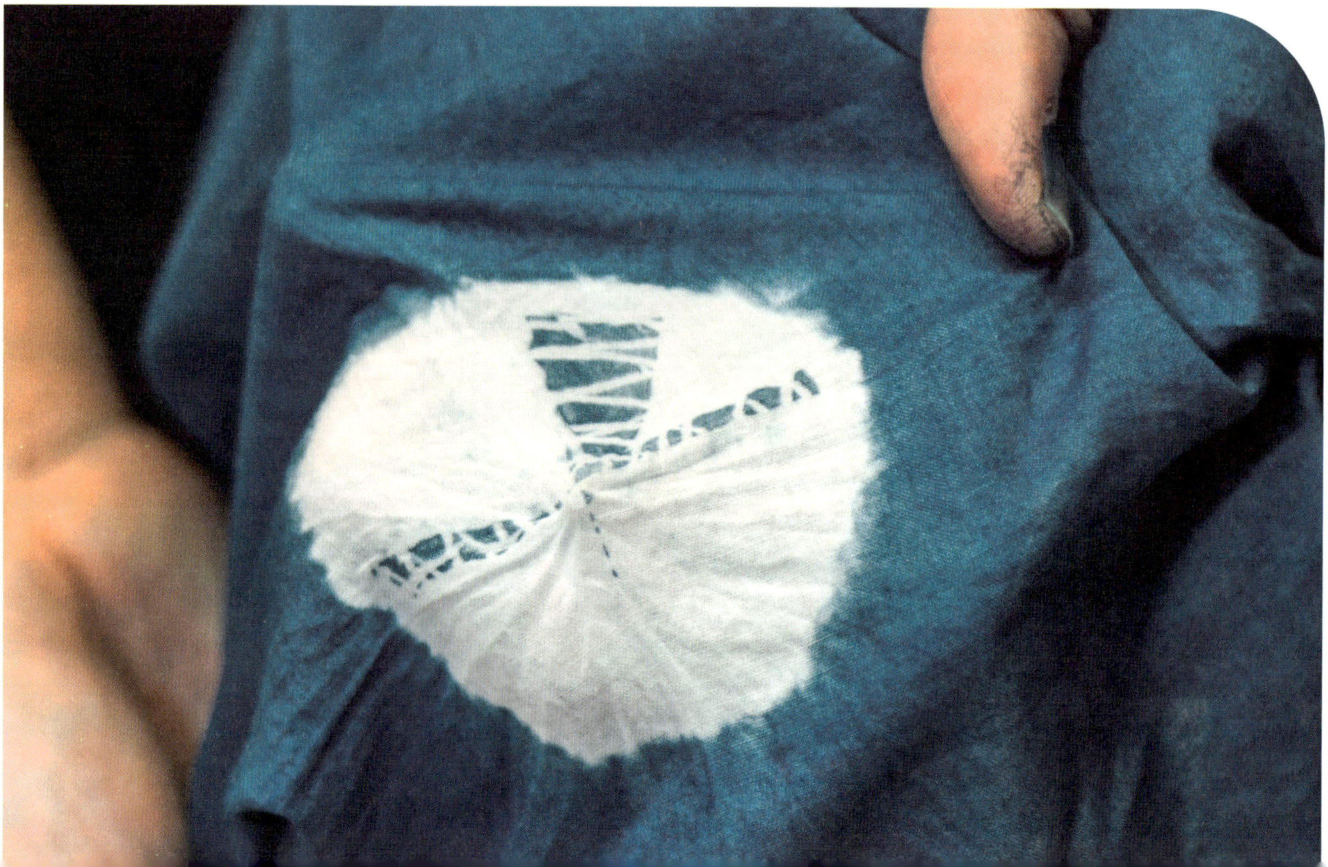

Indigo-dyed fabric

Hisaka Island's Gorin Church

> **Combine with FUKUOKA**
>
> *If you're flying from Fukuoka spend an extra night there and enjoy its street food scene (p94). The city is famous for its yatai (food stalls), many of them located at the riverside.*

18

Discover the hidden Christian history of Nagasaki

A visit to the Goto Islands combines gorgeous subtropical scenery with fascinating religious history

MAKE IT HAPPEN

The Goto Islands are located roughly 100 km (60 miles) west of Nagasaki city, off the island of Kyushu.

The islands are linked by a high-speed ferry service.

Book a ferry to the islands from Nagasaki or Sasebo, or fly to Fukue from Nagasaki or Fukuoka.

In the 16th century, Catholics' missionary zeal reached Japan. An eager few made their way here, hoping to find converts, and some were successful. But it was risky, and many of the missionaries ended up on the wrong side of the shogun. In the 17th century, Japan's government curtailed trade with the outside world – and banned Christianity. Still, in parts of Japan's far southwest, notably the subtropical Goto Islands, a few adherents continued to practise their faith in secret, protected by their remoteness. They passed down Bible stories orally, and hid or disguised Christian images; "Maria Kannon" statues present Mary as the Buddhist deity of mercy, for example. Finally, the ban was lifted in 1873, and after 250 years of hiding their faith, the *kakure kirishitan* (hidden Christians) could build churches and worship openly.

Fukue's Dozaki Church, built in 1908, has a museum about the history of Goto's Christians, so it's a great one to start with. Then, head to the four other churches from UNESCO's 2018 list of Hidden Christian Sites in the Nagasaki Region: Gorin Church on Hisaka Island; Egami Church on Naru; and Kashiragashima and Nozaki churches, best reached from Nakadori. Most are in stunning settings and, whether of grand or humble design, each church speaks to the endurance of faith and the power of hope.

TIMELESS JAPAN

19

Watch a colourful kabuki performance

Experience the most lively of classical Japanese performing arts

A man stands on stage, his face contorted into a fearsome expression. His mouth turns sharply down, his eyebrows are raised and his eyes bulge from their sockets. Dramatic make-up (lines of black and white) exaggerates his features into a mask. His shaggy rug of hair flies around as he flicks his head from side to side. With each flick, his arms move, flowing to one side and the other before stopping suddenly, each finger precisely placed. He shifts from foot to foot, at times raising one leg into a bird-like posture. Music swells – wailing flutes and a crescendo of taut drum beats. A few wooden clacks sound out and he assumes one last pose. A final note rings out, and the curtain falls: the act is over. Attend any kabuki show and this is what you can expect.

Kabuki has been around for roughly 400 years, since a shrine maiden, Izumo no Okuni, danced and sang on a dry riverbed in Kyoto, inventing a whole new artform. Not long after, the government decreed that only adult men could appear on stage, and to this day, kabuki is an almost entirely male affair. Japan is home to many historical kabuki stages, but one of the best places to get your performance fix is Tokyo's revered Kabuki-za theatre. Whether you stay for an entire performance or opt for a one-act ticket (plays are usually five acts long), you're assured of atmospheric music, sumptuous costumes and high drama.

A kabuki performance at Tokyo's Kabuki-za theatre

MAKE IT HAPPEN

 Tokyo's Kabuki-za theatre is centrally located in the swanky Ginza neighbourhood, not too far from the transport hub of Tokyo station.

 Buy single-act tickets on the day; book other types of tickets ahead (kabuki-za.co.jp). Some performances offer helpful English audio guides.

 The nearest public transport station to Kabuki-za is Higashi-Ginza; this is served by the Hibiya and Asakusa metro lines.

20

Dig into Jomon life at Sannai-Maruyama

This archaeological site and museum are a must-visit for history buffs

In 2021, Japan gained its 20th UNESCO World Cultural Heritage Site: the Jomon archaeological sites of Hokkaido and Northern Tohoku. The Jomon civilization – named for its distinctive pottery, which was decorated by pressing cords into clay – was around from 14,000 to 300 BCE. Of the 17 Jomon sites recognized by UNESCO, Sannai-Maruyama in Aomori is undoubtedly the best developed. Local knowledge of the site stretches back centuries, but it was only in the 1990s that excavation began in earnest, and archaeologists realized that they had an incredible find on their hands (or rather, under their feet) – one of the largest and most complete Jomon-period villages ever unearthed.

Today, the site contains some of the original dig sites, preserved to show the process of excavation, plus reconstructed buildings, including thatched houses; and a huge, multi-level structure, which may have been a watchtower or lighthouse. There's also a museum, which holds many objects the Jomon either made or discovered, including 2,000 clay figurines. And if all that doesn't paint a picture of what life was like during this period, eat a meal at the restaurant, which will feature Jomon-appropriate ingredients like red rice and chestnuts. However you spend your time here, you'll leave with a fascinating insight into an ancient culture.

MAKE IT HAPPEN

Sannai-Maruyama archaeological site is located in Aomori city in the broader Aomori Prefecture, found in the far north of Honshu Island.

Check hours and infrequent closures on *sannaimaruyama. pref.aomori.jp*. It gets very cold exploring the outdoor portion of the site in winter, so dress accordingly.

Take the Tohoku *shinkansen* from Tokyo to Shin-Aomori station, then take a local train to Aomori station. From here, it's a 20-minute bus ride to Sannai-Maruyama.

TIMELESS JAPAN

> **Combine with TOWADA CITY**
>
> *Also in Aomori prefecture is Towada city – less ancient, more modern. Take the shinkansen to Hachinohe then a bus ride, and you'll reach one of Japan's best contemporary art museums: Towada Art Center (p208). Explore the museum's bold pieces, then check out the artworks dotted through the city as part of a community revitalization project.*

Left Remodellings of pillar-supported buildings
Above A clay figurine displayed at the museum
Below Reconstructed dwellings

21

Celebrate Ryukyuan culture in Okinawa

From textiles to music, the subtropical archipelago's culture is rich and fascinating

The Okinawan archipelago has a long, proud history. The Ryukyu Islands united to form the Ryukyu Kingdom in the 15th century, and trade with surrounding nations such as China and Korea enriched the local culture. From the 17th to the 19th centuries, the Ryukyu Islands were a vassal state of the Japanese Shimazu clan, but they retained their own monarchy, language and way of life. In the 1800s, Japan annexed the islands, forcing the Ryukyuan people to assimilate and renaming the archipelago Okinawa.

Though the assimilation policy – and the loss of around a third of the local population in World War II – means that much of the Ryukyuan people's traditional culture has been lost, there are robust efforts to keep what remains alive. Not far from the Okinawan capital, Naha, you'll find Ryukyu-mura (Ryukyu Village), an open-air museum containing several farmhouses brought from the islands. Here, artisans work on local crafts such as vibrant *bingata* textiles and fearsome *shiisa* figurines, prepare traditional foods, and perform Eisa dances and music. Visit Okinawa in late summer and you can join in the fun at the raucous Eisa Matsuri (festival), during which the lively, rhythmic Eisa folk dance – traditionally performed by young people and intended to pay tribute to the performers' ancestors – takes over the streets.

MAKE IT HAPPEN

 Okinawa is a group of subtropical islands in Japan's far south. Ryukyu-mura is on the west coast of Okinawa Honto, the archipelago's main island.

 There's an entry fee for Ryukyu-mura, but there is no need to pre-book tickets. Check for irregular closures and details of events on the website (*ryukyumura.co.jp*).

 There are frequent flights to Naha, the capital of Okinawa, and regular ferries. From Naha, the best way to reach Ryukyu-mura is by bus.

Eisa drummers and dancers performing at Ryukyu-mura

TIMELESS JAPAN

Combine with OKINAWAN CUISINE

Okinawa has a disproportionately high number of centenarians, and it seems that the traditional Okinawan diet (p98) is part of the reason. While you're on the islands, be sure to try local delicacies like goya (bitter melon), umi budo ("sea grapes", seaweed with a caviar-like texture) and fresh fish.

Soak in Kinosaki Onsen's welcoming springs

Immerse yourself in Japan's refined hot-spring bathing culture in a scenic town

A cicada buzzes lazily in the still evening air. A couple in *yukata* (robes) emerge from a café, pushing aside the hanging *noren* (curtain) as they leave. Steam drifts from behind a tiled roof, dissipating above a shrine. And a group of friends approaches a bathhouse, the tick-tocking sound of their *geta* (wooden sandals) on the street punctuating the quiet scene. It's a typical night in Kinosaki Onsen, one of Japan's most enjoyable *onsen* (hot spring) towns.

Like all such resorts, the town of Kinosaki Onsen grew up around its mineral-rich, geothermally heated waters. People have been bathing in those waters for as long as they've been there, developing a culture that celebrates the health, relaxation and even social benefits of bathing. In Kinosaki, the spring feeds an impressive seven public baths, all of which welcome tattooed guests – a rarity in Japan. It's also notable for its especially scenic townscape, crisscrossed by canals lined with willow and cherry trees, and for its unusual approach to the "resort" idea.

The tourism-oriented businesses work together to create a sort of town-wide *ryokan* (traditional Japanese inn): all the facilities guests could want are spread out, so rather than just one or two hotel owners benefitting, the whole town does. They encourage "hot spring hopping", so guests visit different parts of Kinosaki and see the variety of shops and cafés (most businesses close over dinnertime, then reopen for the evening bath rush). The needs of people living in Kinosaki are considered, too – for instance, the hotels don't offer private, in-room *onsen*, so as not to deplete the spring.

The spring around which the town grew is said to have been discovered 1,300 years ago. The monk Dochi Shonin sat in prayer for 1,000 days, after which a healing spring burst forth, allegedly on the site of the still-operating public bath, Mandara-yu. Onsen-ji, the Shingon Buddhist temple Dochi Shonin founded, keeps watch over the town from the mountainside, and is still the focus of the community. Because of the sacred origins of Kinosaki's waters, the town baths prefer not to artificially cool them. You'll feel the effects as you go *onsen*-hopping – Yasugi-yu is known to have the hottest water (often over 40°C/104°F), but they all get the blood flowing.

Everyone has their favourite *onsen*, so what will be yours? Luckily, you don't have to choose. Beyond relaxing in Gosho-no-yu's *rotemburo* (outdoor bath) and enjoying Ko-no-yu's quiet surroundings, there's joy to be had in making the most of what the town has to offer. Walking between the baths and *ryokan*, stopping at restaurants, artisan workshops and meditation classes as you go, is part of the experience. So stroll around town in your *yukata* and see where the evening takes you.

— MAKE IT HAPPEN —

The town of Kinosaki Onsen is near Toyooka City, in western Honshu's Hyogo prefecture.

If you're staying at a *ryokan* in Kinosaki, you'll receive a free pass to all seven baths. For those not staying here, you'll have to purchase a ticket for each *onsen*; this can be done via the front desks or vending machines at each *onsen*. The town also has an English-speaking tourist information point, located in front of Kinosaki Onsen station; the staff here can help with booking workshops, tours and classes, and also offer information on transport.

You can access Kinosaki Onsen by JR San'in main line train from Kyoto or Osaka, which takes around 2.5 hours. You can use your JR Pass or a JR West Rail Pass to reach Kinosaki, and seats should be reserved in advance. It's also easy to reach the town via Zentan Bus, the main local bus service that operates in and around the town, from Osaka or Kobe.

Right One of the town's many hot springs
Left Strolling through the town of Kinosaki Onsen in *yukata*
Below The scenic town

Three golden rules of onsen

············ 1 ············

Baths are enjoyed naked
You wouldn't wear swimwear to bathe at home, and you don't at an onsen. If you have tattoos, they will of course be visible at the baths, so check the onsen's policy – tattoos may be fine, allowed if covered with an adhesive seal, or outright banned.

············ 2 ············

The water stays clean
It's not just swimwear that stays out of the water – it's everything but your body. Shower first, and rinse off all soap and shampoo; if your hair is long, put it up; and either put your small towel aside or on top of your head.

············ 3 ············

It's a bath, not a pool
Onsen are for relaxing and healing, so don't splash, swim or shout. Just soak, rinse, soak again, and enjoy the benefits.

23

Appreciate the beauty of Motonosumi Inari Taisha

Visit one of Japan's most beautifully located shrines, with 123 red torii

When you enter a Shinto shrine in Japan, you'll always pass through a torii (gate). But some shrines don't stick to just one or two torii. They have dozens, even hundreds, mostly painted a bright, orange-red vermilion. The vermilion gates are typical of shrines dedicated to the mischievous Inari fox spirit. Originally linked to rice and sake, the spirit's symbolic domain now includes agriculture, fishing, fertility, and general success and wellbeing.

While Kyoto's Fushimi Inari, with its 10,000 gates, is doubtless the most famous example, there's no beating Nagato's Motonosumi Inari Taisha when it comes to location. Its 123 bright red torii snake along a clifftop path, creating a dramatic contrast with the sea below. Motonosumi Inari Taisha was established in 1955, after an Inari is said to have appeared to a local fisherman and told him to build a shrine here. If you're hoping to receive the Inari's blessing yourself, try your luck with the shrine's unusual *saisenbako* (offertory box); it's fixed to the top of a torii, so you'll need to throw your five-yen coin (deemed lucky, *p36*) 5 m (16 ft) into the air to make your wish. Whether or not you get your coin into the box, simply being here – and soaking up the beautiful views – is reason enough to count yourself lucky.

MAKE IT HAPPEN

 The shrine is in a fairly remote location in Nagato, northern Yamaguchi prefecture, in far southwestern Honshu. It's 40 km (25 miles) west of the castle town of Hagi.

 Given the remote location, it's wise to bring snacks. Stock up at the station or head to Senzaki's Senzakitchen roadside station, two stops east on the JR San'in line.

 The nearest *shinkansen* stop is Asa. Take the JR Mine line from there to Nagatoshi, then JR San'in line to Nagato-Furuichi, and a taxi to the shrine.

The red torii gates of Motonosumi Inari Taisha

TIMELESS JAPAN

A beautifully detailed piece of Arita porcelain

Combine with FUKUOKA

Arita-ware was cutting-edge technology when it was created – a meeting of nature, science and artistic sensibility. To experience where art and technology meet today, explore the interactive, immersive digital world of teamLab Forest in Fukuoka (p151).

24

Admire intricate Arita porcelain

Pick up some high-quality local souvenirs in Arita, or make your own unique pieces

Japan has dozens of centuries-old local pottery traditions, from the iron-rich reds of Okayama's Bizen-ware to Kutani-ware's riot of colours. But Arita-ware is probably the best known, prized for its translucent lightness, durability and delicately painted blue designs. Also known as Imari-yaki, it was the first porcelain made in Japan. In around 1600, masters of complex techniques such as coloured overglazing were forcibly brought from Korea to Japan to share their skills, leading to the development of Arita porcelain.

The town of Arita, in Kyushu, developed into a centre of production, and Imari-yaki is still its most famous product by far. To explore its wares, visit any one of the dozens of specialist shops here, looking out in particular for blue-and-white floral patterns. If you're in town during Golden Week, spend time at the Arita Ceramics Fair; at any other time, add some adrenaline to your shopping experience with Kouraku Kiln's Treasure Hunting experience – one warehouse, one flat fee and 90 minutes. Whatever fits in your basket is yours to keep.

Arita is also a great place to try making pottery. Classes are offered by many studios such as Rokuro-za, which provides English-language instruction and international shipping. Arita-ware made with your own hands? That's something to be proud of.

— MAKE IT HAPPEN —

Arita is on the southern island of Kyushu, in the western Saga province.

There's no need to pre-book Kouraku Kiln Treasure Hunting (kourakukiln.com).

Fly into Kyushu's city of Fukuoka from Tokyo or Osaka, then take a JR local or limited express train to Arita.

Feed your spirit with a temple stay

Even a short time in a Zen temple can be restorative and insightful

The life of a Zen monk is simple but rigorous. Zen is a branch of Buddhism that became established in Japan around the 12th century and found favour with its samurai leaders due, in no small part, to its focus on discipline as a path to awakening. For monks, this path is paved with *zazen* (seated meditation), chanting, work and chores, in the belief that approaching any activity diligently, even the most mundane, can cultivate mindfulness.

Intrigued? Many temples offer *shukubo* (temple stays), so visitors can benefit from these practices too. One of Japan's best temple stays takes place at Eihei-ji, a sprawling temple complex founded in the 13th century by legendary monk Dogen.

On Eihei-ji's overnight Sanzen programme, bed down in communal accommodation, sit *zazen* several times, eat only *shojin-ryori* (Buddhist vegetarian cuisine) and wake up before 4am. But if you're not quite up to the physical privations, you can book a stay at the Hakujukan, an affiliated hotel nearby. Here you'll get a private room, *nihonshu* (sake) with your *shojin-ryori* and a lie-in, but also the option to join the temple's morning service and try spiritual practices like *zazen* and copying out Buddhist sutras.

Many visitors find *shukubo* fulfilling – being welcomed into a spiritual practice feels profound. It also serves as a reminder to slow down and pay attention to the spiritual foundations of Japanese society.

— MAKE IT HAPPEN —

Eihei-ji is in central Honshu's Fukui prefecture, in the mountains near Fukui City.

If staying at the Hakujukan, book any experiences at the temple slightly in advance. Eihei-ji is a working temple, so be respectful.

Get a train from Osaka or Kyoto to Fukui station, then take a 30-minute bus to Eihei-ji.

The working temple of Eihei-ji

Relax and recharge at a ryokan

The spirit of Japanese hospitality runs through these traditional inns

If travel in Japan is defined by one thing, it's *omotenashi*. This principle, which is at the core of traditional Japanese hospitality, has a deceptively simple translation – roughly, "welcoming guests". But layers of meaning have accrued over the centuries, so *omotenashi* today implies a no-less-than laser focus on the guest's comfort, continuous attention to their needs and a whole-hearted willingness to work hard for them. The culture of *omotenashi* runs so deep that you'll see it in all kinds of settings, both modern and traditional. But to fully immerse yourself in *omotenashi*, there's nothing better than a stay in a ryokan. These traditional Japanese inns live and breathe the concept, with everything specifically designed for the guests' experience.

Unlike in typical Western high-end hotels, relaxing at a ryokan isn't about doing whatever you want, whenever you want – dinner is at a set time, for instance, and breakfast usually finishes at a single-figure hour. Instead, it's about trusting the ryokan to know what will replenish you, body and soul. After all, many of these inns have had a lot of time to figure it out. Founded in 718 CE, Hoshi Ryokan (in Awazu Onsen) is both one of the world's oldest hotels and the world's oldest business continually run by the same family. As you'd expect from so many years of practice, the staff at Hoshi Ryokan know exactly how to help guests recharge. Rather than offering every facility under the sun, they focus on what makes them special: mineral-rich hot springs, exquisite seasonal Japanese food and meticulously maintained gardens. It's simple, but wholly effective.

As at other top-tier *ryokan*, much of the service at Hoshi is designed to go unseen – return from dinner, and you'll find your futon bed laid out on the tatami floor and the lights dimmed, as though by magic. But even in these invisible actions, the staff's warmth and attention to detail shines through. Overseas visitors can be mystified by some aspects of the *ryokan* experience, but having friendly staff on hand to answer your questions (do I wear my yukata to dinner? Should I bring a towel to the *onsen*?) makes it easier to sink into the experience, and let the beautiful surroundings soothe your spirits.

While Hoshi Ryokan is one of the most highly regarded *ryokan* in Japan, there are plenty of these traditional inns dotted around the country, each offering their own perks. Many are expensive (the indulgence is undoubtedly worth it), but there are budget varieties, too. And while these may lack some of the frills seen in pricier options, the service is always second to none – and that, in the end, is what *omotenashi* is all about.

MAKE IT HAPPEN

Hoshi Ryokan is in Awazu Onsen, Ishikawa prefecture, located down the coast from Kanazawa. Awazu is one of four hot-spring villages in the resort town of Kaga Onsen.

To book a stay at Hoshi Ryokan, reserve a room via the *ryokan*'s website (ho-shi.co.jp). Though Hoshi does, many *ryokan* don't have websites, so you'll usually need to make a reservation by phone or through a travel agent. If you have tattoos and are staying at a *ryokan* with hot springs, always check in advance whether you can use the baths, and if so, whether you'll need to cover your tattoos with adhesive patches.

The four Kaga Onsen villages are connected by the Can Bus network. Awazu Onsen is accessible by Can Bus from Kaga Onsen, a stop on the Hokuriku *shinkansen* line. There are also taxis and some buses from Awazu, a stop on the IR Ishikawa train line.

TIMELESS JAPAN

Combine with EIHEI-JI

To experience a different side of Japanese hospitality, join the Zen Buddhist monks at Eihei-ji (p73) for a shukubo (temple stay). The temple is accessible from Fukui, a stop on the Hokuriku shinkansen line not far from Kaga Onsen.

Above left A cup of green tea
Above right Scenic surrounds of Hoshi Ryokan
Left Beautiful views from a traditional *ryokan*

A bedroom overlooking gardens in a traditional *ryokan*

"Basho remained a humble man who lived a simple life, often travelling the country on foot."

27

Commune with the haiku master in Iga-Ueno

Matsuo Basho's hometown is full of places to learn more about the man and his art

The old pond;
A frog jumps in —
The sound of the water.

This poem, probably the world's most famous haiku, neatly illustrates the form's key characteristics: brevity, references to nature and seasonality, and a blend of sensitivity and humour. In Japanese it has 17 syllables, as is the tradition for haiku. Written by Matsuo Basho (with the translation above by Robert Aitken), the poem was a hit as soon as it was published in 1686. Despite being famous for his *hokku* (now called haiku) and *renku* (witty, collaborative linked verses), Basho remained a humble man who lived a simple life, often travelling the country on foot, writing as he went.

You can gain an insight into Basho's formative years in Iga-Ueno, his hometown. Basho's Birth House contains the room in which he composed his first verse; the Basho Memorial Museum has texts and maps linked to his work; and the small house of Minomushi-an is preserved as it was when he used it as a retreat. Basho remained startlingly prolific until his death in 1694 – and, of course, he left with a poem: *on a journey, ailing / my dreams go wandering / on a withered moor.*

The house of Minomushi-an in Iga Ueno

MAKE IT HAPPEN

 The city of Iga-Ueno is located in Mie prefecture, in the southern part of Honshu between Tokyo and Kyoto.

 You can buy a joint ticket for Minomushi-an, the Basho Birth House and the Basho Memorial Museum (*basho-bp.jp*).

 Take a JR train from Kyoto, Osaka, Nara or Nagoya to Iga-Ueno, then take a short trip to Ueno-shi station on the Iga Railway.

TIMELESS JAPAN

> "Painted for the people, ukiyo-e often captured everyday scenes and lively characters."

Above Transferring a colour image to a woodblock
Left Green colourant used in printing
Right Yoshiwara, from Utagawa Hiroshige's *Fifty-three Stations* series

28

Get to grips with the art of woodblock prints

Discover the history and craft of this popular art form in Shizuoka

When you think of Japanese art, chances are you're picturing ukiyo-e. Literally meaning "pictures of the floating world", these woodblock prints were hugely popular in Japan from the 17th to 19th centuries. Though many – including Hokusai's famous *The Great Wave off Kanagawa* – are now on display in world-class art galleries, ukiyo-e were originally developed as accessible and affordable pieces of mass media. Painted for the people, they often captured every-day scenes and lively characters common in Japanese culture. In-demand geisha, famous Kabuki theatre stars, top-class sumo wrestlers and stylish *oiran* (court-esans) were perennially popular subjects. And just as penny dreadfuls and pulp novels sold by the boatload in Europe and the US, so did woodblock depictions of erotic scenes and scary stories in Edo-era Japan.

The best place to learn about the history and styles of ukiyo-e is the Tokaido Hiroshige Museum of Art, in the city of Shizuoka. Named after one of the last great masters of the art, Utagawa Hiroshige, the museum hosts a significant collection of his work. Rather than the more lurid subjects chosen by many ukiyo-e artists, Hiroshige preferred to capture natural landscapes through fine lines and the subtle use of colour. The beautiful gradations of colour he achieved in pieces like *The Plum Garden of Kameido* (a piece that was a major influence for Vincent Van Gogh) highlight Hiroshige's dedication to his craft – the process to achieve this colour gradation (the *bokashi* technique) was incredibly labour-intensive and involved painting a precise wash of colour by hand for every single print.

It's a process that's best left to the masters, but you can still try out simpler ukiyo-e techniques at the museum and create your very own colourful prints. Hiroshige isn't the only artist represented here, either. Works by numerous ukiyo-e creators are on display, with explanations of the nifty optical tricks, visual puns and political commentary you can find in some of the pieces.

The museum is located on the Tokaido, the Kyoto–Tokyo route travelled by every-one from merchants to warlords in the Edo era. Hiroshige is best-known for depicting the post towns along the route in his *Fifty-three Stations of the Tokaido* series, and you can still see some of the scenes he painted today. It's well worth stopping at Mariko, the 20th station, to eat some *tororo-jiru* (grated yam served over barley rice) at Choji-ya – you'll recognize the restaurant from Hiroshige's print; it still looks just like it did when he painted it.

—MAKE IT HAPPEN—

The museum is located just north of Shizuoka city, along the coast southwest of Tokyo. The post town of Mariko is just southwest of Shizuoka, across the Abe River.

There's no need to pre-book tickets for the Tokaido Hiroshige Museum of Art; check the website (*tokaido-hiroshige.jp*) for hours and entry fees. The same applies to the Choji-ya restaurant (*chojiya.info*). If you'd like to walk part of the Tokaido route, try the short but scenic stretch from Mariko to Okabe (a former post town).

Shizuoka is connected to Tokyo and Kyoto by the Tokaido *shinkansen* line (the journey from Tokyo to Shizuoka takes just over an hour). The museum is then a 25-minute walk from Yui station, a few stops from Shizuoka on the regular JR Tokaido line.

A journey through traditional Japan

SUGGESTED DURATION 10 days **START** Kyoto, a 4–5 hour *shinkansen* from Tokyo **GETTING AROUND** Use regular and bullet trains **END** Tono; JR trains link it to the closest major airport, Hanamaki-kuko (flights go to Osaka, Fukuoka, Nagoya and Sapporo), as well as Shin-Hanamaki station, where a *shinkansen* goes to Tokyo

Area of map

One of the most intriguing aspects of Japanese culture is its preservation of centuries old traditions – the tea ceremony, the ritual of the *onsen* and so on – and that's exactly what this itinerary explores. The tour, all of which can be completed by rail *(p16)*, kicks off in Kyoto, that ancient capital, then ventures from Honshu's southwest up to its northeast, stopping off at hot-spring towns and ancient capitals, dramatic coastlines and rural idylls. In each of the route's destinations, you'll have the chance to experience aspects of Japan's traditional culture, from famed literary locations to artisanal craft workshops. In the end, you'll be left with a real sense of how tradition is not only surviving but evolving in modern Japan.

2. KINOSAKI ONSEN
It's a 2.5-hour train ride from Kyoto to Kinosaki Onsen, a renowned hot spring town *(p68)*. Book into a *ryokan* and hop between *onsen*, cafés and meditation classes before bedding down for a restful night.

1. KYOTO
What better way to start your tour than in Kyoto, Japan's old imperial capital, where scores of the country's famous monuments are preserved. Try a weaving workshop, visit Zen gardens or experience a geisha show.

START

3. UJI
Fully rested, return to Kyoto then take a day trip to Uji *(p56)*, a town famous for its tea. Enjoy a tea ceremony, then it's back to Kyoto (via a 20-minute train).

5. ATAMI
After spending the night in Shizuoka, make your way to Atami in the Izu peninsula via a 30-minute *shinkansen*. Book into another *ryokan* here and spend the day dipping into the MOA Museum of Art, Atami Castle and the city's hot springs.

6. KAMAKURA
Next stop is Kamakura, a 1.5-hour JR train away from Atami (with a change in Ofuna). Admire traditional Japanese garden design at Zuisen-ji and delve into the city's crafts scene – Kamakura is known for its lacquerware. Then it's on to Tokyo.

9. TONO
Another JR train whisks you away to your final stop Tono, via Hanamaki, in two hours. Immerse yourself in atmospheric folk tales and learn about *mingei* (folk crafts) in the Tono Valley's (p90) rural surroundings.

8. HIRAIZUMI
Journey to Hiraizumi (around three hours from Tokyo) to see the town – with fine temples, gardens and archaeological sites – that inspired the iconic Matsuo Basho (p79) to write haiku in the 17th century.

4. HAMAMATSU AND SHIZUOKA
From Kyoto, board a 1.5-hour *shinkansen* to Hamamatsu for a *chusen-zome* dyeing workshop. In the afternoon, take a 30-minute *shinkansen* to Shizuoka to learn about woodblock prints (p81).

7. TOKYO
After a restful sleep, spend a couple of days seeking out the city's traditional corners. Try your hand at arts like calligraphy, watch kabuki theatre (p63), and see where traditional and contemporary aesthetics meet at spots like the Nezu Museum.

CULINARY

JAPAN

Fresh sushi, hearty ramen, fine cuts of wagyu beef: Japan is the ultimate foodie destination. And that's not forgetting the drinks, from flavourful sake to ceremonial green tea. Get ready to indulge.

ON THE MAP
CULINARY JAPAN

- **29** Eat like a Buddhist monk with *shojin-ryori*
- **30** Enjoy fairy tales and farm-fresh food in Tono
- **31** Sample the goods in a *depachika*
- **32** Take a *wagashi*-making class
- **33** Tuck into street food at a *yatai*
- **34** Aim for a hundred with Okinawan cuisine
- **35** Try the three great noodles of Morioka
- **36** Sip sake in Niigata
- **37** Indulge in a multi-course *kaiseki* meal
- **38** Splash out on succulent wagyu
- **39** Browse Kyoto's beloved Nishiki Market
- **40** Drink 'til the small hours in *izakaya* and *yokocho*

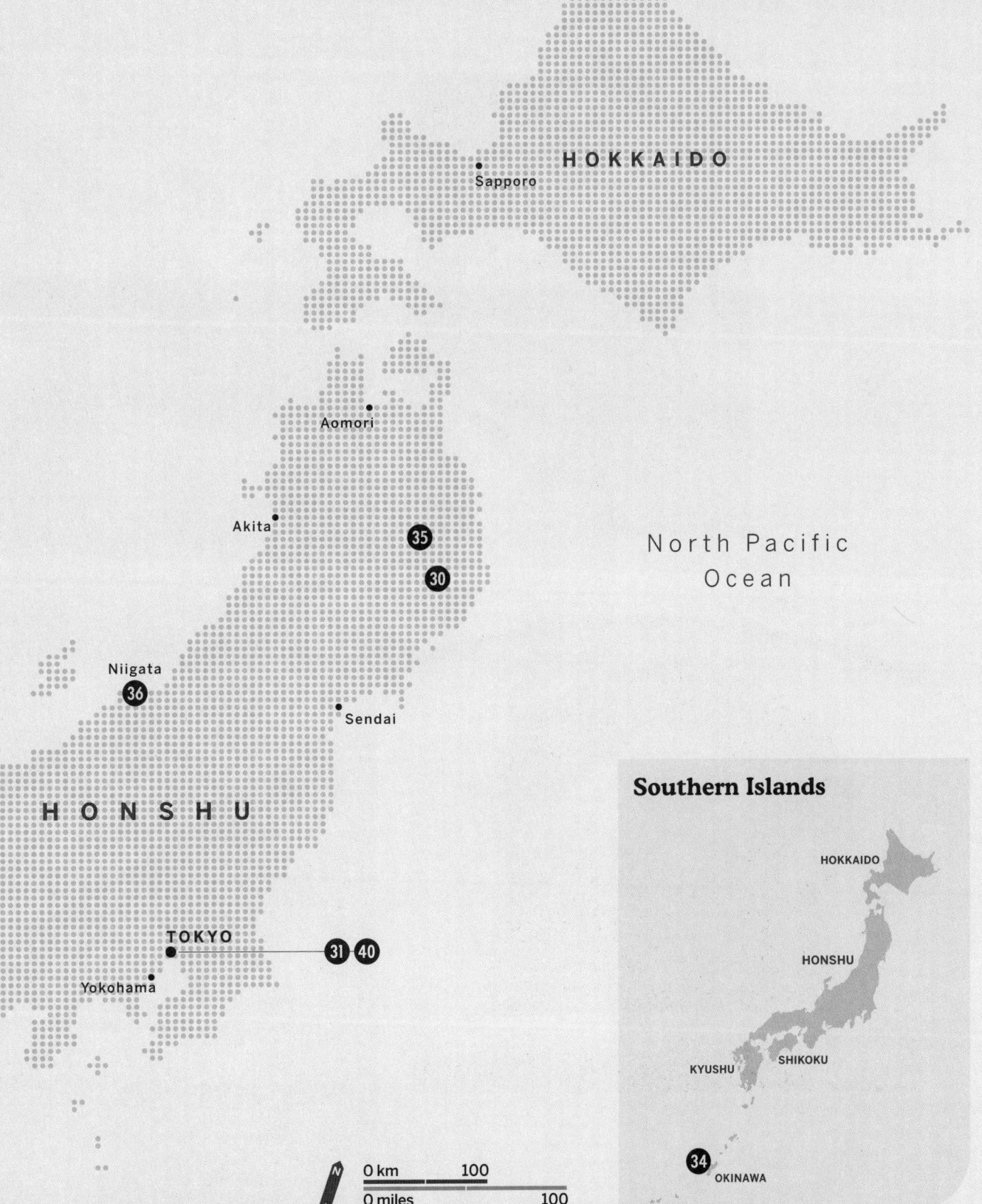

CULINARY JAPAN

Top A *shojin-ryori* dish
Bottom Sesame tofu
Right Delicately plated *shojin-ryori* at Kakusho

Eat like a Buddhist monk with shojin-ryori

Takayama is a great place to sample this ancient yet inventive cuisine

Takayama's over 200-year-old Kakusho restaurant calls *shojin-ryori* the ultimate slow food, reflecting the "spirit-progressing" cuisine's focus on seasonality, mindfulness and minimizing waste. Set in a traditional house and gardens near the picturesque temple-filled neighbourhood of Higashiyama Teramachi, it's an atmospheric place to try *shojin-ryori*, under the watchful eye of the restaurant's 12th-generation owner and head chef.

Though Kakusho's specific form of *shojin-ryori* derives from *chado* (p56), *shojin-ryori* in general came from Zen Buddhism, which became well established in Japan from the 12th century and prohibits monks from eating meat or fish. Zen grew popular with the ruling samurai class, so the temples gained power and resources, and developed a highly refined plant-based cuisine. Along with classic dishes like *goma-dofu* (sesame tofu), vegetable tempura and *nasu dengaku* (aubergine with a sweet-salty miso glaze), there are also creative faux-meat dishes *(modoki ryori)* such as *unaju* (a sweet potato-based alternative to *unagi*). Whether it's a simple lunch in a temple or an elaborate multi-course meal at a restaurant like Kakusho, trying *shojin-ryori* will give you a taste of Japan's spiritual past and present.

MAKE IT HAPPEN

 The town of Takayama is located in the mountainous Hida region of the Gifu prefecture, near the Japan Alps (the name Takayama means "tall mountain").

 Try *shojin-ryori* at restaurants and temples throughout Japan. Takayama's Kakusho *(kakusyo.com)* has both lunch and dinner sets; make a reservation ahead.

 The JR Takayama railway line connects Takayama with Toyama and Nagoya, from both of which you can catch the Tokaido *shinkansen* to Tokyo.

30

Enjoy fairy tales and farm-fresh food in Tono

Experience true farm-to-table eating in this mysterious rural corner of Japan

The Tono Valley is a curious place. At first glance, it's a normal area of Japanese countryside, its uneven patchwork of fields punctuated by small clusters of houses. But look more closely, and you'll start to spot unusual things, such as statues of turtle-like humanoid creatures with a shallow depression on top of their heads. These are *kappa*, a well-known creature from Tono's rich and varied local legends. Most famously chronicled in folklorist Yanagita Kunio's *The Legends of Tono* collection (1910), Tono's tales served both to relay knowledge (amphibious *kappa* are said to eat children, a warning to kids to avoid deep water) and to pass the long, dark evenings when snow fell thick and fast. It's easy to imagine how they developed: surrounded by the mountains of northeastern Honshu, Tono feels remote and apart from the rest of Japan – a world in need of another lore entirely.

While there are some fascinating folk museums and villages offering insight into the area's history and traditional ways of life (such as the well-preserved Furusato Village), perhaps the best way to immerse yourself in Tono's culture is by visiting a farm, and ideally staying overnight. Agriturismo Omori-ke, just north of the main town, is one of the most popular small farms open to visitors. Here, guests can join the family in picking vegetables and fruits from the fields by the house, then cooking them up in the home kitchen and sharing the meal together with other guests. The methodical work of picking peppers, tomatoes and corn will give you a glimpse into the daily life of generations of Tono farmers, and your dinner will taste even better with the knowledge that you contributed so directly to it. While menus are seasonal depending on the harvest, guests can expect delicious dishes like *hittsumi* (a warming noodle soup), fiery padrón pepper green curry and plenty more home-grown vegetables cooked in a variety of ways. And for dessert, there's refreshing ice cream, homemade using the fruit you harvested earlier in the day.

Once satiated, there's no better way to end the day than by sharing stories over some sake or homemade tomato juice. Your hosts may even regale you with a few Tono tales of tricksy shape-shifters, terrifying monsters and roaming shamans, too. And don't worry if you hear scampering feet and mischievous giggles overhead – that'll just be a *zashiki-warashi*, a cheeky child spirit that brings good luck to a house. After all, in the Tono valley the spirit world is never far away…

— MAKE IT HAPPEN —

The Tono Valley is located inland of the east coast in the Tohoku region, north of Sendai and Hiraizumi but south of Morioka.

Omori-ke *(en.stayjapan. com/area/iwate/tono/pr/767)* offers overnight stays, plus agriculture and cooking experiences. In the winter season, planting and harvesting fruits and vegetables is replaced with an *ikkanbari* (lacquered paper and bamboo) craft experience.

The Tohoku *shinkansen* between Aomori and Tokyo stops at Shin-Hanamaki, from where you can take the JR Kamaishi line to Tono. As it's a rural area, the attractions are quite spread out. There are some buses, but it's a rewarding area to explore by bike or e-bike – you can hire one at the tourist office or rental shops near the station.

CULINARY JAPAN

"Here, guests can join the family in picking vegetables and fruits from the fields by the home."

Harvesting tomatoes in Tono

CULINARY JAPAN

31

Sample the goods in a depachika

Food halls in department stores are great places to try high-end food

Japan does food well – and not just Japanese food. As you explore the country, you'll encounter a huge array of cuisines, some adapted to local tastes and others so authentic you may wonder if you've somehow left the country altogether. This dizzying amount of choice can be stressful – after all, it's just not possible to try everything. That's where *depato* (department store) food halls come in. Usually sprawling across an entire basement floor – hence the nickname *depachika*, a portmanteau of *depato* and the word for underground – they have everything from delicate fruit tarts to fresh-baked, crusty French bread and eye-wateringly expensive melons, beribboned and ready to be gifted. Best of all, a lot of the counters offer tasty samples, ideal for trying lots of different cuisines and dishes.

For one of the best, look no further than Tokyo's Daimaru. First of all, it's a huge space, with glass cabinets bursting with every food imaginable. It's also conveniently connected to Tokyo Station, and bucks the trend by having a ground-floor food hall as well as basement – meaning quicker access to the trains after you've picked up food for the journey (and likely snacked on too many samples).

— MAKE IT HAPPEN —

Daimaru is attached to Tokyo station, near Yaesu North Exit.

Tokyo station is a maze, so be sure to get your bearings first if you plan to catch a specific train after visiting Daimaru.

Tokyo station is connected to several train lines, including the cross-country *shinkansen*.

Combine with NISHIKI MARKET

Also heading to Kyoto on your tour of the country? Pay a visit to Nishiki Market in downtown Kyoto (p107) for more epic snacks. This venerable covered shopping street sells plenty of traditional foods, including kyo-tsukemono (lightly salted pickles), plus modern treats like soy doughnuts.

Delicatessen booth at Tokyo's Daimaru

A delicately sculpted work of *wagashi*

32

Take a *wagashi*-making class

Try your hand at making Japan's traditional sweets in historic Kanazawa

— MAKE IT HAPPEN —

Kanazawa is the prefectural capital of Ishikawa, on the coast near the Japan Alps.

There are several classes available in central Kanazawa, for example at the Ishikawa Local Products Centre (*kanazawa-kankou.jp/en*).

Kanazawa is on the Hokuriku *shinkansen* line between Tokyo and Tsuruga.

Wagashi are works of edible art. Carefully sculpted traditional sweets, typically served during tea ceremonies, these Japanese confectioneries come in all shapes and sizes. Some are akin to jewels, with deep colours and a glossy shine. Others re-create natural scenes in miniature, maybe a red and orange maple leaf or a koi carp swimming through clear blue waters. There are plenty of simpler, everyday varieties, too – a soft, plump *mochi* (rice cake) filled with red bean paste or fruit, perhaps, or a *manju* steamed bun with a warm centre of red beans or black sesame. But it's well worth seeking out the more elaborate varieties, which are sold at speciality *wagashi* shops.

You could take things one step further, however, and make your own. Historic Kanazawa, a city that works hard to maintain and promote its traditional culture, is a great place to discover the art of *wagashi* making. In just an hour or so at a local workshop, you can learn how to make two or three *jo-namagashi* – the soft, unbaked style of sweets shaped into seasonal motifs. It's a memorable, meaningful way to discover the hard work and creativity that goes into this eye-catching delicacy (as you'd expect, it's no easy task). And – if you can withhold from eating them yourself – these perfectly formed sweet treats make for a lovely souvenir from your trip.

33

Tuck into street food at a yatai

Fukuoka is famous for its bustling late-night roadside stalls – an exciting culinary experience not to be missed

Imagine: steaming bowls of Hakata ramen, with chewy noodles in a rich, pork-based soup. Creamy *mizu-take*, its hefty chunks of meat and vegetables served in a chicken broth simmered for hours. *Goma-saba*, or ultra-fresh mackerel sashimi with a sweet-but-salty sesame sauce. Tender, nutty, deep-fried burdock served on bouncy udon noodles in *goboten udon*. There's no argument: Fukuoka, on Kyushu island, is one of Japan's great food cities.

Though it has plenty of excellent high-end restaurants and a thriving café culture, it's the hearty, everyday food that is the headliner here. And there's nowhere better to try it than at the city's beloved *yatai*, or food stalls. There are around a hundred in total, though they're not usually all open at once. The *yatai* are independently run and the owners may choose not to open some evenings if the weather is bad – or if they just want a break. You'll see the stalls being set up as evening begins, the most popular attracting crowds of locals and visitors who linger in front of them well before opening. Once ready, the owner ushers in as many people as can fit around the counter, everyone squeezed together behind a *noren* curtain.

The feeling of cosiness and camaraderie while you eat is part of the fun. As you knock elbows with your neighbour, you'll probably end up exchanging a few words, whether it's simply raising your *chu-hai* (a highball made with Kyushu's popular *shochu* spirit) for a quick *kanpai* (cheers) or a longer chat about where you're from and whether you're enjoying your trip to Fukuoka. You may even pick up some of the local Hakata-ben dialect, as your fellow diners take an especially succulent bite and sigh "*umaka*" ("delicious") or perhaps "*bari umaka*" ("very tasty").

Ultimately, however, it all comes back to the food. Settle in somewhere with a varied menu, or spend the evening hopping from one specialist stall to the next. Follow your nose and you'll find local favourites like *motsu-nabe* (tripe stew); its grilled counterpart, *yaki-motsu*; and *hito-kuchi* (one bite) gyoza, super-crispy dumplings small enough to eat in one go. There are Japanese classics here, too, such as sushi, tempura and yakisoba, plus stalls specializing in the likes of Italian, French or fusion dishes. Fukuoka is its own culinary world, and there's no better way to truly immerse yourself in it than by exploring it via the *yatai*.

— MAKE IT HAPPEN —

The compact city of Fukuoka is located on the coast in the northwest of Kyushu island. The *yatai* are dotted around the city, but most are clustered along Nakasu's riverside; around the intersection of Tenjin-nishi-dori and Showa-dori; and on Watanabe-dori.

The *yatai* generally start opening from around 6pm and close as late as 2am. Reservations aren't accepted (so if there's a queue you'll have to wait or move on) and many are cash only.

Fukuoka's main train station, Hakata, is on the *shinkansen* line, which heads south to Kagoshima and north to Hiroshima and Osaka (with some trains continuing on to Kyoto, Nagoya and Tokyo). The city is also accessible by air and sea. Buses and a subway make getting around easy.

CULINARY JAPAN

Right A *yatai* in Fukuoka
Below left Serving up street food at a *yatai*
Below right *Yaki-motsu* on the grill

"The feeling of cosiness and camaraderie while you eat is part of the fun."

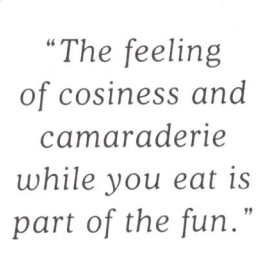

95

A bustling street of food stalls, Fukuoka

34

Aim for a hundred with Okinawan cuisine

The subtropical archipelago of Okinawa has the world's highest proportion of centenarians

Stretching across the Pacific Ocean in a delicate string, the Okinawa (or Ryukyu) archipelago exerts a powerful pull. People from Japan and far beyond make their way here to laze on white-sand beaches, swim in sapphire waters, and explore jungles and mangroves. Researchers are also drawn here by one question: why do people here live so long? There are proportionally more people over the age of 100 in Okinawa than anywhere else in the world.

There are several answers to this question, but many point to the Okinawan diet, something you can experience while visiting. Okinawans traditionally view food as part of healthcare – one of the words for food is simply "medicine" *(kusuibun)*, after all – and many ingredients native to the archipelago are nutritionally dense. Be sure to try *goya* (a bitter gourd) in the region's much-loved stir-fried dish, *goya champuru*. Also on the centenarians' menu is *mozuku*, a superfood seaweed often served vinegared or as tempura; *shikuwasa*, a slightly tart citrus used in desserts, drinks and condiments; and sweet potatoes, which traditionally formed the bulk of the Okinawan diet. Seek out all these and more at restaurants, cafés and hotels throughout the prefecture, and see if you can taste all that goodness – holidays are the perfect way to rejuvenate, after all.

MAKE IT HAPPEN

 The subtropical archipelago of Okinawa is in the far south of Japan. The capital, Naha, is on the largest of its islands, Okinawa Honto.

 Look for Okinawan cuisine specifically, as mainland Japanese and Western cuisines are now common in the archipelago, since the mid-20th century.

 Okinawa is easily reached by air, with flights from other parts of Japan and Asia. Ferries go from Kagoshima (southern Kyushu) and Taiwan.

A stir-fry dish of goya champuru

CULINARY JAPAN

Okinawan ways of life

1
Eat with intention
The traditional Okinawan diet is largely plant-based, and takes a hara hachi bu approach – eating until you're 80 per cent full.

2
Get physical
Make like Okinawa's centenarians and stroll around the islands, take up gardening or do some light calisthenics of a morning.

3
Embrace socializing
Community is very important to the traditional Okinawan way of life. Yuimaru (mutual aid) is also important – strong social support, in the good times and the bad.

35

Try the three great noodles of Morioka

This northern city's *sandaimen* (three great noodles) draw in food fans year round

Between its castle ruins, lively summer festivals and local crafts (including iron kettles and colourful textiles), Morioka is a charming place to spend a couple of days. But this laid-back city in northeastern Honshu is actually most famous for its food – more specifically, its noodle dishes. It has three very different local varieties, and it's well worth trying them all if you can.

First up is hearty *jajamen*, made with thick, bouncy noodles similar to udon. They're served with brown miso paste, aromatics and minced meat; refreshing toppings like sliced cucumber, spring onions and pickles; and extras like chilli oil or vinegar to taste. The flavour profile reflects the dish's Chinese origins – its inventor adapted it from the *zhajiangmian*, "noodles served with fried bean sauce". When your noodles are almost finished, you can opt to have *chiitantan* as well, which involves cracking an egg into the bowl, adding hot water, and mixing in extras like miso or ginger to make a creamy, flavourful broth to round out your meal.

If *jajamen* is the heartiest of Morioka's "three great noodles", *reimen* is the most refreshing. A classic summer meal, *reimen* is a cold noodle dish and a twist on Korean *naengmyeon*, "cold noodle soup". Here, the noodles are semi-translucent, and have a satisfyingly chewy texture because of the addition of potato flour. They're served in a light, chicken- and pork-based broth, and come with a fun mix of toppings – usually kimchi, boiled egg, sliced meat and seasonal fruit.

Completing the trio is *wanko soba*, which depending on your perspective is either a meal to be enjoyed or a challenge to be faced. The name means "small-bowl buckwheat noodles", and that's the heart of it: you'll receive small servings of soba in a light broth, quickly replenished by an encouraging server until you can stomach no more. While the noodles come with an array of optional toppings, including wasabi and tuna, many people ignore these, laser-focused on slurping down as many bowls of noodles as possible instead. Serving sizes differ, but roughly 8–15 dishes of *wanko soba* equal one regular bowl, and your server won't stop bringing noodles over until you firmly place the lid on top of your bowl (the only acceptable marker that you've finished). Most restaurants will give you a commemorative wooden plaque if you reach 100, a far cry from the current record that stands at well over 500 – not that it's a competition.

— MAKE IT HAPPEN —

Morioka is a city in northeastern Honshu's Iwate prefecture.

There are several restaurants around the city specializing in one or other of the three noodle dishes. Some require reservations, especially for *wanko soba*. Note that while it's easy to get caught up in the competitive atmosphere of *wanko soba*, remember that it's not a race, and you'd be wise to pace yourself.

Morioka is on the Tokaido *shinkansen* line between Tokyo and Aomori, and the Akita *shinkansen* line between Tokyo and Akita. The *shinkansen* journey time from Tokyo to Morioka is just over two hours. It's easy to get around central Morioka on foot, by bike (there are numerous hire shops), or on the Dendenmushi loop bus.

CULINARY JAPAN

"Your server won't stop bringing noodles over until you firmly place the lid on top of your bowl."

Attempting to complete the wanko soba challenge

36

Sip sake in Niigata

With more breweries than any other prefecture, Niigata is a *nihonshu* paradise

Japan's most famous drink is undoubtedly sake, or to use its proper name, *nihonshu* (literally "Japanese alcohol"). It's made with a method similar to beer: combine high-quality rice and pure water, ferment it (using *koji* mould as a starter) and press it. Niigata's fertile farmlands and crisp meltwater from snowy mountains are a winning combination, something recognized centuries ago. Today, the prefecture has some 90 breweries, many of them open to visitors.

Yoshinogawa, opened in 1548, is the oldest. The brewers spend their winters making *nihonshu* and their summers in the fields, growing the perfect rice for their smooth, clean-tasting drinks, some of which are sold only at the brewery. Established as a sake shop in 1767 and a brewery from the late 19th century, Imayo Tsukasa is a relative youngster, but its brewers still pour generations of knowledge into their work. It's a great option for a tour – the quirky building is in the centre of Niigata city, and it runs English-language tours and free and tastings. To try *nihonshu* from different breweries, you'll find what are effectively sake vending machines at Kikizake Bansho in Niigata station's Ponshukan. Buy a cup and some tokens, and you're ready to drink your way around Niigata – but as *nihonshu*'s average ABV is 15 per cent, you're unlikely to manage all 90 breweries in one visit.

MAKE IT HAPPEN

 Niigata prefecture is located on Honshu's northwest coast. Yoshinogawa is in the Settaya district of Nagaoka city, an hour from the capital.

 Yoshinogawa's hours vary so check online before visiting (*yosinogawa.co.jp*). Make sure to pre-book tours for Imayo Tsukasa (*imayotsukasa.co.jp*).

 To reach Yoshinogawa, take the train to Nagaoka, then a local train to Miyaura. Imayo Tsukasa is near Niigata station, the end of the Joetsu *shinkansen* line.

Pouring a cup of Japanese sake

CULINARY JAPAN

Unique sakes

1

Ine Mankai

Mukai Shuzo, in the seaside town of Ine (Kyoto prefecture), produces an unusual nihonshu, Ine Mankai. It's made with red rice, which lends it a gorgeous colour and rich flavour. It was created by Mukai Kuniko, who became Japan's first female head brewer in 1999.

2

Mizubasho Pure

An early member of Japan's national Awasake (sparkling sake) Association, Nagai Sake – in Gunma prefecture – pioneered the use of an in-bottle secondary fermentation to create a natural, silky-smooth sparkling nihonshu, Mizubasho Pure.

3

Komyo

The more you polish the rice, the smoother and more refined the nihonshu. In Yamanashi, the team at Tatenokawa took that to the extreme, polishing the rice down to 1 per cent for the Komyo sake.

"Local produce, personal care and incredible artistry – the kaiseki experience at its best."

Greenling soup, a common dish in *kaiseki* meals

CULINARY JAPAN

Indulge in a multi-course kaiseki meal

Japan's traditional haute cuisine is a delight for all the senses

As Japanese cuisine has gained popularity worldwide, restaurants have popped up from London to Lima serving the likes of sushi, ramen and okonomiyaki. But if you want to try it in its most elevated form, find time for *kaiseki*. This ultra-refined cuisine is the apotheosis of Japan's food culture, and as there are so few *kaiseki* restaurants outside Japan, you need to go to the source.

Multi-course *kaiseki* meals are all about bringing out the flavour of the very best local and seasonal ingredients. The dishes – usually ten to twelve – are served in a set order, broadly from lightest to heaviest. The meal starts with a small appetizer, followed by a clear soup and then the *hassun* course, a selection of seasonal delicacies. Next up is sashimi, then simmered, grilled, fried and steamed dishes, before something sharp and vinegary to cleanse your palate. The meal wraps up with pickles, miso soup and rice – so integral that the course is called *shokuji* ("a meal" in itself) – and a small dessert.

While the flavours are central to *kaiseki*, there's no denying that presentation and performance matters, too. Each morsel is served on carefully chosen tableware, often locally made, and garnished with seasonal blooms, foraged herbs and even gold leaf. All your senses are indulged. Dishes are often cooked at the table, the bubbling of broth providing a soothing backdrop. Rough ceramics and smooth lacquerware provide tactile variation, as do the textures of the dishes, from velvety tofu to crisp tempura. And the smells? Tantalizing. Removing the lid from your miso soup, for example, releases a warm, earthy aroma.

Needless to say, the art of *kaiseki* has been honed over centuries. The likes of Kyoto and Nara have a concentration of generations-old restaurants, but you can find exquisite *kaiseki* throughout Japan. And like so much here, chefs are finding ways to combine age-old principles and cutting-edge techniques. Take Oryouri Fujii, which received two stars in Michelin's special 2021 Hokuriku guide. Chef Fujii trained in Tokyo, Kyoto and Kanazawa, before returning to his native Toyama for its abundance of farm-fresh vegetables and the bounty of Toyama Bay. His meals are high-end but never over-complicated – summer *ayu* (sweetfish) is simply charcoal-grilled and served in a nest of fresh bamboo leaves. *Nihonshu* (sake), made just down the road, is served in artisan-crafted cups. Local produce, personal care and incredible artistry – the *kaiseki* experience at its best.

— MAKE IT HAPPEN —

Oryouri Fujii is in Toyama city's Iwase district, near the coast. Toyama is on the Japan Sea coast in central Honshu.

Oryouri Fujii is closed on Mondays. Like most *kaiseki* restaurants, reservations are required *(oryouri-fujii.jp or pocket-concierge.jp)*. Check with restaurants in advance if there are foods you want or need to avoid, and clarify whether you can have dashi (fish stock) and soy sauce if vegetarian or gluten free.

Oryouri Fujii is ten minutes' walk from Higashi-Iwase and Keirinjo-Mae tram stops. The tram goes to Toyama train station, a Hokuriku *shinkansen* stop, and has other lines connecting you to Gifu, Takayama and the Tateyama-Kurobe Alpine Route. There's also a boarding point near the restaurant for the Fugan Suijo Line canal cruise between Iwase and Kansui Park.

CULINARY JAPAN

38

Splash out on succulent wagyu

Heralded around the world as one of the finest varieties of beef, Kobe isn't the only wagyu worth trying

Wagyu has become a global phenomenon, the gold standard for beef among food lovers. Though some outlandish rumours have sprung up to explain its deliciousness (the cows receiving daily beer massages is a popular one), the real secrets of wagyu are more prosaic: careful breeding, a precisely balanced diet, and plenty of room to roam and graze.

Though Kobe beef steals the limelight, there are actually several types of wagyu, which simply translates to "Japanese beef". In fact, many connoisseurs rate varieties such as Matsusaka and Omi even more highly than Kobe itself. Omi beef is known for its exceptional tenderness, marbling and the low melting point of its fat. It's rare, too: only 6,000 cattle are raised annually for Omi beef, so if you want to try it, go straight to the source in Shiga prefecture. There are plenty of places serving it here, from guesthouses on the shores of Lake Biwa to *kaiseki* restaurants *(p105)*; the lakeside prefectural capital of Otsu, historic castle town of Hikone or scenic canal-threaded Omi-Hachiman have the most options. By the way, be prepared to splash some serious cash. Wagyu is highly prized for good reason, and has a hefty price tag to match.

— MAKE IT HAPPEN —

Shiga prefecture borders Kyoto, Mie, Gifu and Fukui.

Visit the Omi Beef Association website *(oumiushi.com)* for a list of places serving Omi.

The Tokaido *shinkansen* line from Tokyo stops at Maibara, near Hikone, and Kyoto, near Otsu.

Cooking wagyu on a barbecue grill

Grilled eel at Nishiki Market

39

Browse Kyoto's beloved Nishiki Market

This covered shopping arcade is home to the city's best food market, known as Kyoto's Kitchen

MAKE IT HAPPEN

Nishiki Ichiba is in central Kyoto, just off the covered Teramachi shopping street north of Shijo-dori.

Most of the shops are open 10am–6pm, but may close earlier if they sell out.

There are several bus stops nearby, plus Shijo station on the Karasuma subway line.

Fresh fish skewers sizzling on a charcoal grill. Hulking wooden barrels filled to the brim with colourful pickles. The aroma of soy-milk doughnuts cooking in the fryer, almost ready to be eaten warm from a paper bag. Nishiki Ichiba is a feast for all the senses, and taste above all. Known as Kyoto's Kitchen, this covered market contains over 100 shops, squeezed down a narrow shopping street. And like so many places in Kyoto, it's been here for centuries too, beginning life as a fish market and later expanding to sell all sorts, from local food produce to beautiful, handmade kitchenware. Indeed, some of the stalls have been here for generations.

Today, it's all about the food, making it a great place to explore the city's diverse cuisine. Many of the shops offer tasty samples, so visitors can try Kyoto specialities like *Kyo-tsukemono* (Kyoto-style pickles) before they buy. Others sell snacks in small portions, making it easy to pick up some tempura vegetables at one stall, crunchy miso-flavoured *senbei* (rice crackers) at another, then a tempting array of *mochi* (soft, chewy rice cakes) at a third. Just remember that eating while walking is frowned upon in Japan – it's best to enjoy your spoils right there, standing or sitting by the stall and taking in the sights, sounds and smells of this historic market.

Drink 'til the small hours in izakaya and yokocho

Japan's traditional late-night food and drink spots shine a light on Japan's social scene

Bars, clubs, karaoke rooms ... there are countless ways to spend an evening in Japan. But if you want to experience a long-established evening out, Japanese style, you need to find an *izakaya*. These traditional spaces (a bit like the European pub) focus on food, drink and conversation.

For the uninitiated, chain *izakaya* such as Uotami (which specializes in seafood), Akakara (known for its spicy hotpot) and Torikizoku (with its popular 360-yen menu) are a good place to start; all are more likely to have English menus, so you can get acquainted with typical *izakaya* dishes. Once your confidence is boosted, it's time to hit something more local and independent. Decor in these *izakaya* tends towards Japanese style, often with tatami mats, and you'll likely spot a *kamidana* (small Shinto altar) or *ofuda* (talisman) on a shelf. The drinks are plentiful, ranging from highballs and beers to *nihonshu* (sake). The walls will probably be plastered with strips of paper or wooden plaques bearing bold black calligraphy – also known as the menu. Don't be intimidated, though. Order classics such as *hokke* (grilled mackerel), *tamagoyaki* (Japanese omelette) and *yakitori* (chicken skewers), and you can't go wrong, or why not ask the waiter for recommendations by asking "*osusume wa?*"

Whether you're looking for *izakaya* specifically or just unique, atmospheric venues for a late-night snack or friendly drink, you'll likely end up in a *yokocho*. Roughly translating to "alleyway", *yokocho* are narrow streets crammed with tiny eateries and bars, often with neon signs stacked high.

One of Tokyo's most famous is Omoide Yokocho ("Memory Lane"), a Shinjuku staple with about 60 hole-in-the wall restaurants. With its softly glowing red lanterns and drifting charcoal smoke, it feels like you're stepping back into the Tokyo that existed before the skyscrapers. Nearby Golden Gai is another time-warped neighbourhood. This pocket of low-rise buildings near Shinjuku Station somehow survived postwar redevelopment and remains a charmingly ramshackle cluster of over 200 minuscule bars. Each one feels completely different, with the decor, menu and music often reflecting the owner's obsession – be it punk rock, classic films or plastic models. Some Golden Gai bars are members-only and some charge for entry, but most are free and open to visitors. Totobar is a great option for *nihonshu*, dragon_i is a welcoming, LGBTQ+-friendly spot and Pitou has an impressive selection of natural wines.

— MAKE IT HAPPEN —

Izakaya are found all over Japan, with many close to train stations. Golden Gai and Omoide Yokocho are ten minutes' walk from each other in Tokyo's Shinjuku. Golden Gai is east of Shinjuku and Seibu-Shinjuku stations, while Omoide Yokocho is right by Shinjuku-Nishiguchi station.

Many *izakaya* serve an *otoshi* (small snack), which will appear on the bill like a table charge. Members-only Golden Gai bars have closed doors and signs saying "regulars only" or "no tourists". Photography is prohibited in Golden Gai without permission. Note that many bars and *izakaya* allow smoking.

Any station in Shinjuku will work for accessing Golden Gai and Omoide Yokocho. Try to check the best exit in advance if using Shinjuku station – it's the world's busiest railway station, so it's easy to get lost.

CULINARY JAPAN

Top left Eating at an *izakaya* in Tokyo's "Memory Lane"
Top right A bustling *yakitori* spot in Shinjuku
Left Gathered at a tiny *izakaya* in "Memory Lane"

A food lover's tour of Japan

SUGGESTED DURATION 10 days **START** Miyazaki; fly in from Tokyo or Osaka, or get here by *shinkansen* from Kyushu destinations **GETTING AROUND** Complete this itinerary by JR and bullet trains **END** Morioka; this major city is a stop on the Tohoku *shinkansen* line between Aomori and Tokyo, so it's easy to return to the capital

Area of map

If your idea of the perfect trip revolves around food and drink, then this is the itinerary for you. Here you'll eat and drink your way around Japan, visiting convivial *yatai* (street food stalls), tiny *izakaya* (traditional pubs), refined Michelin-starred restaurants and lively *yokocho* (drinking alleys). On the menu? As well as the classics you'd expect like sushi (which will be some of the freshest you've ever tasted), expect regional delicacies like Hiroshima-style okonomiyaki, Kobe's world-class beef and locally brewed whisky and sake. Just be sure to save room for Morioka's "three great noodles" at the end for the ultimate foodie challenge.

3. FUKUOKA
From Beppu, take a two-hour JR train to this lively city and spend an evening *yatai-* (street food stall) hopping (p94), snacking on spicy *mentaiko* (marinated pollock roe) and noodles.

4. HIROSHIMA
Take a one-hour *shinkansen* to this city (p32), then seek out a Hiroshima-style okonomiyaki, made with layers of pancake batter, fried noodles, cabbage and meat or seafood, slathered in an umami-rich sauce.

2. BEPPU
The sulphurous hot-springs of Beppu (p188) are put to good use making *onsen* specialities, from eggs to fish, steamed over the springs. Spend a night here, eating and relaxing.

1. MIYAZAKI
Home to many popular regional dishes, this prefecture is the ideal place to start. Try chicken nanban, fried chicken topped with tartar sauce, and "Egg of the Sun" mangos, a sweet variety only grown here. Then it's on to Beppu, about 3.5 hours away via Oita.

5. KOBE
For meat eaters, Kobe's famous beef (p106) is sure to be top of the to-taste list. It's an easy train journey here from Hiroshima; leave enough time in Kobe for yoshoku dishes, too.

START

8. TENDO
Take a three-hour *shinkansen* to Tendo, where you'll find some of Japan's best *nihonshu* (sake). Breweries around Tendo produce traditional styles, seasonal specials, naturally sparkling varieties and aged sake. Stay the night, then hop on a two-hour JR train to Sendai (via Uzenchitose).

10. MORIOKA
End your trip on a high with Morioka's "three great noodles" *(p100)*, of which *wanko soba* is a must-try. Not that it's easy to finish – these noodles are served in small bowls that prompt an all-you-can-eat challenge, since the tiny portions just keep coming.

END

9. SENDAI
This city does comfort food exceptionally well, with hearty specialties like *gyutan* (grilled beef tongue) and *aoba* gyoza (fried green dumplings) on menus far and wide. Thirsty? Check out the Nikka whisky distillery and the winery in Akiu Onsen.

6. TOBA
This beautiful spot by Ise Bay is well-known for its *ama*, free-diving women who harvest oysters, abalone and other seafood in the surrounding waters. It's worth the journey here to meet them and try their fare; take trains to Toba via Shin-Osaka and Nagoya (just under four hours).

7. TOKYO
After a JR train to Nagoya (two hours), then a *shinkansen* (just under two hours) to Tokyo, you'll be hungry. This buzzing city has plenty to offer foodies, so spend at least two nights here indulging at *izakaya (p108)* and Michelin-starred spots.

OUTDOOR
JAPAN

Stretching from the edge of Siberia down to the tropics, this archipelago of thousands of islands is home to an incredible array of landscapes – cities, volcanoes, beaches, lush valleys. Now's your chance to explore them all.

ON THE MAP
OUTDOOR JAPAN

- **41** Walk through ancient forests in Yakushima
- **42** Explore remote Rishiri-Rebun-Sarobetsu National Park
- **43** Heal your spirit with forest bathing in the Sayama Hills
- **44** Be awed by the volcanic power of Sakurajima
- **45** Dive in the waters of the Yaeyama Islands
- **46** Seek serenity in Kyoto's classic gardens
- **47** Bow to the sacred deer of Nara
- **48** Live like the mountain monks of Dewa-Sanzan
- **49** Admire the details in Adachi's great garden
- **50** Get back to nature on the Ogasawara Islands
- **51** Ride the rapids on the Kitayama River
- **52** Stroll through Kyoto's bamboo groves

Walk through ancient forests on Yakushima

On this mysterious island off southern Kyushu, discover ancient cedar trees older than some civilizations

Yakushima is an ancient and powerful place. An island of granite to the south of Kyushu, its 505 sq km (195 sq miles) are crowned with peaks and draped in dense rainforest. There are trees here that have seen empires rise and fall, and beaches where sea turtles return generation after generation to lay eggs in the same spot. Time is almost tangible here, hanging in the air like the clouds perpetually wreathing the mountains. Hayao Miyazaki, the visionary founder of Studio Ghibli, sought inspiration in Yakushima's lush, living landscapes for his environmentalist epic *Princess Mononoke*. It's easy to see why – stepping into the forest here, you feel closed off from the outside world, plunged into a reality distinctly different from the everyday. Your eyes will be drawn up to the dripping canopy, then back down to the undulating roots that emerge from the path, before a bird call or the distant roar of a waterfall pulls your attention elsewhere.

Hiking is, as expected, one of the main reasons to come to Yakushima. While the island's settlements are strung around the edge, connected by one winding road, the interior is given over entirely to mountains, forests and waterfalls. There are several trails to follow; some of the easiest are at Yakusugi Land, a forest reserve (reachable by bus) with a few loop trails. Even on a 30-minute walk you'll see some awe-inspiring scenery, and get a chance to marvel at Yakushima's biggest draw: the *yakusugi*, cedar trees that are at least a millennium old. Now protected from logging, these ancient trees are dotted through the forest, each one an ecosystem in its own right. Just 6 km (3.5 miles) west of Yakusugi Land is the 3,000-year-old Kigen-sugi (the oldest trees are named), which has a circumference of over 8 m (26 ft) and hosts an abundance of epiphytes such as Japanese rowan and Yakushima rhododendron.

The most spectacular *yakusugi* are found deep in the heart of the forest. There's the Jomon-sugi, named after the Jomon era (14,000–300 BCE) during which it likely began growing. Its gnarled, mossy trunk is twice the circumference of Kigen-sugi and calls to mind fossils and striated rock as much as living wood. To reach it, you'll need to walk for five hours along the Anbo and Okabu trails (perhaps unsurprisingly, it wasn't discovered until 1968).

From coastal mangroves to hot springs revealed only at low tide, the island's natural bounty is overwhelming. To make the most of it, all you need to do is embrace Yakushima time – slow down, breathe and take in the ancient world around you.

— MAKE IT HAPPEN —

Yakushima is in Kagoshima prefecture, and sits 60 km (37 miles) off the south of Kyushu island.

Yakushima is the rainiest place in Japan, so pack accordingly. You should expect snow in the interior over winter, too. There are very few international ATMs on the island, so it's best to bring plenty of cash. Wild camping is not allowed, but there are several huts and campsites in the forest, and a good range of accommodation on the coast.

Yakushima has an airport with flights to Kagoshima, Fukuoka and Osaka, plus two ports, Miyanoura and Anbo, with jetfoils to Ibusuki. There's also a car ferry to Kagoshima. Buses follow the island's coast road (except the narrow west-coast section from Nagata to Okonotaki) and connect to some spots in the interior.

OUTDOOR JAPAN

Right A wild Yakushima deer
Below left The ancient Kigen-sugi tree
Below right A macaque

OUTDOOR JAPAN

"Rebun-to has a number of hiking routes, the most scenic being the Momoiwa trail."

Rebun-to, famous for its beautiful flora and coastal scenery

42

Explore remote Rishiri-Rebun-Sarobetsu National Park

Japan's northernmost national park contains two beautiful islands and a protected wetland area

In the far north of the far north, you'll find some of Japan's most remote and remarkable natural landscapes, and among the best are those in Rishiri-Rebun-Sarobetsu National Park. This sprawling protected area is divided into three sections: the Sarobetsu Plain, on the coast of Hokkaido's main island; Rishiri-to, an elegantly cone-shaped volcanic island; and Rebun-to, a wedge-shaped island just northwest of Rishiri-to.

Though the region follows Japan's usual four-season pattern, at this latitude things look very different. In the cool, dry spring and autumn months, bird-watchers settle into the waving grasses of Sarobetsu Plain to spy migrating bean geese, tundra swans and the critically endangered yellow-breasted bunting. As summer approaches, cheerful yellow *ezo-kanzo* (day lilies) bloom in Sarobetsu, delicate *Rishiri hinageshi* (tiny yellow and green flowers) open near Mount Rishiri's summit, and native flowers like the rare, edelweiss-like *Rebun usuyukiso* blossom on Rebun-to's gently undulating topography.

With this abundance of flora and fauna, hiking is the best way to explore and get to know the landscape. Rebun-to has a number of hiking routes, the most scenic being the Momoiwa trail. This popular path weaves along the island's rugged, windswept cliffs, winding past colourful alpine flowers and offering spectacular views of Rishiri-to, just across the water. More spectacular hikes await on this wild island, home to the dormant Mount Rishiri, one of Japan's 100 Famous Mountains (*hyakumeizan*). If you're up for a challenge, set aside a day to summit its North Peak (1,719 m/5,640 ft) via the slightly easier Oshidomari Route or the quieter but more technical Kutsugata Course. Whichever road you choose to take, expect out-of-this-world views from the summit above the clouds. Alternatively, rent a bike and explore a 20-km (12-mile) cycle route along the island's northwest coast, stopping at scenic Hime Pond, from where you can hike to Mount Pon (444 m/1,457 ft) in 90 minutes.

During the long winters, the landscapes fall quiet under a thick layer of snow, occasional skiers slicing through the powder while white-tailed eagles and Steller's sea eagles circle overhead. Few people venture here due to the often harsh conditions – the mountainsides are very exposed – but those who do are rewarded on calmer days with pristine backcountry terrain. This is Rishiri-Rebun-Sarobetsu National Park at its most wild.

— MAKE IT HAPPEN —

The Sarobetsu Plain is on the northern tip of Hokkaido, between Wakkanai and Horonobe. Rishiri-to is 20 km (12 miles) west, and Rebun-to a further 10 km (6 miles) northwest.

On Rishiri-to, rent bicycles near the ferry ports or often through your accommodation. There are minimal facilities on the Rishiri-to trails, so pack the necessary equipment (including a portable toilet). When walking, always stick to the trails to avoid damaging fragile wildflowers.

Wakkanai has an airport, and is also on the Japan Rail line from Sapporo via Asahikawa (where you may need to transfer). Regular ferries link Wakkanai, Rishiri-to (Kutsugata port on the island's west coast, Oshidomari on the north) and Rebun-to.

OUTDOOR JAPAN

43

Heal your spirit with forest bathing in the Sayama Hills

Get back to nature, even just for an afternoon, in the landscapes that inspired *My Neighbour Totoro*

Japan has always understood the power of forests, developing specialized vocabulary – like *komorebi*, the dappled light of the sun through trees – and building shrine gates to mark sacred groves. In the 1980s, this knowledge was combined with modern psychological research to create the concept of *shinrin-yoku* (forest bathing) – essentially walking in the woods, mindfully. As digital technologies have become increasingly enmeshed in our lives, *shinrin-yoku* has been embraced as a way to unplug and reset.

And there's no better place to do it than in the Sayama Hills. This welcome pocket of green is located on the outskirts of Japan's bustling capital, Tokyo. It's also known as Totoro's Forest, in tribute to Studio Ghibli's beloved 1988 film *My Neighbour Totoro*, which used this lovely, leafy scenery as inspiration for its setting. As you walk the quiet paths, listen to the crunch of twigs and leaves underfoot and the trilling calls of the birds in the canopy. Run your hand over bark. Focus on the rich scent of soil after rain, or the fresh coolness of autumn as you breathe in. This sense of being present in nature will have you feeling calm in no time. And when you're ready to return to the rush of Japan's megacities, you'll do so with a peaceful heart.

— MAKE IT HAPPEN —

Sayama Hills is west of the Tokyo metropolitan area, on the border with Saitama.

You can see a map of all the Totoro's Forest sites at *totoro.or.jp/national_trust*.

Depending on which part you want to explore, head to Kotesashi, Shimoyamaguchi or Seibukyujo-mae station.

Combine with SHIKOKU

Embrace the spiritual side of shinrin-yoku on a pilgrimage. The section of the Shikoku Henro (p191) between temples 11 and 23 has some lovely forested stretches.

Sayama Hills

Mount Sakurajima

44

Be awed by the volcanic power of Sakurajima

With its near-constant plume of smoke, there's no doubting the power of this stratovolcano

— MAKE IT HAPPEN —

Sakurajima is in Kagoshima Bay, on Kyushu island.

You can check the volcanic activity level on the Japan Meteorological Agency's website *(jma.go.jps)*.

Take the *shinkansen* from Osaka to Kagoshima-chuo station, then catch a ferry to Sakurajima.

While there's no doubt Mount Fuji is Japan's most famous volcano, it's certainly not its most active. If you truly want to appreciate Japan's powerful peaks, you'll need to head south to the island of Kyushu, where the country's most active volcano sits just 4 km (2.5 miles) across a bay from the 580,000 residents of Kagoshima city.

This is Sakurajima, a 1,117-m- (3,665-ft-) high stratovolcano with an almost constant thread of ominous smoke rising from its jagged crater. While *"-jima"* means "island", Sakurajima is actually located on a peninsula (thanks to the 1914 eruption that sent pyroclastic flows to the mainland, creating a land bridge). That same eruption almost buried a 3-m- (10-ft-) tall torii, which you can still see today.

Due to its explosive tendencies, the volcano is largely off limits to the public, but venture to Yunohira Observation Deck, on the west side of Sakurajima, and you'll find epic views of its peak. Or, head across the bay to the manicured gardens of Sengan-en (the historic residence of the powerful Shimazu samurai clan) to take in the volcano's distinctive silhouette. Whether Sakurajima is silent, simmering or on the edge of erupting (there are small eruptions every day), it's sure to stop you in your tracks with its subtle power and brooding beauty.

Marine life to look out for in Yaeyama

1
Hammerhead sharks
Up to 100 hammerhead sharks migrate by Irizaki, on Yonaguni's western side, between November and April each year.

2
Sea turtles
Kuroshima, southwest of Ishigaki, is the only place in Japan to see nesting green, hawksbill and loggerhead turtles.

3
Reef manta rays
The Yaeyamas are the best place in Japan to see the world's largest ray species gliding through the water.

45

Dive in the waters of the Yaeyama Islands

This remote archipelago teems with diverse and beautiful marine life

White sandy beaches, crystal-clear waters and a subtropical climate might seem like a clichéd image of paradise, but if anywhere lives up to that cliché we all dream about, it's the Yaeyama Islands. In the southwest of Okinawa, these faraway islands offers beauty in spades. Yet it's what's beneath that crystal-clear water that makes the Yaeyamas so special.

A haven for divers, these islands promise coral reefs, underwater hot springs, huge rock formations and schools of tropical fish, just offshore. The main island of Ishigaki is a great starting point for underwater adventures. At one popular dive site, near Yonehara, colourful butterfly fish, sea goldies and even sea turtles flit about the reef. Over on the island's southeastern coast, Shiraho-no-umi is home to one of the largest Ao coral (a rare type of blue coral) networks in the world. And at Manta Scramble, in northwestern Ishigaki, majestic manta rays glide serenely through the sea.

More experienced divers should head to the secluded island of Yonaguni, where the mysterious Yonaguni Monument beckons beneath the waves. This huge rock formation is so angular and precise that some people argue it's the remains of a civilization thousands of years old. Whether you choose to believe it or not, it's a fascinating, and completely unique, place to explore.

Snorkelling over a coral reef in the Yaeyama waters

MAKE IT HAPPEN

The Yaeyamas are in southwestern Okinawa prefecture and encompass Japan's southernmost and westernmost inhabited islands.

There's good diving year-round, but the main diving season is May to November, when the water is warmest and mantas tend to appear.

The best-connected airport is Ishigaki, one of the islands in the Yaeyamas, with links to Tokyo, Osaka and Naha. The islands are all linked by ferries.

Gorgeous white sands and blue waters on Ishikagi, Yaeyama Islands

Tenryu-ji's serene garden with colourful autumn leaves

46

Seek serenity in Kyoto's classic gardens

Get to know the various Japanese garden styles in the ancient capital

— MAKE IT HAPPEN —

Kyoto is in the Kyoto prefecture in the Kansai region.

Most gardens have an entry fee, but don't require booking.

Kyoto is on the Tokaido *shinkansen* line between Tokyo and Shin-Osaka, and several local train lines. Get around the city by train, bus, subway or on foot

Japanese gardens aren't your average green spaces. Though undoubtedly beautiful, these tranquil spots are cherished for the spiritual and philosophical ideas behind every design element. There are various garden styles – dry, stroll and tea the most common – but many share components and principles: plantings are subtle, winding paths aid concentration and water is regarded as purifying, for starters.

One of the best places to see such flawless landscape design is Kyoto, a city of myriad gardens. While it's hard to choose a favourite, there are those that stand out. Ryoan-ji's 15th-century dry garden is a meditative space of pared-back beauty, with its precisely placed rocks and raked gravel. Then there's the verdant traditional gardens of Okochi Sanso, a labour of love by one of Japan's early *jidaigeki* (period drama) film stars. Yet for many, the garden at Tenryu-ji (Japan's first designated Site of Special Historic and Scenic Importance) is the most impressive. While the temple buildings have been repeatedly destroyed and rebuilt, the grounds have remained remarkably intact since the 1300s, making them possibly Japan's oldest surviving stroll garden. You'll quickly understand that term as you explore, your pace slowing as you follow the edge of the pond and absorb the perfectly curated views along the way.

Bow to the sacred deer of Nara

Japan's 8th-century capital has some 1,200 cheeky but charming resident animals

For most wildlife experiences, you'll need to venture deep into nature, but not so in Nara. This scenic city is most famous for its wild (and often rather cheeky) deer, who roam freely around the historic streets. Legend has it that Takemikazuchi, a deity enshrined in Nara's 8th-century Kasuga Shrine, arrived here riding a sacred white deer. Thus, the animal came to be seen as a messenger of the gods and was given the run of the city – though naturally deer tend to stick to the wooded hills of Nara Park. As you head there from the bustling city centre, you'll start to spot the deer napping under trees, peeking through railings or nonchalantly holding up traffic.

Once in the park, you'll see dozens of them, unphased by tourists proffering *shika-senbei* (deer crackers). Many have learned that a quick bow seems to result in food – and of course, it's only polite to bow back – but some take a more direct approach, poking twitching noses into bags and pockets.

This cheeky behaviour mostly happens at the park's busiest times, so to avoid it (and to enjoy a calmer experience), stay overnight in Nara. Wake early to watch herds of deer emerging from the morning mist or linger at dusk to see them lit by the glowing lamps of the ancient shrines and temples. You might start to wonder if they truly are holy messengers.

MAKE IT HAPPEN

Nara Park stretches east from Nara city centre.

Nara's deer are technically wild, so exercise caution around them. Only feed them *shika-senbei* sold by street vendors near the park.

Kintetsu-Nara station and JR Nara station are both within walking distance of the park.

A Nara deer roaming in Nara Park

48

Live like the mountain monks of Dewa-Sanzan

The *yamabushi* tap into ancient spiritual practices in Japan's wild, mountainous landscapes

There's something special about Japan's mountains. Just ask the *yamabushi*. Meaning "one who bows down to the mountains", these reclusive monks practise Shugendo, an ancient form of mountain worship centred on ascetic practices and a deep, direct connection with nature. This syncretic religion emerged from a combination of Buddhist, Shinto and folk beliefs around the 7th century and was later banned by the Meiji government between 1872 and 1947 due to its amalgamation of religious practices. Though there are few adherents today, Shugendo still exerts a powerful pull on the Japanese imagination. Just as New Yorkers might dream of escaping to the sunny coast of California and Londoners of running a farm in the countryside, burned-out Tokyo office workers fantasize about escaping to the mountains to lead a quiet and frugal life. Luckily, there's a way to do that (at least temporarily): join a retreat with a *yamabushi*.

The *yamabushi* were once active throughout Japan, but now the main centre of activity is Dewa-Sanzan, the three sacred peaks in Yamagata where Shugendo is said to have first developed. Here, visitors can take part in the practice to varying degrees, from joining guided hikes and meditations over three days to escaping on a week-long stay eschewing all modern comforts.

Whichever transformational retreat you embark on, the rules are the same. Firstly, mobile phones, watches and books are locked away to help focus on the present moment. You'll dress in the same pure white clothes and soft split-toed shoes the *yamabushi* wear, carry a wooden walking stick, sleep in temples or pilgrims' huts and eat simple meals made from local ingredients. Every day is an early start, and the hours pass on sacred trails around the mountains and practising the likes of *takigyo*, a form of meditation under a waterfall that aims to purify the body and focus the mind. Throughout it all, the only sounds you'll hear are those of nature, the haunting call of the conch shell the *yamabushi* use to summon the gods and your own response to instructions: *uketamo*, I humbly accept – the only words you'll utter.

And after spending however many days wandering around the mountains, you'll take a sense of calm and focus back home with you. With the indomitable spirit of the mighty mountains held close, the chaos and the noise of modern life won't feel quite so unmanageable.

— MAKE IT HAPPEN —

The three peaks of Dewa-Sanzan – Haguro-san, Gassan and Yudono-san – in Yamagata prefecture, northern Japan, are in the northernmost part of Bandai-Asahi National Park.

Most *yamabushi* courses are only available between June and September, as heavy snowfall makes the mountains inaccessible – or at least unsafe for inexperienced visitors – for the rest of the year. Book your experience through Yamabushido (yamabushido.jp), which offers multi-day, multilingual experiences with the Dewa-Sanzan *yamabushi*.

The city of Tsuruoka is the main access point for the three peaks of Dewa-Sanzan, and the meeting point for many *yamabushi* courses. It's accessible by train from Niigata, a stop on the Joetsu *shinkansen* line.

OUTDOOR JAPAN

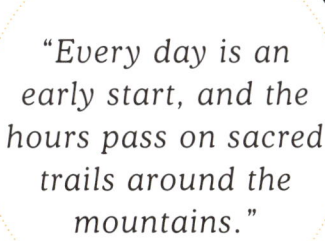

"Every day is an early start, and the hours pass on sacred trails around the mountains."

Top Split-toed *yamabushi* shoes
Above *Yamabushi* walking through thick snow, Yamagata
Left A snow-dusted pagoda on Haguro-san, one of the Dewa-Sanzan peaks

129

49

Admire the details in Adachi's great garden

This meticulously crafted showpiece of design is Japan's number one garden

A quiet rural area in Shimane might not be the most obvious location for Japan's best-loved garden, but this is where you'll find it. The garden at the Adachi Museum of Art has been voted the country's favourite every year since 2003, a remarkable feat considering how new it is. It's the vision of Adachi Zenko, a local man of humble origins who became a major collector of Japanese art. Wanting to add to the cultural scene of Shimane, he opened this fascinating art museum and its gardens in 1970. Adachi had begun landscaping the museum grounds two years earlier, claiming "the garden is also a canvas". The gardens were his passion, and a huge achievement given he was in his late 60s when he started, continuing the work until his death at 91.

The six areas showcase different styles of Japanese gardening, from the elegant moss garden to the clever incorporation of nearby peaks as "borrowed scenery". Their precision is almost unreal: not a pebble is out of place in the dry landscape garden; the lawns are so vibrant and painstakingly trimmed that they look like rugs; and the windows inside the museum frame the views of each area to create "living paintings", showing the synchronicity between the grounds and the museum. If you can only visit one garden in Japan, make it this one.

The artfully designed Pond Garden at the Adachi Museum of Art

---

MAKE IT HAPPEN

 The Adachi Museum of Art is located near Yasugi in Shimane prefecture, east of Matsue and Izumo on the JR San'in main line.

 The museum is open daily; check hours at *adachi-museum.or.jp*. There's discounted entry for overseas visitors. English audio guides are available.

 There's a free shuttle bus from JR Yasugi station; get there a bit early to queue for it, and pick up your timed return ticket at the museum.

OUTDOOR JAPAN

Japan's "Three Great Gardens"

.... **1** ....

Kanazawa Kenrokuen
Though its origins are hazy, Japan has had a widely accepted list of the Three Great Gardens since at least the 19th century. First up is Kanazawa's Kenroku-en, a stroll garden with an array of interesting features – ponds, bridges, stones, teahouses and precisely pruned trees.

.... **2** ....

Koraku-en
Koraku-en in Okayama, also designed in the stroll garden style, presents different views to visitors as they slowly walk around. Okayama Castle, peering over the trees from across the river, is used as shakkei (borrowed scenery).

.... **3** ....

Kairaku-en
Kairaku-en (p236) in Mito, the third Great Garden, began as a park. It still has a more laid-back, unstructured feel than the other two gardens, its groves of plum, bamboo and cedar inviting visitors to relax in their shade.

OUTDOOR JAPAN

50

Get back to nature on the Ogasawara Islands

Japan's farthest-flung and UNESCO-protected islands teem with fascinating life

The world's largest metropolitan area by population, Tokyo encompasses densely packed skyscrapers, quiet backwaters, a mountain or two, and – most surprisingly – the idyllic Ogasawara Islands. Yet while this archipelago is administratively part of Tokyo, it's a good 1,000 km (600 miles) away; in fact, the islands are so remote that plant and animal life here has followed unique evolutionary pathways. This fascinating ecology, paired with the lack of tourists willing to venture this far, make the Ogasawaras a hugely rewarding destination.

Wildlife is undoubtedly the highlight on the islands. Travellers can delve into the subtropical forests for a chance to see rare endemic Bonin flying foxes, green and yellow Bonin white-eyes, and Japanese wood pigeons. You can also join a guide at night to seek out the bewitching glow of bioluminescent mushrooms (*Mycena chlorophos*). Offshore, grab a snorkel to explore the rich marine life surrounding the archipelago's coral reefs, or board a boat for all but guaranteed sightings of playful bottlenose and spinner dolphins and majestic humpback whales. The Ogasawaras are also the largest green sea turtle breeding ground in Japan – they come ashore to lay their eggs (Mar–Sep) under the light of the stars, a sight well worth staying up late for.

— MAKE IT HAPPEN —

The Ogasawaras are south of Tokyo Bay. The largest island is Chichijima, the second-largest Hahajima.

To protect the islands' biodiversity, off-trail hiking and camping are prohibited.

The only access is by boat. The Ogasawara-maru ferry leaves Tokyo every three to six days.

Humpback whale breaching off the Ogasawara Islands

Rafting down the Kitayama River

51

Ride the rapids on the Kitayama River

Hold on tight for a wet and wild *ikada-kudari* log raft ride on scenic waters

MAKE IT HAPPEN

The Kitayama River is in Yoshino-Kumano National Park, in the eastern part of Wakayama prefecture.

Ikada-kudari only takes place May–Sep; book your spot online (kumano-travel.com).

Get the morning bus from Kumano city to Okutoro-Koen then a shuttle bus to the river.

A land of steam-shrouded hot springs and densely wooded peaks, the mountains of the Kii peninsula harbour pockets of ancient Japanese culture. Here you can make the pilgrimage along the Kumano Kodo's sacred trails (p170) or hunker down in one of Koya-san's atmospheric temples. If you're looking for more of an adrenaline rush, however, head to the choppy waters of the Kitayama River. Here, and only here, can you try the ancient art of *ikada-kudari* (log rafting).

The *ikadashi* (helmsmen) have traversed the rapids of this steep, narrow river for centuries. Before roads opened up the mountains, log rafting was the only way to transport cypress and cedar logs to the coast: the 30-m (100-ft) rafts were flexible enough to snake around bends and over rapids. Today, their purpose is a little less practical. As a means of keeping these ancient rafting skills alive, *ikadashi* now transport tourists down the rushing river instead. It's a heart-pumping, hour-long ride, with the *ikadashi* steering the rafts around rapids and through churning white water, before floating into quieter sections to allow travellers a moment to contemplate the beautiful surroundings of the Kii peninsula. And it's entirely safe, with life jackets provided and sturdy rails to hold onto. Still, for many, it's the most thrilling experience you can have while in Japan.

OUTDOOR JAPAN

Combine with KYOTO

Immerse yourself in another of Kyoto's (p247) natural scenes by taking a train through the "maple tunnel", where autumnal red leaves surround the Eizan train as it heads north.

52

Stroll through Kyoto's bamboo groves

Let the ancient capital's dreamlike bamboo forests soar and sway above you

In 1996, Japan's Ministry of the Environment listed the 100 Soundscapes of Japan. Each sound was chosen to reflect the unique natural and cultural features of a specific place, ranging from temple bells to the lazy drone of summer cicadas. Kyoto's defining sound? The whistling breeze and wind-chime-like knocking of the city's bamboo groves.

Kyoto's most famous bamboo grove is undoubtedly Sagano Bamboo Forest, in historic Arashiyama. It's a beautiful place, the overhanging stalks freshly green and shiny, and the dried grass fencing carefully chosen to blend in with the surroundings. Beautiful, yes, but popular, too. The forest is no secret, and visitors shuffle through shoulder-to-shoulder all day long.

Surprisingly, there's a quieter bamboo forest right next to another Kyoto sight: Fushimi Inari Taisha (p37). Approach the main entrance, where the famous path of red shrine gates sets off up the mountain, but instead of entering the torii tunnel, take a right. After a few minutes, this tranquil path will lead you to an often-deserted bamboo grove, wilder but no less spectacular than those in busy Arashiyama. As you breathe in the fresh forest air and listen to that iconic whistling breeze, you'll feel like you're miles from the Fushimi Inari Taisha crowds, even if you're not.

The towering stalks of Sagano Bamboo Forest

MAKE IT HAPPEN

 | |

Sagano Bamboo Forest is located in Kyoto's Arashiyama district, in the foothills west of the city. Fushimi Inari Taisha is in the city's southeast. | Sagano Bamboo Forest is open 24 hours; avoid the biggest crowds by going at dawn. Fushimi Inari Taisha is also open all day. | Saga-Arashiyama (JR Sagano line) is closest to Sagano Bamboo Forest. Fushimi Inari Taisha is near Fushimi-Inari station (Keihan line).

Island hopping in the south

SUGGESTED DURATION 14 days **START** Nagasaki; arrive via plane from Tokyo or Osaka, or take the train from Fukuoka **GETTING AROUND** This journey relies on planes and boats **END** Yonaguni; fly from Yonaguni to Naha. From there, you'll find flights to Honshu and Kyushu

Area of map

Japan's southern islands are home to some truly spectacular scenery, from rainforests and mangroves to beaches with rare star-shaped sand. On top of that, there are amazing wildlife-watching opportunities, too – this is where to go if you'd like to see nesting sea turtles or watch manta rays glide past coral reefs.

This itinerary takes you from Kyushu down to the subtropical Okinawan archipelago, giving you the chance to experience each area's distinct climate and beautiful landscapes. As you explore these regions and take part in myriad outdoor activities, make time to learn about their fascinating histories, too, from the powerful Kagoshima samurai who led a rebellion against the Meiji government in the 1870s to the story of the independent Kingdom of Ryukyu.

7. ISHIGAKI
Take a one-hour flight from Naha to Ishigaki (p123) to go walking in the shade of palm trees, kayaking through mangroves and snorkelling off idyllic beaches.

8. TAKETOMI
Just a 15-minute ferry from Ishigaki is tiny Taketomi. Spend a day cycling through its village of red-roofed houses with a pitstop on its white-sand beaches before heading back to Ishigaki to catch a ferry to Iriomote.

10. YONAGUNI
Reach the end of the line at Japan's westernmost island (p123) via plane from Ishigaki. Experienced divers can see migrating hammerheads and fascinating rock formations, while hikers will share the pastureland with endemic Yonaguni horses.

9. IRIOMOTE
It's worth spending a couple of nights on wild, undeveloped Iriomote island for the chance to spot the rare Iriomote cat. No luck? Enjoy river kayaking and hiking in forests and mangroves.

END

START

1. NAGASAKI
Spend your first day in this port city getting a sense of the south's history at the former Dutch enclave of Dejima and the Peace Park. Then it's on to the Goto Islands, just over an hour away by ferry.

2. GOTO ISLANDS
These scenic islands are known for their churches, linked to the "hidden Christians" (p61). Enjoy exploring this intriguing part of Japan's history, and perhaps go kayaking while you're here. Then it's back to Nagasaki for your onward journey.

3. KAGOSHIMA
The south's main transport hub, Kagoshima is where boats for Yakushima and Sakurajima depart and return, so you'll spend a lot of time here on this itinerary. Luckily, there's plenty to do: admire the smoking Sakurajima volcano from the waterfront, take in the view from mountaintop Shiroyama Park and soak in hot springs.

4. SAKURAJIMA
It's an easy day trip from Kagoshima to Sakurajima (p121), one of Japan's most active volcanoes. Take one of the frequent ferries across the bay (it's a 15-minute trip) and spend the afternoon hiking and soaking in hot springs, then get the ferry back to Kagoshima for the night.

5. YAKUSHIMA
Take a two- to three-hour high speed boat from Kagoshima to see trees older than the Roman Empire on this lush, rainforest-covered island (p116). Explore its mangroves and watch quietly as sea turtles nest on its beaches before returning to Kagoshima.

6. OKINAWA HONTO
It's a one-and-a-half-hour flight from Kagoshima to Naha, Okinawa Honto's capital. Base yourself in Naha (p66) and spend a couple of days exploring the island: walking coastal and forest trails, finding waterfalls and seeing the remains of grand Ryukyuan castles and royal residences.

FUTURISTIC
JAPAN

It might be a land of tradition, but Japan is also forging the future, one new technology at a time. For every temple, there's a skyscraper; for every tea ceremony, a new online obsession. Prepare to experience a new world.

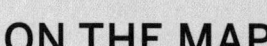

ON THE MAP
FUTURISTIC JAPAN

- **53** Luxuriate in high-end Tokyo at Azabudai Hills
- **54** Optimize your rest in Akasaka's sleep lab
- **55** Wonder at Yusuhara's old-meets-new architecture
- **56** Let the lights of Yokohama Bay wash over you
- **57** Answer nature's call in high-tech style
- **58** Embrace your inner child at teamLab Forest
- **59** Seek out Japan's weird and wonderful vending machines
- **60** Glimpse the fascinating future of train travel
- **61** Enter a new reality at Tokyo Tower's digital amusement park
- **62** Consider Japan's industrial past and future in Nagoya
- **63** Meet the friendly and adorable robots of Tokyo
- **64** Explore Osaka's skyscraper sandbank

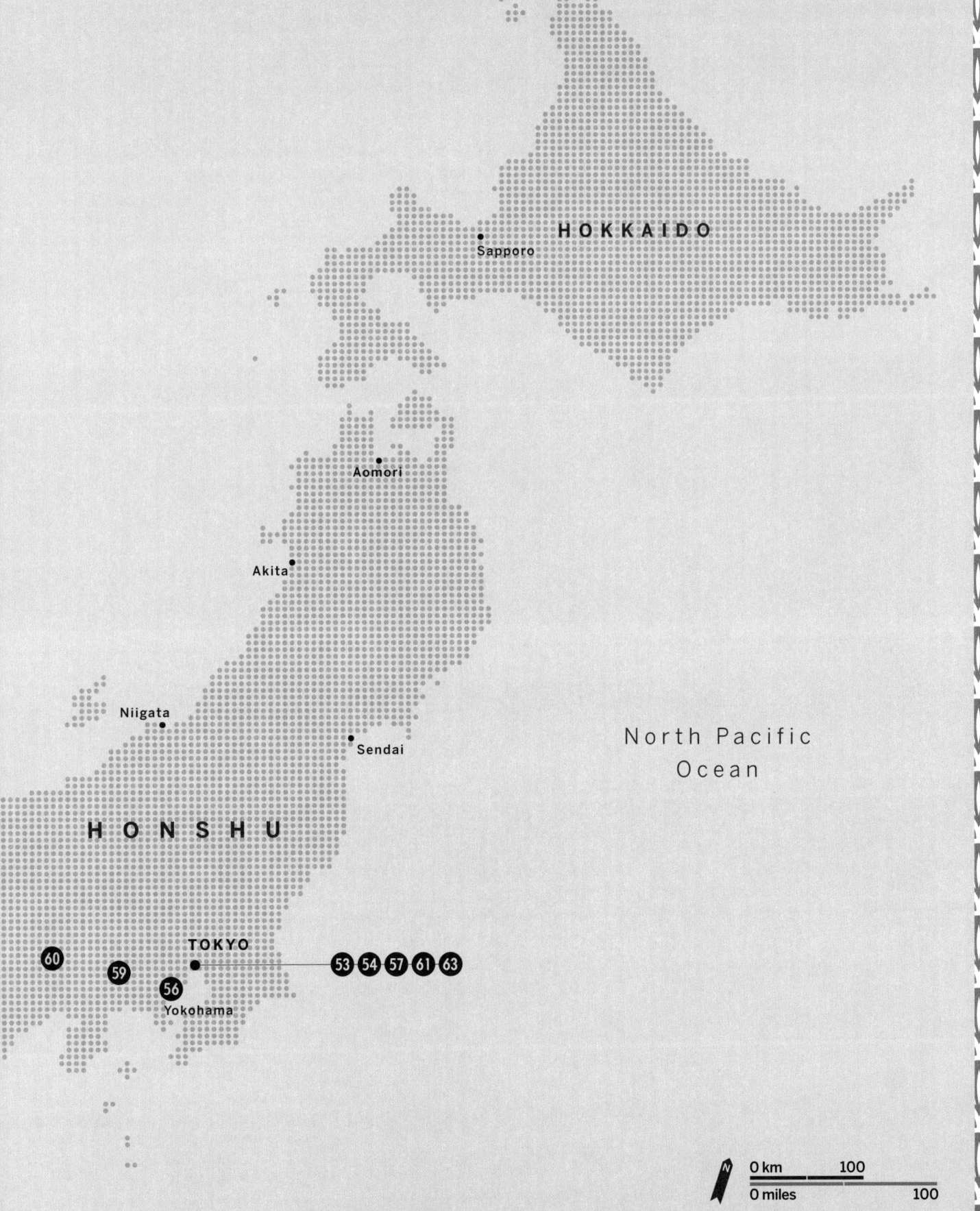

Luxuriate in high-end Tokyo at Azabudai Hills

This development, right by the iconic Tokyo Tower, showcases the city's unique style and architectural innovation

Tokyo has changed radically over the centuries. Once a fishing village, it grew into a capital city after 16th-century land reclamation, and swathes were rebuilt after the Great Kanto Earthquake of 1923 and then World War II. By the time the new millennium rolled around, it had become the consummate modern metropolis, with sleek skyscrapers and urban sprawl as far as the eye could see. Azabudai Hills, an 8-ha (20-acre) development in central Tokyo, encapsulates a new approach to this ever-continuing growth – one with sustainability, greenery and a more human scale in mind. Completed in 2023 by some of the world's most pioneering architectural firms, the complex is a shining example of Tokyo's forward-thinking architectural ethos.

Azabudai Hills is packed with high-end stores and lavish facilities. Big spenders can drop by the Garden Plaza's shops – think Dior, Cartier and Bottega Veneta. For a further taste of luxury, premium snacks and the freshest groceries are available at Azabudai Hills Market, an airy, open twist on the classic basement-floor food halls of Japan's department stores. As for cultural highlights, digital art pioneers teamLab (*p151*) moved their Borderless museum here in 2023, and the Azabudai Hills Gallery showcases exhibitions and installations by luminaries such as Yoshitomo Nara and Olafur Eliasson.

Museums and galleries aside, Azabudai Hills is a joy to visit simply because of the space itself. The introduction of natural elements was a key goal of British design firm Heatherwick Studio, which dedicated a third of the street-level space to plant life. Greenery is built into the bones of the Garden Plaza, too, a mesmerizing structure which looks like some fantastical creature rising from the earth. To the west is Mori JP Tower, which at 330 m (1,083 ft) became Japan's tallest building on its completion. As the tower is built to be narrower at the base before curving outwards, there's room for green spaces at ground level.

The Azabudai Hills project spanned over 30 years, and existing residents, landowners and businesses were consulted on their desires for the space – 90 per cent of them returned to the district when it was finished. Perhaps this focus on how people actually want to use the urban environment is what underpins its success. Azabudai Hills is sleek, modern and ambitious, but it also feels organic and human in scale – no mean feat in the heart of such a vast city.

MAKE IT HAPPEN

Azabudai Hills is located in Tokyo's central Minato district, with Roppongi to the west and Tokyo Tower to the southeast. Attractions on the ground level of the development include various shops and restaurants, a square (where events are often held), and a multi-language child-care facility.

Opening hours vary by facility, so check in advance. It's best to pre-book for teamLab Borderless; tickets will give you a timed entry slot *(teamlab.art/e/tokyo)*. The complex as a whole can be explored at any time.

The Garden Plaza area of the development is directly connected to Kamiyacho station on the Hibiya subway line. Roppongi-Itchome station, on the Namboku subway line, is a short walk from the development's western edge.

FUTURISTIC JAPAN

The view east from swanky Azabudai Hills, over the Garden Plaza

Combine with TOKYO SKYTREE

For another brilliantly successful fusion of traditional and modern engineering and design, you need look no further than Tokyo's iconic Skytree tower (p42).

Optimize your rest in Akasaka's sleep lab

Cutting-edge capsule hotel technology helps you hone your sleep routine

Staying in a capsule hotel, where you sleep in an intimate, one-person pod rather than a regular hotel room, is one of those must-try Japan experiences. A night in one of these cosy pods will introduce you to many facets of Japanese society, from the space-saving innovations in densely packed cities to the culture of politeness and consideration when staying in close proximity with strangers.

Capsule hotels were originally developed as a practical and convenient solution to the common problem of missing the last train, often after a late stint in the office (or the karaoke booth). Though the image of low-lit pods stacked on top of each other feels very space age, capsule hotels haven't changed much since their invention way back in 1979.

Design-forward hotel company 9h (nine hours) is changing that. At its Akasaka sleep lab in Tokyo, it's incorporated new technology to give guests a "sleep fitscan", assessing breathing, night movements and more to create a thorough, personalized sleep report. The decor of its lab is minimalist but warm – concrete floors, glossy black walls – and lockers and showers are kept away from the sleeping areas, so you can focus solely on getting a good night's rest. Book a stay: you've never had a night's sleep quite like it.

— MAKE IT HAPPEN —

9h (nine hours) Sleep Lab is in Tokyo's Akasaka district.

Pods can be booked online (ninehours.co.jp/en). Male and female capsules are separate.

9h (nine hours) Akasaka is five minutes' walk from Akasaka (Chiyoda line) and Akasaka-Mitsuke (Ginza and Marunouchi lines).

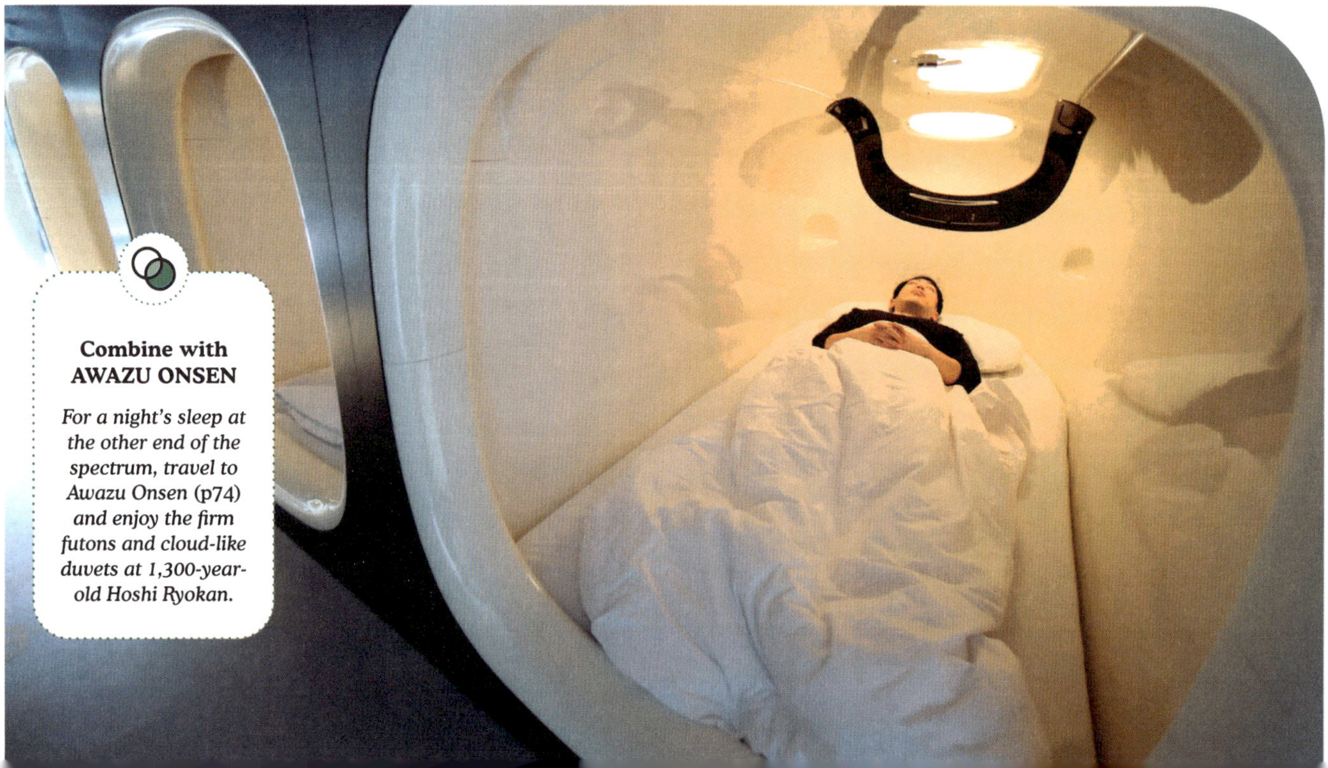

Combine with AWAZU ONSEN

For a night's sleep at the other end of the spectrum, travel to Awazu Onsen (p74) and enjoy the firm futons and cloud-like duvets at 1,300-year-old Hoshi Ryokan.

Getting some rest in a 9h capsule hotel

Yusuhara's Kumo-no-Ue Gallery

55

Wonder at Yusuhara's old-meets-new architecture

This town of the future is an unexpected find in remote Shikoku

— MAKE IT HAPPEN —

Yusuhara is in inland Kochi prefecture, in western Shikoku.

The welfare centre, one of Kuma's buildings, is not open to the public but can be enjoyed from outside.

The best way to reach Yusuhara is by car, or by bus from the JR station in Susaki.

Yusuhara sits in the mountains of Shikoku's interior, its surrounding forests draped in a gossamer scarf of drifting clouds. It's a wonderfully ethereal setting, one where you might expect to uncover a hidden world untouched by the passage of time. You'll be surprised, therefore, to discover that this "town above the clouds" is instead defiantly forward-looking.

At Yusuhara, superstar architect Kengo Kuma has looked ahead to the designs of tomorrow, while celebrating the area's unique heritage. He has designed six of the town's buildings, turning this bucolic settlement into an architectural wonder that continues to attract global attention.

Kuma has designed community facilities that thrill with their elegant, tactile designs – a combined market and hotel, a gallery, a library and a welfare centre. These practical, beautiful buildings lovingly incorporate local materials like fragrant cedar wood, as well as thatching and carpentry techniques that have stood the test of time. By combining these with modern comforts, architectural methods and sustainable technologies like solar power, Kuma and the people of Yusuhara have co-created an enchanting showcase for the idea that, to find our way to a bright future, we need to embrace the wisdom of the past.

56

Let the lights of Yokohama Bay wash over you

Illuminated at night, the skyscrapers of Minato Mirai 21 make for a dazzling picture

The skyline of Yokohama's Minato Mirai 21 area

When it comes to the most famous skylines in Japan, Tokyo's usually comes in first – though only just. Not far behind is another city, Yokohama. Located on the edge of Tokyo Bay, just an hour away from the capital, this bustling port city has long been in Tokyo's shadow (spot the capital's Skytree looming in the distance), but it still manages to hold its own. Yokohama was one of just five treaty ports opened to foreign trade in 1858, after over 200 years of isolationism in Japan, and since then it's become one of the country's most diverse cities (you'll find Japan's largest Chinatown here).

Yokohama is also big, bright and colourful, and nowhere is that truer than on Minato Mirai 21, where skyscrapers like the Landmark Tower rise abruptly by the water. A sleek district of glass and steel in the daylight, this area comes alive at night. The historic Red Brick Warehouse is moodily uplit, the curves of the sail-like InterContinental Hotel are illuminated in warm tones and the Cosmo World Ferris Wheel (once the tallest in the world) turns in every colour of the rainbow. The best way to take it all in? On a nighttime cruise around the bay, the bright lights reflecting in the water. Be sure to have your camera ready.

MAKE IT HAPPEN

 Minato Mirai 21 is in the bayside area of Yokohama. The city is under 30 minutes south of Tokyo by train and is the capital of Kanagawa prefecture.

 For an evening boat ride, hop on one of the Sea Bass ferries (special guided illumination service on Fri, Sat and Sun nights; *yokohama-cruising.jp*).

 You can reach Minato Mirai 21 by subway to Minato Mirai station or via the Akaikutsu bus or Yokohama Air Cabin cable car from Sakuragicho station.

FUTURISTIC JAPAN

> "Tokyo's toilets have been given their moment to shine on the big screen, too."

Top Toilet with transparent walls, by architect Shigeru Ban
Left Jingu-dori Park's toilet by Tadao Ando
Right Kengo Kuma's cedar-clad toilet

Answer nature's call in high-tech style

In one of Tokyo's busiest districts, public toilets are works of art

It may be an unlikely icon, but the humble toilet has become one of modern Japan's star attractions. TOTO is one of very few toilet manufacturers with brand-name recognition, and its Washlet toilet seats – with built-in bidets and much more – are ubiquitous in Japan. They may not be the reason you visit the country, but there's no denying that there's a certain childish glee in walking into a bathroom only to have the seat lift automatically and maybe even light up. For those more accustomed to standard toilets of the tech-free variety, the array of loo-side buttons might be intriguing and intimidating in equal measure. But once you've played around with the many features, you'll be loath to return to standard plumbing.

Of course, the country's toilets are not all quite so high-tech, and you'll still spot squat toilets everywhere from fancy department stores to the deepest countryside. But Japan has certainly leaned into this niche notoriety, leading to brilliant projects like THE TOKYO TOILET. Opened ahead of the 2020 Tokyo Olympics, the toilets – which vary in size from small stalls to larger blocks – are located in busy public spaces, to increase those spaces' accessibility and encourage people to linger in them. But they weren't designed merely to provide a practical service – each one is the creation of a globally renowned architect or artist, and adds a beautiful and unusual structure to the scene. There's an impressive range: the cosy jumble of wood from Kengo Kuma in leafy Nabeshima Shoto Park; the concave white disc of Sou Fujimoto's Nishisando facility; the cheerful, breezy toilet designed by NIGO® to look like a nostalgic house circled by a white picket fence; and more than a dozen others to discover.

Tokyo's toilets have been given their moment to shine on the big screen, too. In 2023, acclaimed director Wim Wenders released *Perfect Days*. The film focuses on the day-to-day life of Hirayama, a THE TOKYO TOILET cleaner, who takes pride in doing his job well and lives simply. It may not be the most romantic line of work, but Hirayama finds solace in his mindful routines. Fans of the meditative film can easily recreate moments from it – giggling when the coloured glass walls of Shigeru Ban's Yoyogi Fukamachi Mini Park toilet turn opaque, perhaps, or taking a moment to watch the leaves dancing through the slats of Tadao Ando's toilet in Jingu-dori Park. As Hirayama knows, there's joy to be found even in life's simplest moments.

— MAKE IT HAPPEN —

The 17 toilets are spread throughout Tokyo's central Shibuya ward, in the Ebisu, Yoyogi and Hatagaya neighbourhoods. There is also an occasional shuttle that takes guests to each of the toilet locations. More information can be found on THE TOYKO TOILET website (tokyotoilet.jp/en).

Every toilet is wheelchair accessible, and several have ostomate facilities. You can check the details of their facilities, and learn about their designs and the artists behind them, on THE TOKYO TOILET website.

Being in the well-connected Shibuya area, all the toilets are within walking distance of a subway station and all are on numerous bus routes. Most are near Hatayama, Ebisu, Yoyogi-koen and Yoyogi-Hachiman stations, and one toilet is a relatively easy walk from the next.

FUTURISTIC JAPAN

Graffiti Nature in a Beating Valley – Symbiotic Lives, A Whole Year per Year, Red List © teamLab

Combine with SETO ART ISLANDS

Continue your mind-expanding adventure by visiting Seto Art Islands (p200), each home to an array of sculptures, installations and art pieces.

Embrace your inner child at teamLab Forest

Immerse yourself in a digital world of fantastical plants and animals

Sometimes, we all need to take a break from the stresses of modern life and embrace our inner child. That's often easier said than done, however. Thankfully, international art collective teamLab are here to help. The group builds vast artistic installations using pioneering digital technology, each designed by an interdisciplinary team of artists, programmers, engineers, mathematicians and architects. They're specialists in creating immersive digital experiences, giving you space to feel an unguarded sense of childlike wonder.

Their self-contained worlds are sprinkled across Japan, from museums like Tokyo's teamLab Borderless: MORI Building DIGITAL ART MUSEUM to the open-air teamLab Botanical Garden in Osaka. In Fukuoka, Kyushu's largest city, you'll find teamLab Forest – SBI SECURITIES Co., Ltd., where visitors are encouraged to explore a vast natural playground. Every detail of this beautiful new world is carefully rendered through innovative digital processes, including screens, projections, phone apps and audio installations.

The first section of teamLab Forest is the Catching and Collecting Forest, which taps into our innate human desire to discover more about our physical environment. Stepping into it, you're surrounded by a colourful, ever-changing landscape projected onto the walls and floors. You might find yourself walking through shimmering blue waters, glittering digital koi carp tracing lazy circles around your feet, or moving your hand through sprays of cherry blossom petals. The forest's creatures react to you differently, some turning to face you and others darting away when you approach. You can work together with other people to direct them where you'd like, and use an augmented-reality smartphone app to capture, learn about and release different animals.

The second area, the Athletics Forest, is more physical. Its multiple spaces are designed to make you engage with the world in imaginative new ways, whether you're jumping between stepping stones that subtly move and change colour as you land on them, or navigating your way through a room filled with gently glowing spheres which hum and change colour as you move through. Each area contains something new, and everyone – regardless of age – will find something that puts a spring in their step and a joyous sparkle in their eye. The groundbreaking designers at teamLab provide us with a welcome opportunity to forget our lengthening to-do lists and to switch off for a while.

— MAKE IT HAPPEN —

teamLab Forest is in the bayside Momochi area of Fukuoka city, on Kyushu's northwestern coast.

There are sometimes tickets (which are timed) available on the door, but it's best to book ahead *(teamlab.art/e/ forest), particularly on weekends or holidays*. The museum is active and interactive, so you're asked not to wear high heels, sandals or clogs. Some, but not all, of the space is wheelchair accessible.

Tojinmachi metro station is about 15 minutes' walk from teamLab Forest, and is directly linked to Hakata station (the city's main transport hub). From Hakata, the Kyushu *shinkansen* line heads south to Kagoshima and the San'yo *shinkansen* north to Osaka, with some through services to Tokyo. There are also buses from Hakata to Momochi.

Retro vending machines in Sagamihara

59

Seek out Japan's weird and wonderful vending machines

A collection of restored vending machines inspire nostalgia and curiosity

Vending machines exist at that intersection between convenience and whimsy that Japan does so well. You'll find them almost everywhere, even on Mount Fuji, dispensing all manner of items. Most of them serve drinks (both hot and cold), but a few minutes of online sleuthing will reveal how much more is available: vending machines offering fresh produce from farms and allotments; hand-cranked *gacha* games that dispense random toys in shopping arcades; and anything from insect-based snacks to tinned bread in local parks and neighbourhoods.

To guarantee something more exciting than canned coffee and Pocari Sweat (a popular sports drink), head to the bafflingly named Rat Sunrise used tyre shop in Sagamihara, where you'll find over 100 painstakingly restored retro vending machines. They're mostly from the Showa era (1926–89), and many Japanese people visit to relive those beloved memories of instant meals, favourite sweets and childhood snacks. But even if you have no fond childhood attachment to Bon Curry or instant *udon* noodles, there's something charming about the loving attention to detail that has gone into the restoration and design of these old machines. And, honestly, fizzy drinks just taste better from glass bottles, don't they?

— MAKE IT HAPPEN —

Rat Sunrise tyre shop is in Sagamihara, a city in Kanagawa prefecture.

Though the tyre shop closes around 6pm, all of the machines are available 24 hours a day.

Access is easiest by car, but you can also take the JR Sagami line to Harataima station.

Glimpse the fascinating future of train travel

See record-breaking magnetic levitation trains in the shadow of Mount Fuji

Levitating vehicles may feel like something from a retro-futuristic 1950s cartoon, but in Japan they're a reality. Though they only hover about 10 cm (4 in) above the ground, these trains have the potential to revolutionize rail travel in Japan and beyond. Development of magnetic levitation (maglev) trains began in earnest in the 1960s, with the first line linking Birmingham's airport and train station in the UK from 1984 to 1995. The technology has now been used in several countries, but Japan can stake a claim to planning the first long-distance commercial route, with the brand new Chuo maglev line between Tokyo and Nagoya (later continuing to Osaka) planned to open in the 2030s. The service will cut the journey time from 90 minutes to just 40.

While this service is in the works, you can see prototypes of sleek trains, learn about superconducting magnetic levitation technology and even ride a mini maglev train at Yamanashi Prefectural Maglev Exhibition Center, in Fuji Five Lakes. You may even be able to watch a speed test – they've been conducted here since 1997, including the 2015 test of an L0 Series SCMaglev train that set the world speed record for any type of train, reaching 603 km/h (375 mph). In Japan, the future of rail travel is within touching distance.

— MAKE IT HAPPEN —

The Yamanashi Prefectural Maglev Exhibition Center is in Tsuru, northeast of Mount Fuji.

The centre is closed on Mondays. Check the website for dates of speed tests (*linear-museum.pref.yamanashi.jp*).

There are regular buses to the centre from Otsuki station.

A maglev train, Yamanashi Prefectural Maglev Exhibition Center

61

Enter a new reality at Tokyo Tower's digital amusement park

Delve into Japan's cutting-edge gaming tech at this family-friendly attraction

With its memorable red and white stripes and Eiffel Tower silhouette, Tokyo Tower has been a beloved symbol of the city since its construction in 1958. Its two observation decks (150 m/490 ft and 250 m/820 ft) are one of the main draws, with their 360-degree views that take in the elegant spire of Tokyo Skytree and – on clear days – Mount Fuji on the horizon.

But the tower's lower levels are well worth exploring, too. They're home to RED° Tokyo Tower, the biggest digital amusement park in Japan, where you can immerse yourself in a vast range of the country's state-of-the-art gaming technologies. The collection is impressive: amusement arcade classics; VR (virtual reality) survival and racing games; AR (augmented reality) dodgeball and climbing; hyper-realistic racing simulators; a devilishly difficult game of *daruma ga koronda* (red light, green light) with strings set up like Mission Impossible-style lasers; and much more. The excitement and adrenaline certainly adds a new shine to this retro Tokyo icon. You'll be hard pressed to leave its thrilling confines.

MAKE IT HAPPEN

 Tokyo Tower is located in the capital's Minato ward, next to Shiba Park and Azabudai Hills. Despite the number of high buildings nearby, it can be seen from surrounding neighbourhoods.

 Tickets cover a specific time period; separate tickets are needed for the observation deck. RED° Tokyo Tower is open daily; check the website for hours (*tokyotower.red-brand.jp*).

 There's easy access to the tower by public transport. The nearest stations are Akebanebashi (on Oedo subway line), Kamiyacho (on the Hibiya line) and Onarimon (on the Mita line).

Playing motor racing games at RED° Tokyo Tower

FUTURISTIC JAPAN

Other immersive experiences

1
Miraikan
At Tokyo's Miraikan (National Museum of Emerging Science and Innovation), you're surrounded by cutting-edge discoveries and tech. The 10 million-pixel resolution in the Dome Theater makes the footage screened feel incredibly real.

2
teamLab
When it comes to digital art, teamLab leads the pack. You can explore their digital worlds in Fukuoka (p151), Osaka and Saitama, but their Tokyo locations are best known. Set aside a few hours to explore the nature-inspired art at teamLab Borderless in Azabudai Hills (p142).

3
Universal Studios Japan
As well as the usual thrill rides, Universal Studios Japan has one or two VR-enhanced attractions. The technology is a fun addition to the park, letting you inhabit your favourite fictional worlds.

Tokyo Tower lighting up the city at night

FUTURISTIC JAPAN

"Nagoya has been driving Japan's economy forward since the 19th century."

Toyopet Crown, Toyota Commemorative Museum of Industry and Technology

Consider Japan's industrial past and future in Nagoya

With its *monozukuri* (manufacturing) culture, this lively city embraces invention and innovation

Nagoya has been driving Japan's economy forward since the end of the 19th century. In the Meiji era (1868–1912), the city became a major centre of ceramic and textile production, developing pride in its culture of making things ("*monozukuri*"). Then in the 1910s, the Toyota Group was founded in the area – firstly as a textile manufacturer, and later expanding into an automobile company. After most of Nagoya was destroyed in World War II, it was rebuilt bigger than ever, contributing its industrial and manufacturing expertise to the postwar Japanese "economic miracle". Toyota became one of the country's leading companies, and the so-called Toyota Way – underpinned by principles like *kaizen* (continuous improvement) – became the focus of global interest.

The Toyota Nagoya office is right in the city centre, in the Midland Square skyscraper opposite the station. The city's tallest building, it has an excellent Sky Panorama observation deck on floors 44 to 46. Look north of the station from there and you might spot an inviting patch of green: this is Noritake Garden, which offers a scenic introduction to Nagoya's *monozukuri* culture. As well as a pretty green space, it includes historic red-brick warehouses where you can buy beautiful Noritake porcelain, discover its production process and even join an expert-led ceramics workshop.

To learn more about Toyota itself, make your first stop the Toyota Commemorative Museum of Industry and Technology, set in one of the company's old red-brick factories. It runs through Toyota's early days, from 1890s looms clanking and rattling in long rows to the robotic arms used by the car manufacturer today. If you have time, add on a visit to the Toyota Kaikan Museum, which showcases the company's new technologies.

You'll see even more technology at SCMaglev and Railway Park, in Nagoya's docklands. Here you can explore real train cars, from steam locomotives to *shinkansen*, and learn all about Japan's rail innovations. You can also try out a train simulator, which leaves kids – and any adults who ever dreamed of being a train driver – giddy with excitement. For more interactive science, drop by the Nagoya City Science Museum. The huge space has hands-on exhibits, a mesmerizing Tesla coil demonstration, and one of the world's largest planetariums. Through each of these institutions, Nagoya celebrates its history of innovation – and by doing so, it aims to inspire the inventors of tomorrow.

— MAKE IT HAPPEN —

Nagoya is the capital of Aichi, a prefecture on the south coast of central Honshu between Tokyo and Kyoto. The Toyota Kaikan Museum is attached to an active factory, just southeast of Nagoya in Toyota city.

All the museums plus Noritake Garden are closed on Mondays, except Toyota Kaikan (closed Sun) and SCMaglev and Railway Park (closed Tue). Individual shops and cafés in Midland Square and Noritake Garden may have different closing days. Check websites for accurate details on tickets, opening and events.

Nagoya is served by Chubu Centrair airport, and is on the Tokaido *shinkansen* line between Tokyo and Osaka. All the museums and sights mentioned are either walkable from Nagoya station, or accessible by public transport from there.

Meet the friendly and adorable robots of Tokyo

From hotel check-ins to anime-style fights, robots pop up in unexpected places

Japan is perhaps equally famous for its glorious history and traditions, and for its pioneering approach to the future. On the one hand you have elegant geisha, imposing castles and sumptuous *kaiseki* cuisine; on the other there are skyscrapers, bullet trains and – perhaps most futuristic-feeling of all – robots. You'll probably encounter some organically on your travels, maybe dispensing information at airports or train stations, or delivering drinks in cafés with a winking cat face.

Humanoid "Pepper" robots have become a fairly common sight across Tokyo, their minimalist white design and placid features making them a popular choice, particularly in hospitality settings. Naturally, you'll meet plenty of Peppers at the city's Pepper Parlor café – the friendly robots trundle between tables to take orders and play games, and chunky little robots periodically put on a dance performance for guests. To guarantee a special robot encounter, book a night at a Henn na Hotel (with locations across Japan), where the check-in counter is manned by an assortment of humanoid, animal and dinosaur robots (and many rooms have robotic smartphones).

Taking robot service even further, Avatar Robot Café DAWN uses OriHime robots – both cute tabletop models and larger ones that provide table service – each piloted by people who can't easily leave their homes and may have limited physical mobility. Not only does this provide steady, flexible employment, but it also helps forge connections between the pilots and customers. You can even try piloting one of the smaller models yourself.

Tokyo's innovative robots aren't used only for serving hungry customers or ensuring a smooth check-in, however. Make for RED° Tokyo Tower (p154) and you face off against a friend in an epic one-on-one battle while wearing and controlling a 15-kg (33-lb) robot suit. It gives you a unique chance to live out your wildest anime fantasies.

Despite its reputation as a pop culture paradise and its "electric town" nickname, the area of Akihabara has surprisingly few robots. But it does provide easy access to Science Square TSUKUBA, a museum that explores the impact of technology and science on daily life. Ranging from care to lab work to hospitality, the fascinating displays give vital insights into how robotics is already touching so many parts of our lives beyond the café or hotel. Though many of the city's friendly robots seem like something of a gimmick, they are a small part of a transformative new era.

MAKE IT HAPPEN

DAWN is in Nihonbashi, Tokyo Tower near Roppongi, and Pepper Parlor in Shibuya. Henn na Hotel has several Tokyo locations, with Robohon available at the one in Maihama (near Tokyo Disney). Science Square TSUKUBA is just outside the city, in Ibaraki prefecture.

DAWN is closed on Thursdays, and requires advance booking for seats in the OriHime Diner section (dawn2021.orylab.com/en). Science Square TSUKUBA is closed on Mondays. The cafés and hotels are open daily.

For step-free access to DAWN, use Mitsukoshimae (Ginza and Hanzomon subway lines) and Kanda (JR Yamanote, Chuo and Keihin-Tohoku lines) stations. Take the Tsukuba Express line from Akihabara to Tsukuba then the Kanto bus to Namiki 2-chome for Science Square TSUKUBA.

FUTURISTIC JAPAN

"Chunky little robots periodically put on a dance performance for guests."

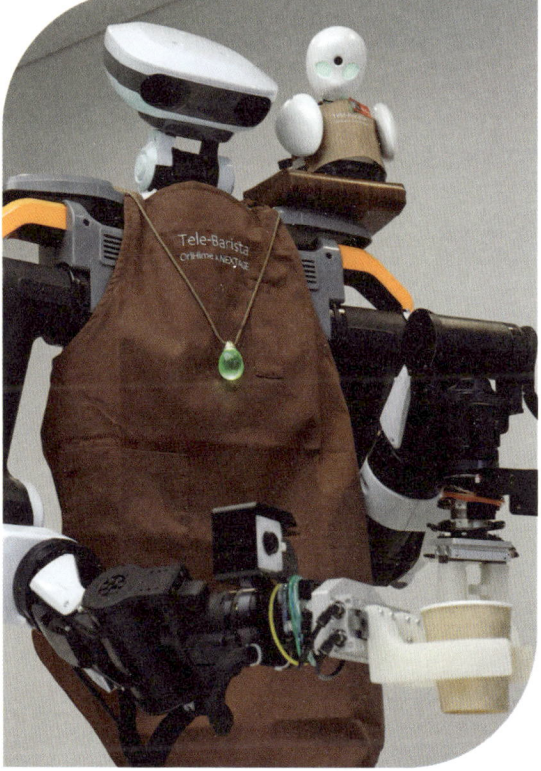

Top A "Pepper" robot
Left Drinks served by an OriHime robot at DAWN
Right A barista robot making a cup of coffee

FUTURISTIC JAPAN

Osaka's futuristic districts

1
Den Den Town
Crammed with electronics shops, anime stores and gaming cafés, Den Den Town is particularly strong on otaku goods. Try your luck at gacha games and claw machines to win figurines, browse shops with rare merchandise and dine at cool themed cafés.

2
Shinsekai
Literally translating as "New World", Shinsekai was designed in 1912 as Japan's vision of the future. At its heart is Tsutenkaku, a tower (with observation deck) that could have been pulled from the pages of a 1950s sci-fi novel, especially when lit up in neon.

3
Umeda
This district of shimmering skyscrapers lies around Osaka station. Whizz up 173 m (568 ft) to the Sky Building's observatory to marvel at the vast expanse of the city below.

64

Explore Osaka's skyscraper sandbank

Meander past some of Osaka's best architecture and museums in Nakanoshima

Japan's vast cities are thrilling, but they can also be a little intimidating, sprawling over huge areas without one clear centre. Osaka is a prime example of this – is it more convenient to stay by Osaka station, or near the *shinkansen* station 3.5 km (2.2 miles) away? Is Osaka Castle "central", or is that the Namba district? Rather than trying to understand how everything fits together, it can be useful to ease yourself in by focusing on one or two neighbourhoods. And in Osaka, Nakanoshima is the best place to start.

This sandbank between rivers measures just 3 km (2.2 miles) end to end, and 300 m (1,000 ft) at its widest point, but it packs a lot into the space. Head to its eastern end and you'll see that it's been a centre of commerce and modernization since the turn of the 20th century: the grand Bank of Japan, Neo-Classical Prefectural Library and Neo-Baroque Central Public Hall are still impressive today. You'll also see futuristic marvels from more recent years, including the spiky steel sculpture around the National Museum of Art Osaka's entrance, the matte black cube of the Nakanoshima Museum of Art (NAKKA), and of course plenty of skyscrapers – head up to Festival Tower West's 40th floor for a cocktail with a sweeping view. A microcosm of the wider city, Nakanoshima is the perfect place to get your bearings, while experiencing the ultra-modern buzz that makes Japan's metropolises so dynamic.

National Museum of Art Osaka

MAKE IT HAPPEN

Nakanoshima divides the Tosabori and Dojima rivers. It's south of Umeda, west of Osaka Castle and north of Shinsaibashi and Namba.

Most of Nakanoshima's museums are open around 10am–5pm, and closed on Mondays (Tue if Mon is a national holiday).

Nakanoshima is very well connected with the rest of Osaka. There are four stations on the island, all on the Keihan Nakanoshima line.

A contemporary architecture odyssey

SUGGESTED DURATION 10 days **START** Tokyo; fly in to one of the city's international airports, Narita or Haneda **GETTING AROUND** This itinerary relies on regular and bullet trains **END** Karuizawa; the town is served by bullet and regular trains that go to Nagano and Tokyo

Area of map

Japan's taste for the future isn't just seen in robots and gadgets – it's visible on streets across the country, where architects have designed cutting-edge buildings that elicit gasps of wonder. And that's exactly what this itinerary will have you doing. This tour takes you on a loop from Tokyo, up through Shikoku's north coast and Kyoto, and along the Hokuriku region, giving you a small sample of some of the country's most forward-thinking projects by exciting architects. And it's not just revolutionary buildings that you'll come across; even our most basic urges are aided by hot new technologies, with artfully designed sleep laboratories monitoring our slumber and high-tech public toilets taking convenience to new heights.

5. IMABARI TO ONOMICHI
Take a two-hour JR train from Takamatsu to Imabari, where you can rent a bike to cycle across the bridges of the Shimanami Kaido *(p178)*. Finish your cycle in Onomichi, where you'll find the 17 outdoor sculptures of the Shimagoto Art Museum, including the geometric metal Belvedere Setoda, which stands in the water of the Seto Inland Sea.

6. KYOTO
Two *shinkansen* get you to Kyoto, a city that blends the old with the new perfectly. Focus on the modern side while you're here, visiting the glass-and-steel hall of Kyoto station and cutting-edge museums like the sleek National Museum of Modern Art.

3. OSAKA
Get a one-hour *shinkansen* to Osaka and explore the skyscrapers and museums on the Nakanoshima Sandbank *(p162)*. Head up to the Umeda Sky Building's Floating Garden observation deck for an impressive view over the city.

4. TAKAMATSU
Take a *shinkansen*, then a JR train, to Takamatsu, the biggest city on the island of Shikoku. As well as being a hotspot for modernist architecture, like Kenzo Tange's Kagawa Prefectural Government Office, the city also has contemporary stand-outs like the Takamatsu Symbol Tower to explore.

7. KANAZAWA
This city might be known for its traditional Japanese architecture, but the 21st Century Museum of Contemporary Art gives it a modern edge. To see the experimental works of art, design and architecture here, take two trains from Kyoto.

8. TOYAMA
Just 20 minutes from Kanazawa is this former castle town turned modern city. Explore the beautifully preserved (and re-interpreted) traditional buildings of the Iwase district, and the sleek modern structures of the Glass Art Musem and the Museum of Art and Design.

9. KARUIZAWA
End your tour in affluent Karuizawa, a 1.5-hour *shinkansen* ride from Toyama. Nature might be the main draw to this town, but around its wildlife-rich forests are innovative buildings, including the undulating Stone Church and Hiroshi Senju Museum.

END

START

2. NAGOYA
Nagoya's modern cityscape is peppered with intriguing structures like the twisted Mode Gakuen Spiral Towers and the Nagoya Science Museum's planetarium *(p159)*, a huge metal ball that seems to float in the air. Get here via *shinkansen* from Tokyo.

1. TOKYO
It's only right to start your tour in Japan's most futuristic city. See how Tokyo takes architecture to new heights with impressive skyscrapers like Tokyo Tower *(p154)*, ambitious projects like Azabudai Hills *(p142)* and even architect-designed public toilets *(p149)*. Then, bed down at 9h (nine hours) Akasaka sleep lab *(p144)*.

JOURNEYS

IN JAPAN

Japan is made for epic journeys. Over the centuries, paths have been worn over its mountains and along its valleys, and an excellent transport system has ensured that it's always about the journey, not the destination.

ON THE MAP
JOURNEYS IN JAPAN

- **65** Trace the sacred trails of the Kumano Kodo
- **66** Follow exiled emperors and intellectuals to Sadogashima
- **67** Ride the rails beneath the sea to Hokkaido
- **68** Drive through the clouds on the Bandai-Azuma Skyline
- **69** Cycle the Shimanami Kaido over the Seto Inland Sea
- **70** Hike up holy Mount Daisen
- **71** Walk the Michinoku Coastal Trail's path to recovery
- **72** Traverse the majestic Northern Japan Alps
- **73** Drift off on Japan's last sleeper service
- **74** Catch the slow boat to Beppu
- **75** Ride a *mama-chari* across the Kibi Plain
- **76** Become an *ohenro-san* on Shikoku's ancient pilgrimage route

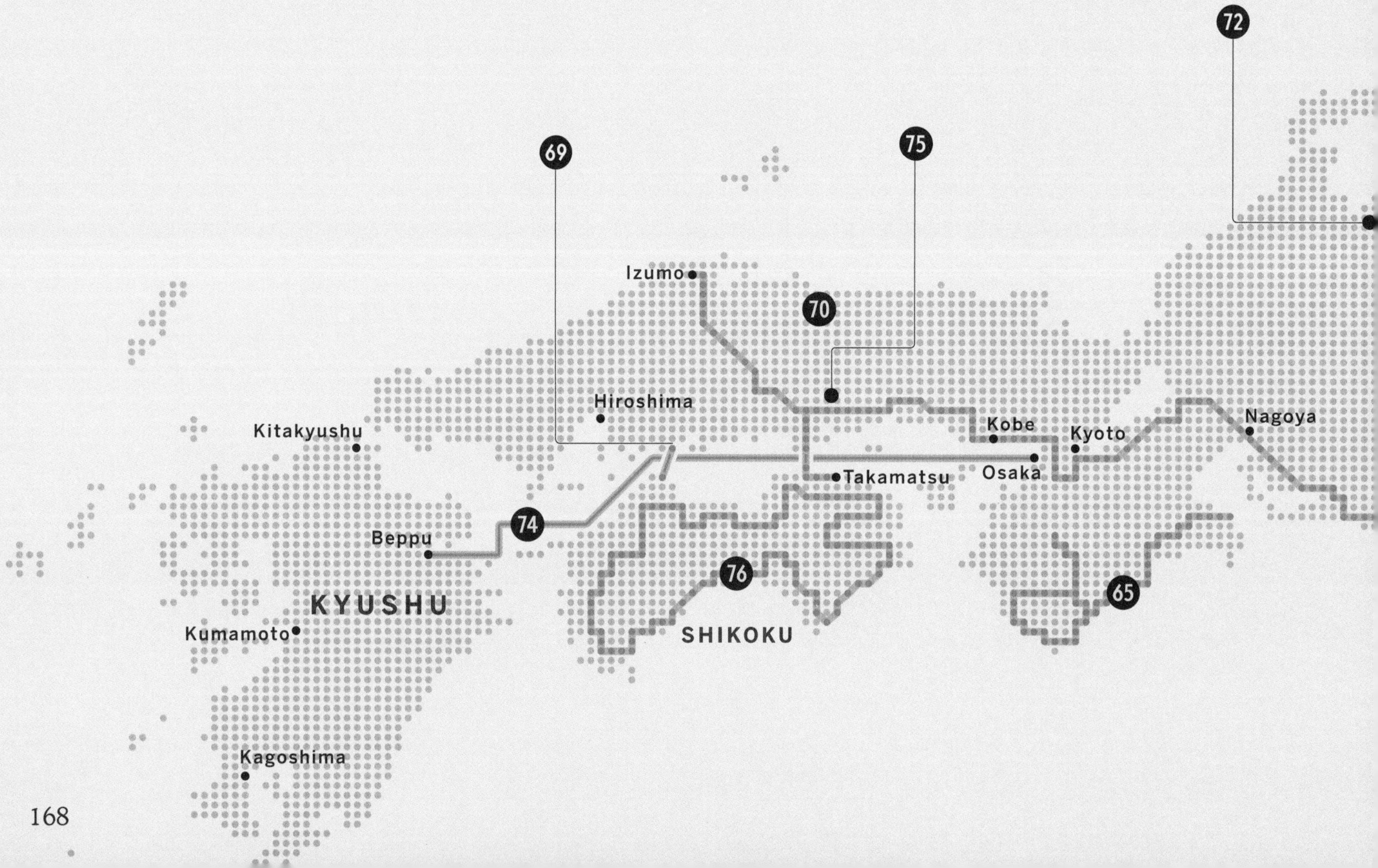

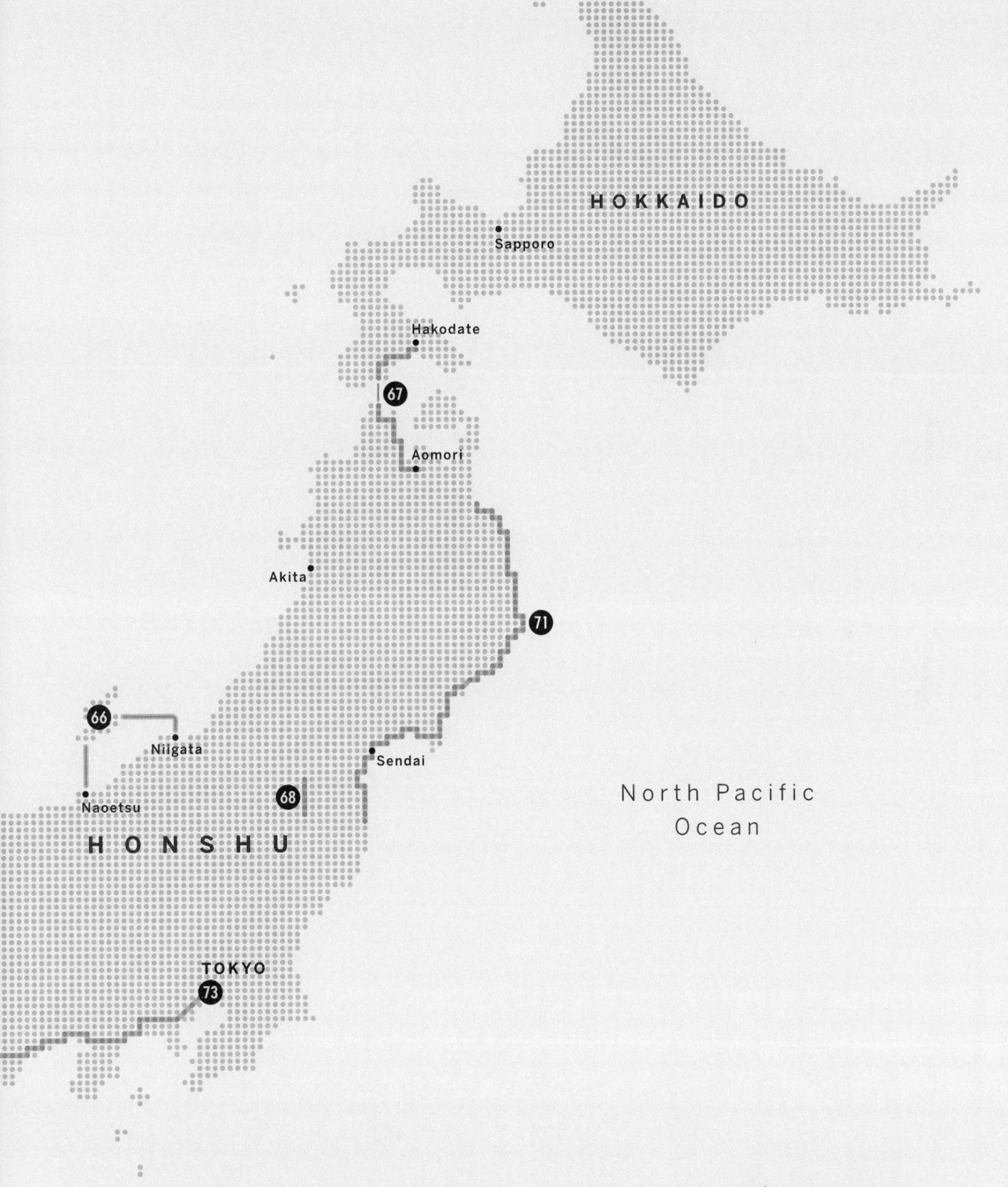

Trace the sacred trails of the Kumano Kodo

One of the world's two UNESCO-listed pilgrimages, this route weaves through the spiritual heartland of Japan

Thundering waterfalls, misty forests, ancient hot springs… The trails of the Kumano Kodo pilgrimage route pass through the mysterious and wild landscapes of the Kii peninsula. It's an area known as the "land of the gods" (in the Shinto belief system, deities reside in every tree, river and waterfall here) and pilgrims have been following these ancient routes for more than 1,000 years. Four of the paths remain, all of which lead to the Kumano Sanzan shrines, some of Japan's most important Shinto shrines.

The Iseji is the longest of the Kumano Kodo's trails, winding its way east for 170 km (105 miles) to Ise-jingu, a major shrine linked to the Imperial Family. With its length comes diversity – mountain passes, cobbled paths, rice paddies and bays – and it's easy to pick out a couple of sections to focus on for a few days. The coastal Ohechi offers a shorter adventure. Featuring impressive sea views and passing through a series of resort towns and fishing villages, this ancient route gives you a chance to experience the local culture and hospitality. The trail's most beautiful areas are at its western end and include the Tonda-zaka section, which takes you through pine forests and up to the Ohechi's highest point: Agotsujimatsu Pass.

It's the two inland routes, though, that promise the most spectacular scenery of the Kumano Kodo. The most popular is the Nakahechi, which starts at the Ohechi's western end, heads up to Kumano Hongu Taisha, then branches into two. One section leads to Nachi Taisha and the eastern Ohechi, the other to Kumano Hayatama Taisha at the Iseji's southwestern end. It's possible to complete the whole route in a week, thereby seeing all three of the Kumano Kodo's main shrines. The scenery is stunning: the vermilion pagoda of Nachi Taisha standing guard by its namesake falls, at 133 m (436 ft) the highest single-drop waterfall in Japan; the blue thread of the Kumano River; and the steaming, soothing hot springs of Yunomine Onsen.

The final route of the Kumano Kodo, the Kohechi, is the most challenging and the least-travelled. Leading from Hongu Taisha through the heart of the mountains to the holy peak of Koya-san, its leg-busting path rewards hardy hikers with breathtaking scenery and hours of quiet immersion in nature. The route includes several passes over 1,000 m (3,300 ft), and the Kumano Kodo's highest point – Mount Obako, at 1,344 m (4,409 ft). And having started at one of Japan's most holy Shinto sites, walkers can finish at the headquarters of the Shingon Buddhist sect on Koya-san, even staying overnight with a *shukubo* (temple stay) – just like the pilgrims did a century or so ago.

— MAKE IT HAPPEN —

The Kumano Kodo trails traverse the southern end of the Kii peninsula – south of Kyoto and Osaka – in Wakayama, Nara and Mie prefectures.

For details about routes and accommodation, *tb-kumano.jp/en* is a useful resource. Always check the weather and ensure you have proper equipment, no matter which section you're walking. Some parts of the trails, especially the northern Kohechi, have to close mid-December to mid-March due to heavy snowfall.

Most of the railway stations on this mountainous peninsula are located on the more developed coastline. Kii-Tanabe is the most convenient station for the western ends of the Nakahechi and Ohechi routes; Kii-Katsuura and Nachi serve the eastern end of the Ohechi and Nakahechi; and Shingu is good for eastern Nakahechi and the southwestern end of the Iseji.

JOURNEYS IN JAPAN

"In the local Shinto belief system, deities reside in every tree, river and waterfall."

Top left Yunomine Onsen
Top right The sacred site of Kyo-san
Left Nachi Taisha pagoda, with its falls in the background

171

Follow exiled emperors and intellectuals to Sadogashima

Today an island paradise, Sadogashima has a fascinating and dark history

In centuries gone by, Sadogashima, or Sado, was a place of exile. Anyone causing trouble to the powers that be risked being sent here – a rugged, remote and isolated island from which you might never return. Among the ranks of the dissidents and disruptors sent here were some towering historical figures: Nichiren, the philosopher-priest who founded a school of Buddhism; Zeami Motokiyo, a master of Noh theatre; and even a 13th-century emperor, Juntoku. In 1601, gold and silver were discovered in the north of the island, and the type of exile changed from the politically powerful to Edo-period convicts sent to work. In the 20th century, labourers from occupied Korea were forcibly brought to work in the mines, which eventually closed in 1989.

While living conditions during exile were harsh, life wasn't devoid of culture. Many artists and workers brought their own traditions with them, from Shogunate-assigned government officials who promoted Noh performances to shipmen who introduced folk songs that were sung in the mines. This cultural legacy remains today, with Japan's highest number of Noh theatres per capita and festivals featuring *okesa* folk songs. It's this, along with Sado's natural beauty and subtropical climate, that has made it a popular place to live and visit.

The difference today, however, is that the journey to Sado is a cheerful one; either take a ferry (with typical Japanese touches like an arcade, vending machine restaurant and designated floor space for napping) or enjoy a high-speed jetfoil, which feels as though it's flying over the water. As the island begins to emerge on the horizon, its hulking silhouette still looks undeniably intimidating. Some places feel slightly ominous, too, like the pockmarked lava fields of Ogi and the concrete ruins of Kitazawa Flotation Plant being reclaimed by nature. Yet the spectacular coastline, lovely villages and wooded interior give the impression of a paradise, not a prison, today.

It's a feeling that's sustained when exploring Sado's headline attractions, many of which are clustered around the coastline. Take the area around Ogi, a port town in the southwest that's home to the humble *taraibune*, or "tub boat", a small vessel originally made by cutting a barrel in half. *Spirited Away* fans might recognize the rustic craft, which is steered by twisting one squeaky oar in a figure of eight, but anyone can appreciate it as a scenic (and unusual) way to see the harbour. Once you're back on land, catch a Noh performance before bedding down in a *ryokan*, drifting off to the sound of the sea lapping at the shore.

— MAKE IT HAPPEN —

Sadogashima is in central Japan's Niigata prefecture, around 35 km (22 miles) from the coast of Honshu, and is Japan's sixth-largest island.

Sadogashima is quite large, so it's worth staying overnight to explore the island's farther-flung corners.

There are regular ferries from Naoetsu to Ogi (late April to mid-November only), in Sado's southwest, and from Niigata to Ryotsu (year round), in the east. Note that jetfoils (year round; reservations required) only cover the Niigata to Ryotsu route. The Joetsu *shinkansen* line from Tokyo stops at Nagaoka (from where the Shin'etsu main line goes to Naoetsu) and Niigata. Buses service the island, but can be infrequent and slow, so it's worth hiring a rental car to get around. Most car outlets are found in Ryotsu Town, the island's main town.

JOURNEYS IN JAPAN

Top Leafy Sado Island
Left Taking in the island scenery on a local tub boat
Right Fishing on a tub boat

JOURNEYS IN JAPAN

67

Ride the rails beneath the sea to Hokkaido

A marvel of construction, the Seikan Tunnel connects Honshu and Hokkaido

At the Tsugaru peninsula's northern tip, in a quiet area dense with evergreens, clattering freight trains and sleek *shinkansen* enter a perfectly normal-looking tunnel. The forested landscape into which they emerge, though, is on a different island: Hokkaido. Until the 1980s, the only way to make this journey was by boat – sometimes a risky endeavour, as Typhoon Marie tragically highlighted in 1954 by sinking five ferries and causing 1,430 people to lose their lives. Constructing an undersea tunnel was a mammoth undertaking, but finally in 1988 the Seikan Tunnel opened.

It's still remarkable today: the world's longest tunnel with an undersea section; second-longest railway tunnel; and deepest undersea railway tunnel. As of 2016, even high-speed *shinkansen* can pass through it, taking just 20 minutes to traverse the Tsugaru Strait and link Honshu's laid-back city of Aomori with Hakodate. This pretty port city is a great introduction to Hokkaido, with its international atmosphere, delicious dairy and seafood, and well-preserved historic buildings. Take the streetcar to the Museum of Northern Peoples to learn about the history of Hokkaido's Indigenous Ainu people, and the impressive network of trade routes they maintained – even without the benefit of an undersea tunnel – before Hokkaido was annexed by Japan in 1869.

Hakodate from above

MAKE IT HAPPEN

 The Seikan Tunnel links the Tsugaru peninsula in Honshu's far northern Aomori prefecture with the southernmost part of Hokkaido.

 There are plans to extend the *shinkansen* line to Hokkaido's capital, Sapporo, in the 2030s. Until then, it terminates in Hakodate.

 The Tohoku *shinkansen* line becomes the Hokkaido *shinkansen* in Aomori; there is no need to change trains if coming from Tokyo.

Drive through the clouds on the Bandai-Azuma Skyline

Nicknamed "the road that runs across the sky", this is one of Japan's most scenic routes

Each April, the slopes of Fukushima city's Hanamiyama blush as 700 cherry trees come into bloom. It's an indicator that spring has arrived, and with it, the prefecture's Bandai-Azuma Skyline has reopened after its winter slumber. But no matter when you drive this route – in the spring, when walls of snow still linger; in the summer, when green leaves cover the mountains; or in the autumn, when the trees are a coppery hue – you're guaranteed a beautiful journey.

Starting at the hot-spring resort of Takayu Onsen, this alpine road crisscrosses the Bandai-Asahi National Park for 29 km (18 miles). Along the 90-minute drive, the path hits an average elevation of 1,350 m (4,400 ft), so spectacular views are a given. The first epic overlook, around 15 minutes in, is the elegant Fudosawa Bridge, where wispy clouds drift down to Tsubakuro Valley and Fukushima city is visible in all its glory. A little further on you'll reach Jododaira, a scenic signal that you're halfway along the route. It's the perfect point to stretch the legs, either taking a nature walk along subalpine marshes or hiking to the active volcano crater of Mount Azuma-Kofuji. After the road's end point at Tsuchiyu Pass, wind your way to Tsuchiyu Onsen for a steaming hot-spring bath.

MAKE IT HAPPEN

The route is in the easternmost section of Tohoku's Bandai-Asahi National Park, about 30 minutes' drive west of Fukushima city.

The road is closed mid-November to early April. There are few hotels along the route, but plenty in Fukushima city and the onsen towns.

The route links Takayu Onsen in the north to Tsuchiyu Pass near Mount Azuma-Kofuji. Fukushima is on the Tohoku and Yamagata *shinkansen* lines.

Bandai-Azuma Skyline in the autumn

JOURNEYS IN JAPAN

Three onsen by Bandai-Azuma

·········· **1** ··········

Takayu Onsen
The milky, blue-tinged waters of Takayu Onsen, at the northern end of the Bandai-Azuma Skyline, are drawn from nine different sources. The resort is home to 11 bathing facilities, traditional ryokan and no souvenir shops in sight.

·········· **2** ··········

Tsuchiyu Onsen
Near the southern end of the route is Tsuchiyu Onsen, a laid-back hot-spring resort with access to great hiking in the surrounding mountains. Try your hand at making kokeshi (cylindrical wooden dolls) here with a local artisan.

·········· **3** ··········

Iizaka Onsen
Iizaka Onsen completes the trio of hot-spring towns around Fukushima city, sitting just to its north. It's a great spot for classic onsen resort activities, like enjoying hot spring-steamed cuisine at an izakaya.

JOURNEYS IN JAPAN

69

Cycle the Shimanami Kaido over the Seto Inland Sea

Weaving between idyllic islands, this easily accessible cycle route is deservedly famous

One of Japan's most spectacular cycling routes takes you through two prefectures, over eight small islands, and along 70 km (43 miles) of road as it crosses the Seto Inland Sea. This is the Shimanami Kaido, an expressway built to connect the islands of Honshu and Shikoku, and it's made up of both a car toll road and a cycle toll-free road. It's the cycling highway that's garnered the most attention, though, and it's no understatement to call it Japan's most famous cycle route – an accolade it fully deserves.

Taking the cycle path gives you enough speed to cover plenty of ground and enough flexibility to stop whenever you'd like and take in your stunning surroundings. The six white bridges connecting the islands are not only elegant and eye-catching, they're also smooth and well-marked, making them a joy to cycle on. Naturally, ocean views are a big draw, but take the time to explore the islands and you'll also find charming small-town scenes and rural spots. There's incredible food along the way, too, making use of local ingredients like lemons from the groves of Ikuchijima, sea salt – try *shio* (salt) ramen or *shio* ice cream – and of course plenty of fantastically fresh fish. You can cycle the route in a day, but embrace the slow travel ethos and stay overnight on one of the islands if you can.

— MAKE IT HAPPEN —

The route starts in Onomichi (Hiroshima prefecture) in Honshu and finishes in Imabari (Ehime prefecture) in Shikoku.

Rent bikes and gear at either end of the route, and drop them off at your arrival stop.

Onomichi has a *shinkansen* and a regular train station. Imabari is on the JR Yosan line.

Combine with KIBI PLAIN

For a more leisurely cycle in the same area, head for the Kibi Plain (p189) near Okayama, where you can spend an afternoon admiring pretty rural scenery from the saddle.

Cycling part of the Shimanami Kaido

Walking a Mount Daisen trail

70

Hike up holy Mount Daisen

The Chugoku region's highest peak has some excellent trails

— MAKE IT HAPPEN —

Mount Daisen is in Daisen-Oki National Park, in western Honshu's Tottori prefecture.

Check the weather in advance. Winter hiking, snowshoeing and skiing are possible.

There are buses to Daisen-ji from Yonago and Daisenguchi stations (both JR San'in line).

Given that a good three quarters of Japan's landmass is mountainous, it stands to reason that it has some impeccable hiking. Mount Daisen, with its diverse and well-signposted network of trails, is a great example. At 1,729 m (5,673 ft), it's the highest peak in the Chugoku (western Honshu) region, and is considered sacred to multiple religions. It's one of the most important sites for adherents of Shugendo (a syncretic mountain-worship religion), whose sacred paths laid the foundations of many of the mountain's modern trails. It's also home to a number of religious sites, including Ogamiyama-jinja Okumiya, a peaceful Shinto shrine in the woods on Daisen's northern face, and Daisen-ji, a Tendai-sect Buddhist temple founded in the 8th century at the base of the mountain. And it's from Daisen-ji that many of the mountain's popular walking trails begin. Routes include the two-hour out-and-back walk to the wooded valley of Motodani; the challenging Utopia Course, where you can rest at a mountain hut in a field of flowers; and the popular five-hour Natsuyama loop, which leads up stone steps and through ancient beech forests to Daisen's highest accessible point, Mount Misen, at 1,709 m (5,608 ft). Whether you reach the summit or not, you'll be rewarded with breathtaking views.

JOURNEYS IN JAPAN

Museums about the 3/11 disaster

·········· **1** ··········

Kesennuma City Memorial Museum
This moving museum is a school that has been mostly kept as it was after the tsunami, with books and debris strewn about, and a tangle of rubble and cars wedged between buildings.

·········· **2** ··········

Iwate Tsunami Memorial Museum
Inside this museum are sensitive displays and videos with English explanations. Outside in the peaceful park, where tens of thousands of pine trees once stood, are the preserved remains of one tree, stark and beautiful.

·········· **3** ··········

MINAMISANRIKU 311 Memorial
The Kengo Kuma-designed space focuses on first-hand accounts. Visitors are asked to listen, and to consider how they might face something similar. It's thoughtfully done, and the interactivity helps the important lessons stick.

71

Walk the Michinoku Coastal Trail's path to recovery

This long-distance trail bears witness to nature's power and humanity's resilience

You may not know it when looking at the verdant lawns of the Tanesashi Coast or the red pines clinging to the craggy Kitayamazaki Cliffs, but this stretch of coastline was a site of devastation in 2011. On 11 March, a 9.0-magnitude earthquake struck off Honshu's northeastern coast, triggering a major tsunami that swept through sea defences. It's estimated that 450,000 people were displaced and almost 20,000 lost their lives due to the disaster.

In its wake, there was a recovery effort on a massive scale. A new national park was created, the Sanriku Fukko (Reconstruction) National Park, with the aim of both sharing the coast's spectacular beauty and educating people about disaster preparedness. Running the length of the park and more – it's 1,025 km (637 miles) end to end – the Michinoku Coastal Trail immerses you in beautiful landscapes, from white sand beaches to island-studded bays. But walking the route is about so much more; it also gives you opportunities to meet local residents. As well as learning about the 3/11 disaster, by patronising local businesses and buying local products you'll be contributing to the ongoing recovery effort. And that's certainly a journey worth taking.

> *"By patronising local businesses and buying local products you'll be contributing to the ongoing recovery effort."*

A serene beach along the Michinoku Coastal Trail

MAKE IT HAPPEN

 The park stretches from Hachinohe in Aomori down to Kesennuma in Miyagi. The trail continues south to Soma in Fukushima.

 Learn about the trail and source maps at *michinokutrail.com*. You can walk sections independently, or book a guided hike through an operator.

 The city of Hachinohe, at the trail's northern end, is on the Tohoku *shinkansen* line between Tokyo and Aomori.

72

Traverse the majestic Northern Japan Alps

Get unique views of the peaks from cable cars, funiculars and sightseeing boats

The jagged spine of mountains running the length of Honshu reaches its greatest heights in the centre of the island. Here in the Japan Alps you'll find almost all of the country's three-thousanders, towering peaks that reach over 3,000 m (9,843 ft). It's little surprise, then, that this is Japan's most popular area for mountain trekking. But hiking isn't for everyone, and there's more than one way to experience this spectacular alpine scenery. The popular Tateyama-Kurobe Alpine Route comprises multiple modes of transport (such as cable cars and funiculars) that traverse these formidable peaks, offering high-altitude access and epic views along the way. (Yet while they may be nifty, many are closed during winter, roughly November through March, as modern technology is still no match for the deep winters of Japan's Snow Country.)

The route begins in Tateyama (near Toyama), where you board a funicular that whisks you up to the lofty Bijodaira area. Here you can pause to wander through a primeval beech and cedar forest before hopping on a connecting bus that takes you deeper into the mountains. The winding route is especially memorable from April to June, when towering walls of snow up to 20 m (66 ft) tall line the road in a stark white "Snow Corridor". You can disembark at Midagahara to stroll along the boardwalks of the area's wetlands, or at the Alpine Route's highest point, Murodo (2450 m/8040 ft). The latter offers incredible views of the Tateyama mountain range, the peaks already draped in a blanket of snow while the autumn leaves are only just appearing at lower altitudes. Hiking trails abound in Murodo if you're looking for a trip on two feet, but if not, board another bus that travels through a tunnel to Daikanbo (it's a ten-minute drive).

Scenic Daikanbo is the gateway to one of the route's most breathtaking moments: a ropeway that glides through the air for 1.7 km (1 mile), affording sweeping panoramas of the mountains. It ends at Kurobedaira, another spot with jaw-dropping views; from here, a funicular heads to Kurobe Dam, Japan's tallest dam (186 m/282 ft) and one of the country's most impressive feats of engineering. It's your final stop, and after exploring – and paying your respects at the memorial to the 171 workers who died building it – you can retrace your steps to Toyama or head east to Shinano-Omachi by bus.

Eager for more adventures? The Japan Alps are also home to the scenic Kurobe Gorge Railway, which winds its way from Unazuki Onsen to Keyakidaira, and the Kurobe-Unazuki Canyon Route, which carves through the mountains to connect the railway with Kurobe Dam. They're a testament to Japan's technological achievements, giving everyone access to this incredible mountain landscape.

— MAKE IT HAPPEN —

The routes traverse the Northern Japan Alps in Toyama and Nagano prefectures. The Alpine Route heads west to Tateyama or east to Shinano-Omachi; the Gorge Railway runs from Unazuki Onsen to Keyakidaira; and the Canyon Route connects the two via Keyakidaira and Kurobe Dam.

Booking is essential or highly advised (*alpen-route.com*; *www.kurotetu.co.jp*; *canyon-route.jp*). Big bags are not allowed, so use a luggage-forwarding service if you're not doubling back. You can buy tickets for parts of the Alpine Route and Gorge Railway or the whole routes, but Canyon Route tickets are only sold as part of a package with an overnight stay.

You can access the Alpine Route from Toyama (also a *shinkansen* stop) or Shinano-Omachi on the JR Oito line. From Kurobe Unazuki Onsen (a Hokuriku *shinkansen* stop), the Toyama Chiho line runs to Unazuki Onsen, where the Gorge Railway starts.

JOURNEYS IN JAPAN

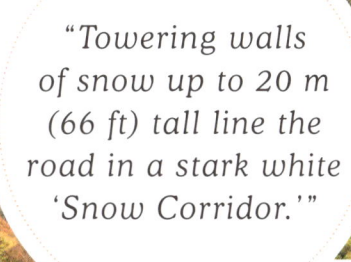

"Towering walls of snow up to 20 m (66 ft) tall line the road in a stark white 'Snow Corridor.'"

Top Cable car travelling along the Tateyama-Kurobe Alpine Route
Left Kurobe Gorge Railway
Right Tateyama's famed "Snow Corridor"

Tulips and cherry blossoms foregrounding the Tateyama mountains

73

Drift off on Japan's last sleeper service

Fall asleep under the bright lights of Tokyo, and wake up to calming rural scenery

From super-speed *shinkansen* to special seasonal services, Japan is famous for its trains, but surprisingly, it has only one regular sleeper left. The little-known *Sunrise Express* runs west from Tokyo station, sweeping from the eastern coast of Honshu island all the way to Okayama, where it splits into the Izumo (the longer journey, with more time to enjoy the scenery and splendid shrines) and Seto services.

While much of the journey consists of rural scenery, your adventure begins in Japan's bustling capital. It's here you'll climb aboard and hunker down in your berth for the night. Cheaper *nobi-nobi* tickets include a semi-private floor space with a blanket, pillowcase and window. If you're willing to splash some cash you can book single or twin berths (with pillows included this time); bag a seat in an upper-deck cabin and your window will curve slightly overhead (perfect for stargazing). There's no entertainment on board, no Wi-Fi and no restaurant car, but you'll soon realize that a window is all you need. As the train trundles out of Tokyo at 10pm, you'll find yourself gawking at the dazzling lights of the capital before being lulled to sleep by the soporific swaying of the train. When you wake up, you can gaze at the scenes rolling by, whether it's snow-covered villages, neatly tessellated rice paddies or the waters of Lake Shinji. And as you pull into Izumo at 10am, you'll find yourself refreshed, ready to explore its winding streets and splendid shrines.

MAKE IT HAPPEN

The *Sunrise Izumo* runs from Tokyo to Izumo, in western Honshu's Shimane prefecture. It's a daily service, and operates in both directions.

Tickets go on sale at 10am a month ahead, and sell fast. Buy in-person if you can; if not, try www.westjrco.jp/global/en/ticket/route_search.

Tickets are sold at JR ticket counters in Japan. You can buy tickets between any stops on the route, not just Tokyo and the terminus.

JOURNEYS IN JAPAN

Combine with SETO NAIKAI

Ride the Sunrise Seto to Takamatsu on Shikoku, and you'll be ideally placed to explore the creative and captivating Art Islands of the Seto Inland Sea (p200).

Above Izumo Taisha, a shrine in the city of Izumo
Below One of the train's sleeping cabins
Left The Sunrise Express sleeper service

Steam rising from Beppu's hot springs

74

Catch the slow boat to Beppu

Travel by sea to arrive in Kyushu's famous hot-spring resort in style

— MAKE IT HAPPEN —

Beppu is in Oita, in eastern Kyushu; Osaka is in Honshu's Kansai region, near Kyoto.

Check details and book tickets at *ferry-sunflower.co.jp*. Arrive at the port an hour early.

The San'yo and Tokaido *shinkansen* lines stop in Osaka. Beppu is on the JR Nippo line.

Beppu is the archetypal *onsen* resort, its cityscape dominated by drifting pillars of steam rising through grates and behind buildings. But it stands out from the rest in its sheer number of hot springs – close to 3,000, which make it one of Japan's most geothermally active areas. The relaxing and maybe even healing properties of Beppu's waters have made it a major holiday destination, popular with both domestic and international tourists.

Most people get there by plane or train, but to arrive in style, book passage on the *Ferry Sunflower* from Osaka, a comfortable and well-designed boat following a particularly scenic route. It departs around 7pm or 8pm, crossing the island-studded Seto Inland Sea and passing northern Shikoku's craggy shores before arriving, 12 hours later, in Beppu. On board, you can indulge at the buffet, watch the sunset or sunrise from the deck and pick up prettily packaged local products. Rooms range from dormitory-style to suite, and include lovely Japanese-style options with *tatami* floors.

After travelling over the water, it's time to get *in* the water. You'll reach Beppu bright and early (7am or 8am, depending on the day), right on time to go for a morning soak at one of the steaming, soothing public baths. What better way to start the day?

JOURNEYS IN JAPAN

Ride a *mama-chari* across the Kibi Plain

This easy cycle route leads through picturesque farmland to historic temples, shrines and burial mounds

With its slower pace of life and seemingly endless green fields, rural Japan was made for leisurely afternoons in the saddle. One of the most serene places to cycle is the Kibi Plain in Okayama prefecture, where a bike route meanders through picturesque flatland for 17 km (11 miles). Unlike a lot of rural Japan, the Kibi Plain has no hills save for the low wooded peaks ringing the plain, which means spending less time changing gears, more time soaking up the scenery. Simply head to a rental shop by the station at either end of the route, pick up a *mama-chari* – literally "mum's bike", an unfussy, economical bicycle with a roomy basket – and you're off.

While it's easy to cross the plain in four hours, don't rush. Get off the saddle to explore intriguing spots, maybe pausing for a picnic in the shade of a tree along the way, and get to know the area's fascinating culture and history en route. Stop off at sights like Bitchu-Kokubunji, a temple with flower-filled grounds and a five-storey pagoda, and grand Kibitsu-jinja, a 15th-century shrine linked to the beloved fairy tale of Momotaro. Then there are the 5th-century *kofun* (burial mounds), which speak to a time when this farmland was the heart of the Kingdom of Kibi; today they serve as excellent viewpoints. Just take your time, and simply enjoy the journey.

— MAKE IT HAPPEN —

The cycle route runs from Bizen-Ichinomiya station in Okayama city to Soja station in the city of Soja.

You can hire a bike at one end, and return it at the other.

Reach Okayama on the JR Tokaido-San'yo *shinkansen* from big cities like Tokyo; from here, get a train to Soja.

Bitchu-Kokubunji in Soja

Combine with KURASHIKI

Leave the Sunrise Izumo sleeper train (p186) in Okayama to spend a glorious day cycling the Kibi Plain, then strolling the lovely Bikan Historical Quarter in Kurashiki.

JOURNEYS IN JAPAN

"It's Japan's longest pilgrimage route, and passes through all four of Shikoku's prefectures."

Ohenro-san pilgrims walking the Shikoku Henro route

Become an *ohenro-san* on Shikoku's ancient pilgrimage route

The Shikoku Henro links 88 historic temples around the island's coast

When you visit Shikoku, the smallest of Japan's four main islands, you might spot distinctive figures picking their way along a mountain trail, or walking by the side of a road. They'll be dressed in white, with a bright sash around their neck, a conical sedge hat on their head and a wooden staff in their hand. As they pass, you might hear the quiet, rhythmic tinkle of a small bell at each step. These are *ohenro-san*, pilgrims walking the 88-temple Shikoku Henro pilgrimage route that circles the island.

Anyone is welcome to join their ranks, whether for the entire route or just one or two sections, and you can even wear the traditional *ohenro-san* outfit to further immerse yourself in the experience. As you walk, don't be surprised if a car pulls up and you're handed snacks through the window, or someone rushes out of their house to offer you freshly brewed tea. These kind acts are *osettai*, a way for people to participate in the pilgrimage by helping pilgrims. Whether it's a cool towel on a hot day or a home-made meal, if you're in a position to accept *osettai*, do so with an open heart and a polite bow.

The full Shikoku Henro route retraces the legendary footsteps of Kobo Daishi, the revered 8th-century monk who founded the esoteric Shingon school of Buddhism. At 1,400 km (870 miles), it's Japan's longest pilgrimage route, and passes through all four of Shikoku's prefectures: Tokushima, Kochi, Ehime and Kagawa. If you don't have months to devote to ticking off all 88 temples, you can just visit a few; the section from Dainichi-ji (temple 13) to Ido-ji (temple 17) is under 8 km (5 miles), so quite achievable in a day. It mostly leads you through rice fields and quiet suburbs, typical scenery along the Shikoku Henro. If you have a few more days to spare you could extend this route in either direction. If you choose to start earlier, at Fujii-dera (temple 11), you'll find yourself tackling mountain passes and walking through quaint villages and swaying bamboo forests on your way to Dainichi-ji. If you'd rather carry on after reaching Ido-ji, you'll discover stunning mountain scenery on the way to Kakurin-ji and Tairyu-ji (temples 20 and 21); this route features a tough but rewarding section known as a *henro korogashi*, or "place where pilgrims fall". If your legs aren't jelly yet, press on for one more day to Yakuo-ji (temple 23). This pretty temple, perched above Hiwasa Bay, is the last in Tokushima prefecture. It's a great place to end your pilgrimage – until you get the itch to come back for temple 24 …

— MAKE IT HAPPEN —

Tokushima prefecture, in the east of Shikoku, is considered the first of the Shikoku Henro's four sections. It represents awakening, and is followed by sections representing ascetic training (Kochi), enlightenment (Ehime) and finally nirvana (Kagawa).

If you plan on walking for several days or in more remote areas, make sure you prepare properly. There are plenty of English-language resources, including henro.org and shikokuhenro.jp, but the most useful remains the *Shikoku Japan 88 Route Guide*, a highly detailed and regularly updated book by Miyazaki Tateki.

Tokushima city has an airport and a ferry port, with connections to Kyushu and Tokyo among other destinations, and there are regular buses from Osaka. Tokushima train station has services to other parts of Shikoku.

A scenic journey through Japan

SUGGESTED DURATION 10 days **START** Tokyo; fly into one of the city's international airports, Narita or Haneda **GETTING AROUND** Use a variety of trains, boats and bikes; you'll also walk some sections **END** Onomichi; the city is served by *shinkansen*, and its closest airport is Hiroshima

It's the journey, not the destination – and Japan prides itself on ensuring the journey is one to remember. The country is renowned for its efficient, comfortable rail network, which ranges from single-carriage "one-man cars" trundling between villages to the record-breaking *shinkansen*. But being made up of islands, parts of the country are only connected by boat. This itinerary makes the most of Japan's varied transport network, taking you from the hyper-fast capital by train to the slower-paced corners of western Honshu and Shikoku, regions that were made for leisurely bike rides and pleasure cruises around scenic bays. These journeys aren't just a means of getting from place to place, but also a way to see the best of what the country has to offer: take a pilgrimage to find meaning or simply marvel at the stunning city, rural and coastal landscapes along the way.

2. IZUMO
Wake up by glittering Lake Shinji with a whole day ahead of you to explore Izumo's gorgeous coastline and important shrine. Avoid travelling again today – grab a leisurely dinner and stay overnight.

3. MATSUE
From Izumo, the retro Ichibata Electric Railway clatters along Shinji-ko's shore for an hour, dropping you in this laid-back castle city for the day.

10. ONOMICHI
From Imabari, hire a bike and hit the road towards Onomichi on the incredible Shimanami Kaido *(p178)*, a cycle route across elegant bridges linking Shikoku with Honshu.

9. IMABARI
Take a two-hour JR train to join the Imabari portion of the Shikoku Henro *(p191)* pilgrimage trail for a couple of days, visiting several temples.

4. KURASHIKI
Reserve a seat on the elegant, modern Yakumo train to Kurashiki (just over two hours from Matsue), where you could spend days exploring the nooks and crannies of the Bikan Historical Quarter – cobbled streets, wooden buildings, traditional restaurants and willow-lined canals.

1. TOKYO
It's not all fast bullet trains in Japan; for an extra special start to your trip, pre-book the Sunrise Izumo (p186), the country's last sleeper service.

START

Area of map

5. SOJA TO OKAYAMA
Take a 15-minute train ride to Soja station, where you can rent a bike. Enjoy a leisurely cycle across the Kibi Plain (p189), with its rice paddies and temples, then drop your bike at the end of the route at Bizen-Ichinomiya station, from where Okayama is under 15 minutes away by JR train.

6. TESHIMA
It's around an hour by JR train (via Chayamachi) or bus to Uno, where you'll catch the ferry to Teshima, one of the Art Islands of the Seto Inland Sea. Once here, rent a bike or walk between the coast, fishing villages and public artworks (p200).

7. NAOSHIMA
From Teshima, take the ferry back to Uno, then get another 20-minute ferry to Naoshima (p200), the most famous of the Art Islands. Spend a day exploring its modern art and beaches.

8. TAKAMATSU
One last hour-long ferry drops you in Takamatsu on Shikoku. Take your time exploring its beautiful garden Ritsurin-koen, seaside castle ruins and views of the Seto Inland Sea.

POPULAR

JAPAN

With its devoted fandoms and endlessly passionate subcultures, Japan truly puts the "popular" in popular culture. If ever there was a time to lean into your inner superfan, it's in Japan.

ON THE MAP
POPULAR JAPAN

- 77 Unleash your inner *otaku* in Akihabara
- 78 Ponder the Art Islands of the Seto Inland Sea
- 79 Strike a pose at the World Cosplay Summit
- 80 Show off your street style in Tokyo
- 81 Feel a sense of wonder at Ghibli Park
- 82 Cheer on a home run at a baseball game
- 83 Visit a community revitalized by art in Towada
- 84 Find everyday beauty in manhole cover art
- 85 Tap your toes to live jazz in Kobe
- 86 Sing your heart out in a karaoke booth
- 87 Show your Pride in Kanazawa
- 88 Meet Japan's favourite mascot in Kumamoto

77

Unleash your inner otaku in Akihabara

Tokyo's Electric Town is a haven for fans of anime, gaming and all things gloriously geeky

All neon lights and buzzing energy, Akihabara is a sensory overload. From billboards high above, J-pop idols sing and dance, catchy jingles advertise trending games and the latest products, and animated figures wave, point and beckon passersby. At street level, in dizzyingly loud arcades, *gachapon* (capsule toy) machines stand side by side with all-night gaming cafés and some of the city's best electronic stores. It's chaotic, but in the best way possible: Akiba (as Akihabara is often called) has an undeniable charm that invites everyone along for the ride.

And that's especially true for *otaku*, those with a deep passion for anime, manga or just about any subject. Akiba is something of an *otaku* paradise, with shops here catering to every whim, from must-have merchandise to hard-to-find fan goods, while themed cafés immerse visitors in their favourite worlds. Not that you have to be a fan to get caught up in it all; if you have even a passing interest in Japan's thriving geeky subcultures, Akiba is a must-visit. Have a go in an arcade or gaming café, belt out anime theme tunes at a karaoke joint, or simply wander through the neighbourhood and take it all in. One last thing: be sure to enter the ticket lottery to attend an AKB48 concert. This pop group phenomenon first started here ("AKB" is short form for Akihabara), and still hold almost daily performances at their dedicated theatre.

MAKE IT HAPPEN

Akihabara is in the northern part of central Tokyo, just two subway stops north of Tokyo station. It's within walking distance of Ueno Park.

Chuo-dori, Akiba's main street, is closed to traffic on Sundays. Apply for lottery tickets for AKB48 concerts online (*akb48.co.jp/theater*).

Akihabara is well connected, with its station a stop on the Hibiya subway line and the JR Yamanote, Sobu and Keihin-Tohoku lines.

The bright lights of Akihabara

Ponder the Art Islands of the Seto Inland Sea

A scattering of idyllic islands between Honshu and Shikoku make an unlikely but magical artistic venue

A polka-dotted yellow pumpkin perched at the end of a concrete pier. A huge, alien-looking white oval peeking out between trees and rice paddies. A sleek, low building tucked into the ruins of a century-old copper refinery. These creative contradictions are at the heart of the Art Islands project, which has been giving new life to the islands of the Seto Inland Sea through contemporary art since the 1980s.

Spearheaded by Benesse Holding Inc., the project was a response to the ecological and economic strife the islands faced in the latter half of the 20th century. Their landscapes and locations are naturally spectacular, but by the 1970s the islands were suffering from post-industrial decline, pollution and even illegal waste dumping. Fukutake Soichiro of Benesse hatched a plan to use art to revitalize the area, starting with the Tadao Ando-designed Benesse House Museum on Naoshima. From there, the project grew and grew, with local and international artists drawing on the nature and history of each island to inspire their work, involving residents and incorporating unused buildings and crumbling industrial monoliths like Inujima's copper refinery. The ever-evolving result is a unique synthesis of art and everyday life, leading curious visitors to places they might never have gone otherwise – and in the process, connecting then with small communities and local businesses.

Half of the joy of a visit here is in serendipitously stumbling upon artworks as you walk or cycle around the islands – perhaps wind chimes hanging in a forest or colourful doodles hidden down a lane in a fishing village. But there are a few permanent sites and pieces around which you can build an island-hopping itinerary. As the origin of the whole project, Naoshima's Benesse House Museum makes a natural starting point. Built out of architect Tadao Ando's signature concrete, it opens up in places to frame stunning sea views or allow the clouds to reflect in a still, oval pool. Also on Naoshima is artist Yayoi Kusama's famous yellow pumpkin, which creates a playful contrast with the shifting greys and blues of the sea behind it. On Teshima, a larger island dominated by a forested mountain, the sinuous shape of Teshima Art Museum calls to mind a drop of water that has rolled down neighbouring rice terraces to pool in a dip by the trees. The third of the main islands, Inujima, is also the smallest. As well as the Seirensho (refinery) Art Museum, it's home to Inujima Life Garden, where an abandoned plot of land is being transformed into an abundant garden, and the Art House Project, where site-specific works are integrated into the village.

The artworks spill out onto other islands, creating a sort of distributed art museum which reminds you to slow down and look around. Countless wonders await.

— MAKE IT HAPPEN —

The art islands are in the Seto Inland Sea (Setonaikai), between southwest Honshu and northeast Shikoku. They're part of Shikoku's Kagawa prefecture.

Most sites on the Art Islands are open year-round. Visit *benesse-artsite.jp* for information on tickets and reservations. The Setouchi Triennale is a major art festival covering the islands (plus several others) and takes place every three years (2025, 2028 etc). During the Triennale, "art passports" are available, offering access to multiple works and sites; passports are cheaper if purchased online in advance (*setouchi-artfest.jp*).

Naoshima serves as a convenient base for exploring the Seto Inland Sea islands. Regular ferries link it with Okayama (on Honshu island) and Takamatsu (on Shikoku island), and connect each of the Setonaikai islands. Inujima also has a link with Hoden port near Okayama.

POPULAR JAPAN

"Half of the joy of a visit here is in serendipitously stumbling upon artworks."

Top left Inujima Seirensho Art Museum
Top right Benesse House
Right Teshima Art Museum, Rei Naito: *Matrix*, 2010

POPULAR JAPAN

Strike a pose at the World Cosplay Summit

Get your costumes ready: every summer, Nagoya hosts the world's largest cosplay event

A combination of the words "costume" and "play", cosplay is exactly what it sounds like: dressing up and having fun. But some people take it deadly seriously, spending hours upon hours crafting perfect replicas of their favourite characters' clothes, styling and even weapons. It's something of an unacknowledged art form, if you think about it, and you can see the masters compete each year at Nagoya's World Cosplay Summit.

Over the course of a week or two, the city is flooded with characters from around the world. It's a joy to spot them in incongruous settings – imagine *One Piece*'s Roronoa Zoro wrangling a huge foam sword down an escalator, or *Final Fantasy*'s Tifa sweeping her hair aside to take a sip of coffee. On stage, though, it's all business, with each competitor showcasing their costume, plus their character's poses and mannerisms. The atmosphere is kept lively with enthusiastic MCs, and performances from idol groups and artists.

Non-competitors are also welcome to dress up as their favourite character from Japanese media (shop-bought costumes are fine). Expect a smile from anyone cosplaying someone from the same media, and maybe a request for a joint photo – striking your character's signature pose if they have one, of course.

— MAKE IT HAPPEN —

The World Cosplay Summit's venue changes, but is always in central Nagoya, the capital of Aichi prefecture.

Buy tickets for the championship online (*worldcosplaysummit.jp*).

Nagoya is on the Tokaido *shinkansen* line between Tokyo and Osaka.

In character at the World Cosplay Summit

Dressed to impress in Harajuku

80

Show off your street style in Tokyo

One of the undisputed fashion capitals of the world, Tokyo's shopping is unmatched

MAKE IT HAPPEN

Koenji is northwest of Tokyo's main sights, Shimokitazawa west, Jiyugaoka southwest. All the other districts are central.

Shops are generally open quite late, and closed on Mondays.

Tokyo has a comprehensive public transport system which connects all these districts.

Whether you're a fan of Uniqlo's no-frills basics, the very frilly Gothic Lolita style, Yohji Yamamoto's low-key luxury or Bape's streetwear, Japanese fashion has probably had an impact on your wardrobe. And there's nowhere better to stock up on staples and spot the next trends than Tokyo.

Depending on your interests, different districts might appeal. In Shibuya and Harajuku, you can take the pulse of the city's youth culture; stroll along Takeshita-dori or visit Shibuya109 mall, and you'll see all the latest weird and wonderful sub-cultural styles. For major brand names, go to glittering Ginza or the tree-lined avenue of Omotesando. Or for a more understated approach to high-end, look around the boutiques in Daikanyama and Kagurazaka, with their faintly European airs, or Jiyu-gaoka, which has more of a Brooklyn vibe. Vintage lovers could while away days in trendy Shimokitazawa or bohemian Koenji.

The real joy of Tokyo's fashion isn't in the vision of any designer or the selection in any shop, though. It's in the fun, creative ways people combine disparate items – luxury, high-street, vintage, repurposed – to create their own, individual style. Cat Street and the other lanes around Omotesando and Harajuku are the place to see this – it's hard not to be inspired by Tokyo's street fashion stars making the pavements their catwalk.

Feel a sense of wonder at Ghibli Park

The fantastical worlds of Studio Ghibli spill off screen in this immersive theme park

The phrase "theme park" might call to mind dodgems, roller coasters and far too much candy floss, but that's not what you'll find at Studio Ghibli's theme park. Instead, it's more of a "themed" park – a huge green area full of buildings, landscapes and characters from the animation studio's beloved films. For fans, it's an unmissable opportunity to step into the movies' exquisitely realized worlds, but even the most casual of watchers will be charmed by the whimsical sights and natural setting.

Located in Nagoya, the park is split into five areas. Up first is the Hill of Youth, based on *Whisper of the Heart* and *The Cat Returns*, and fans are sure to be delighted by the details. As well as the films' World Emporium antique shop and violin workshop, you'll discover the Cat Bureau – peer in to see the cats lounging on squishy red chairs. To the south is the Grand Warehouse. The heart of the park and often its busiest area, it's also the largest covered space, so people tend to linger if it's raining. And there's plenty to keep them busy; the area draws inspiration from 13 films, including the Oscar-winning *Spirited Away*. Step into Yubaba's office, walk between towering flowers (*Arrietty*), enjoy a delicious slice of Siberia Sponge Cake (*The Wind Rises*), and clamber onto Totoro's soft belly or into the fuzzy cat bus (kids only; *My Neighbour Totoro*). The Grand Warehouse is also where you'll find the widest range of food, drinks and souvenirs in the park, plus a beautiful Art Deco-style theatre, which screens exclusive Ghibli short films.

For a quiet interlude, stroll down a tree-shaded path to Mononoke Village, which recreates the Muromachi-era rural landscapes of *Princess Mononoke*. Look out for the sculpture of boar god Okkoto-nushi; made a little less scary than usual, he serves as a slide for kids. You can book a spot on a *gohei mochi* (grilled, skewered rice cakes) workshop here, too.

A few minutes' walk away is the Valley of Witches, Ghibli Park's largest area, which covers films like *Kiki's Delivery Service* and *Howl's Moving Castle*. The flower-hung room in Kiki's childhood home is lovely, and the bakery where she works in the film, Guchokipanya, has *actually* been brought to life, with baked goods galore. You can also explore Howl's titular moving castle, a joyfully higgledy-piggledy space, with balconies providing views of the surrounding park.

The southernmost section is Dondoko Forest, based on *My Neighbour Totoro*. Mei and Satsuki's house has been recreated in loving detail – right down to the slightly rotten wood of the gazebo – and it's thrilling to poke around and discover its nooks and crannies. Not a big Ghibli fan? It really doesn't matter. Spending a day here is a joy regardless.

— MAKE IT HAPPEN —

Ghibli Park is located in the Expo 2005 Aichi Commemorative Park, northeast of Nagoya city.

Visit the park's website (ghibli-park.jp/en/) for opening times, tickets, maps and more. Demand is high (and visitor numbers are kept low to maintain the park's atmosphere) so buy tickets well in advance. Tickets go on sale at 2pm on the 10th of the month, for two months ahead (eg March tickets are available from 10 January and so on). Tickets give a specific entry time for the Grand Warehouse. Only the Premium Pass provides access to everything in the park.

Nagoya is on the Tokaido *shinkansen* line between Tokyo and Osaka. From Nagoya, take the Higashiyama subway line to Fujigaoka, then the Limino elevated train to Aichikyuhaku Kinenkoen station, at the park's northern end. There are also buses from Nagoya's Meitetsu Bus Centre.

POPULAR JAPAN

"Even the most casual of watchers will be charmed by the whimsical sights and natural setting."

Walking past Kaonashi or No-Face from *Spirited Away* at Ghibli Park

POPULAR JAPAN

Three more teams to know

1
Yomiuri Giants
The most famous team in Japanese pro baseball has more championship wins than anyone else. Watch them play in the Pacific League at the swish Tokyo Dome.

2
Yakult Swallows
Another Tokyo team, the Yakult Swallows are in the Central League (like the Hanshin Tigers), and play at the open-air Meiji Jingu Stadium.

3
Fukuoka Softbank Hawks
Down in Kyushu at Fukuoka Dome, this Pacific League team has fought their way to the top of the table several times since 2000.

82

Cheer on a home run at a baseball game

There's nothing quite like seeing Japan's favourite sport played live

Sumo may be Japan's national sport, but in terms of both playing and spectating, nothing comes close to baseball. The game was introduced to Japan in the 1870s, and today it's so popular that the professional leagues aren't enough – even the high school baseball championship is televised, drawing in huge numbers of viewers every August. The quality of play is very high, and players like Ichiro Suzuki and Shohei Ohtani are now household names, even in the US.

If you can't tell one end of a bat from the other, it's still well worth experiencing the unrivalled atmosphere at a game, joining the crowds of fans in team colours keeping the energy levels high. Most enthusiastic is the "cheering section", where everyone chants, sings and dances in unison. The cheering section often travels for big games, but naturally it's at its strongest on home ground.

Chances are, wherever you're travelling, there'll be a stadium nearby. But for the full experience, try to see one of the big teams playing at home, like the Hanshin Tigers at Koshien Stadium. Built in 1924, Koshien is Japan's oldest professional ballpark; it also hosts the summer High School Baseball Championship and has a museum. While you're here, don't miss Koshien's famous foods: yakisoba (fried noodles), yakitori (chicken skewers) and Japanese curry, washed down with a cool beer poured at your seat. It's not a bad way to spend a day, win or lose, sports fan or not.

Settling in for a game at Koshien Stadium

MAKE IT HAPPEN

 Nishinomiya is in the Kansai region's Hyogo prefecture, between Osaka and Kobe. Koshien Stadium is just southeast of the city centre.

 For popular teams like the Hanshin Tigers, it's best to pre-book tickets (koshien.hanshin.co.jp); buy them on the day otherwise.

 Take the Hanshin line from Osaka, Kobe or Nishinomiya (which is also on the JR Tokaido main line) stations to Koshien station for the stadium.

Visit a community revitalized by art in Towada

In this regional city in northern Honshu, you'll find a thriving and unpretentious contemporary art scene

The streets of Towada, an otherwise typical regional city, are home to some curious and unexpected sights – a rearing horse covered in flowers, a stone bench masquerading as a soft pillow, a play house with bulging, marshmallow-like walls. The reason? The Arts Towada project, created in response to the decline of the administrative quarter. Faced with the same creeping depopulation as much of Japan, the city decided it didn't want that to come with a loss of local pride. Instead, the 1.1-km (0.7-mile) street that forms the district's heart was chosen to host an ambitious contemporary art project, in hopes of bringing new life to Towada.

The street, already beautiful each spring due to its avenue of cherry blossoms, now has year-round splashes of colour. They coalesce around the Towada Art Center, which opened in 2008 and is a focal point for frequent community art projects. The sleek white building by Nishizawa Ryue is made up of several sections, connected by glass corridors, and displays both special exhibitions and a permanent collection of around 20 pieces. Some take up entire rooms, while others are others tucked into unexpected corners, ready to delight those who spot them. Highlights include Yoko Ono's *Wish Tree for Towada, Riverbed & Bell of Peace*, a participatory piece which invites visitors to hang their wishes on an apple tree; Kuribayashi Takashi's *Sumpf Land*, in which you clamber onto a table and poke your head through a hole in the ceiling to glimpse a fantastical world; and *Location (5)* by Hans Op de Beeck, which immerses onlookers in a lonely nighttime diner scene.

But the art doesn't end at the museum walls. Across the road is Art Square, with the *Fat House & Fat Car*; vibrant, spotted mushrooms by Yayoi Kusama; and a huge, cartoonishly cute white ghost sculpture, seemingly floating over the lawn. The open space invites kids to play and adults to rest for a moment and enjoy the whimsical surroundings. In the city centre you'll see artistically designed benches and street sculptures, and civic buildings by superstar architects Tadao Ando and Kengo Kuma. You can get a sense of how Towada's residents have embraced living in a "City of Art" by visiting the Takamura Grocery Store, which shows art related to the museum's current exhibition, and the tiny Matsumoto Tea Stall, where the owner will proudly show you both his photos from throughout the Arts Towada project, and the shop's very own installation pieces. It's in these unexpected moments of connection and creativity that the success of the project is clearest, and most joyful.

— MAKE IT HAPPEN —

The small city of Towada is located in northern Honshu's Aomori prefecture, northeast of Lake Towada.

Towada Art Center is closed on Mondays (or Tuesday if Monday is a national holiday). Ticket prices increase during special exhibitions. An English-language audio guide is available for free. Visit towadaartcenter.com/en for more information on opening hours, exhibitions and events.

Shinkansen run from Tokyo to Shichinohe-Towada and Hachinohe stations. Buses run from both to the art centre. From Hachinohe, take either the Towada Kanko Dentetsu bus bound for Hommachi Higashi (about 60 minutes) or the JR Oirase-go bus running to Lake Towada (about 40 minutes). From Shichinohe-Towada, take the Towada Kanko Dentetsu bus bound for Sanbongi Eigyo-sho.

POPULAR JAPAN

Right Yoko Ono *Wish Tree for Towada, Riverbed, Bell of Peace*, 2008
Below *aTTA*, a giant red ant by Tsubaki Noboru at the Towada Art Center, 2008

"*The streets of Towada, an otherwise typical regional city, are home to some curious and unexpected sights.*"

Ghost, Unknown Mass, 2010, by inges idee at the Towada Art Center

84

Find everyday beauty in manhole cover art

Keep an eye out for masterpieces (and memes) under your feet

The usual advice when walking in Japan is to look up, so you don't miss the flashing neon signs, drifting cherry blossom petals or snowcapped mountains on the horizon. But sometimes, it pays to look down. Beneath your feet you might just spot something unexpected: decorated manhole covers. Artistic designs began to appear during a decades-long sewerage overhaul that started in the 1950s; now, over 90 per cent of Japan's municipalities have their own distinctive designs, bringing art into the every day. There are thousands of covers, and with such variety, a new hobby came into being: drainspotting. Fans come from far and wide looking for famous or unusual manhole covers, snapping photos, taking rubbings and picking up souvenirs.

Designs often include local sights or stories, like Osaka's castle with sakura trees, Atami's dramatic scene from the novel *The Golden Demon* and Aomori's *nebuta* festival. Others feature beloved characters like Hello Kitty, Pokémon or Sailor Moon. The regional city of Sakura, between Tokyo and Narita, combines both. In the lakeside surroundings of Sakura Hometown Square, local hero and internet royalty Kabosu is celebrated with a manhole cover. You may not know the name, but you've seen the meme: Kabosu is better known as Doge, the Shiba dog perched on a sofa with demurely crossed paws and serious side-eye. Has drainspotting become your new favourite hobby? You bet.

MAKE IT HAPPEN

Manhole covers are found country-wide. The Kabosu cover is on the edge of Sakura Hometown Square in Sakura city, Chiba prefecture.

Many manhole covers have an associated collectors' card, which lists the cover's coordinates; find a card directory at *gk-p.jp/mhcard*.

From Tokyo, take a Keisei-line train (for Narita Airport) to Keisei-Usui station, then walk, cycle or take the bus to Sakura Hometown Square.

POPULAR JAPAN

"Beneath your feet you might just spot something unexpected: decorated manhole covers."

Top A depiction of Nara deer
Left Design of Osaka's castle
Right Detail of a monkey and Momotaro from a folk tale on a manhole cover in Okayama

POPULAR JAPAN

Other Japanese music styles

1
J-pop
This mega-force of contemporary music kicked off in the 1990s and is closely linked to bubbly chart toppers with an irresistible rhythm. Overseas, the female idol groups are best known, especially AKB48; see them live at the AKB48 Theater in Tokyo's Akihabara (p198).

2
J-rock
J-rock's modern form began to appear in the 1980s Band Boom, during which the glam- and metal-influenced Visual Kei genre emerged. Today, J-rock encompasses everything from punk to indie. See the latest bands at live houses like Koenji in Tokyo.

3
Enka
For a more traditional sound, you can't beat enka, its use of minor scales enhancing its emotional tone. Big-name singers like Ishikawa Sayuri fill major venues on tour.

85

Tap your toes to live jazz in Kobe

The international port city of Kobe is the heart of Japan's thriving jazz scene

From the novels of Haruki Murakami to the soundtracks of shows like *Cowboy Bebop*, jazz has a strong presence in Japan's modern culture. It came into the country through Kobe, a port city that embraced the sudden influx of foreign goods and ideas when the country's borders opened in the late 19th century. In 1923, Japan's first jazz band was formed right here, and the city never looked back, proudly labelling itself the birthplace of jazz in Japan.

If you're a fan of the genre, chances are that you're already planning on visiting Kobe's legendary venues. But even for casual listeners, there's enough variety that it's easy to find somewhere appealing. Sone, established in 1969, offers a timeless experience: settle in at a dark-wood table or on a cosy banquette, and enjoy dinner or drinks while a live band plays. Retro Jazz Café Jam Jam opens earlier in the day, and has a dedicated listening section for patrons who want to enjoy the records without the buzz of conversation. And venues like Basin Street and Great Blue are anchored by accomplished musician-owners (guitarist Kawasaki Tatsuhiko and pianist Andoh Yoshinori respectively), who perform each night with fellow musicians or take a break and just enjoy the show with everyone else. Every October, the city hosts Kobe Jazz Street festival, in which professional and amateur performances spill out of the usual venues – the perfect time to immerse yourself in Japan's City of Jazz.

A performance at Kobe's Sone Jazz Bar

―――― MAKE IT HAPPEN ――――

Kobe is in the Kansai region, near Osaka and Kyoto. Most of Kobe's bars, clubs and music venues are in Sannomiya, Kitano and Motomachi.

Most of Kobe's clubs and many bars have a table charge. You can usually buy tickets on the door, but it's best to check if a big name is playing.

Kobe is on the San'yo *shinkansen* line between Osaka and Hakata (Fukuoka), as well as local JR, Hankyu and Hanshin train lines.

POPULAR JAPAN

86

Sing your heart out in a karaoke booth

One of Japan's most successful cultural exports, karaoke is a national institution

Having fun with friends, cutting loose with colleagues, whiling away the hours after missing the last train… Karaoke ("empty orchestra" in Japanese) is the go-to activity for all kinds of situations in Japan, and a must-try while visiting. There's no need to worry about stage fright, either; in introvert-friendly Japan, the norm isn't singing in front of a rowdy crowd in a bar. Instead, it's heading into a private booth, alone or in a group, so you can belt out your favourite songs without any strangers seeing.

You're bound to come across a branch of Karaoke Kan, Manekineko, Big Echo or JOYSOUND in any large town. Each has its quirks, but the overall experience is the same: guests get a private room with a screen, mics and a snack and drink menu, and often access to costumes and instruments like tambourines and maracas. Queue up your song (the system can usually be set to English), and the lyrics appear on screen, probably over a hilariously unrelated reel of stock footage.

You'll have a great time whichever karaoke booth you end up at. But if you can't decide, put on a pink wig or an inside-out camo t-shirt and queue up "More Than This" at the Shibuya or Shinjuku branch of Karaoke Kan to recreate *Lost in Translation*'s iconic karaoke scene (they were used for interior and exterior shots respectively).

— MAKE IT HAPPEN —

Karaoke Kan's Shibuya and Shinjuku branches are both in the centre of each district.

With so many karaoke places around, you shouldn't need to pre-book anywhere.

Shibuya station's exit A3b and Shinjuku station's exit B18 are the closest to their respective Karaoke Kan branches.

A karaoke session in Tokyo

Tokyo Rainbow Pride, Shibuya, 2016

Show your Pride in Kanazawa

The historic capital of Ishikawa prefecture has become a hub for the LGBTQ+ community in central Honshu

— MAKE IT HAPPEN —

Kanazawa Nijinoma is in the Tatemachi district of central Kanazawa.

Check *kanazawarainbowpride.com* for updates on events including Pride. Kanazawa Nijinoma is closed on Tuesdays and Wednesdays.

Kanazawa is on the Hokuriku *shinkansen* line from Tokyo.

While Japan is a safe destination for LGBTQ+ travellers, its queer scene isn't a huge draw for most visitors. Tokyo's Shinjuku Ni-chome nightlife district has some famous gay clubs and events, and Osaka's venues are becoming better known, but things are generally quite quiet beyond those cities.

That makes it even more impressive that, through years of organizing, the community in Kanazawa has started to put this historic city on the map for LGBTQ+ locals and travellers. Since 2021, they've managed to establish a Rainbow Pride Parade (usually September or October), and in 2023 they even opened a permanent community space – Kanazawa Nijinoma, or Rainbow Room. As well as hosting events, it's open as a café during the day and a laid-back bar on Friday and Saturday evenings. In true Kanazawa style – the city is known for its historical aesthetics and rich traditional culture – it's housed in a 100-year-old Japanese building. Pride flags are displayed by the sliding door at the entrance, and some of the screen doors inside have been painted in muted rainbow tones as well. Whether you'd like to ask for local recommendations, relax in an LGBTQ+-friendly space or just sip a cup of coffee while admiring a traditional courtyard garden, Kanazawa Nijinoma will welcome you with open arms.

Meet Japan's favourite mascot in Kumamoto

You'll come across all kinds of mascots as you travel through Japan, ranging from the adorable to the absurd

A big, soft belly. Round, red cheeks. Wide, unblinking eyes and open-mouthed smile. Meet Kumamon, the bear-like mascot of Kumamoto and a Japanese obsession. Striking that perfect balance between cute and ever so slightly weird, Kumamon makes a memorable and charming face for the prefecture's tourism promotions (the *kuma* is written with the kanji for "bear"). With signature enthusiasm, he introduces visitors to Kumamoto's attractions – among them an imposing castle, Mount Aso's smoking crater, local crafts like *Higo-zogan* (inlay metalwork) and the well-preserved hot-spring town of Kurokawa Onsen (Kumamon is even designated a "hot spring sommelier"). But such is his success that the bear himself has become a draw. Catch a glimpse of him at Kumamon Square, which not only functions as his office for his dual roles as the area's Sales Manager and Happiness Manager, but also as a shop and café selling themed goods, an AR games area, and a performance venue – Kumamon comes out and dances once or twice most days.

And he's not alone. Kumamon is one of many loveable mascots, also called *yuru-kyara* or (roughly) "easygoing characters", found across Japan, all designed to shine a light on the attractions of their area. Visit Kaga Onsen to see Spa Crow-kun, a three-legged crow sporting *onsen*-flushed cheeks and a folded towel on its head. The design draws on the tale of a mystical three-legged crow that healed its wounds by bathing here, and the name plays on "spa crow" and "super crow". In Nara, you'll be confronted with the wide-eyed, unnerving gaze of Sento-kun, a divisive *yuru-kyara* who looks like an infant Buddha with antlers. And in Shimane, you'll spot Shimanekko everywhere – a yellow cat (*neko*) wearing a roof-like headdress and *shimenawa* (sacred rope) necklace, to evoke the prefecture's famous Izumo shrine.

All of these are official *yuru-kyara*, but you might well encounter unofficial ones, too. Head to Hachinohe's huge Sunday-morning market, and you may come across Mama and Papa Ikadon, two locals strolling around in kimono and home-made squid heads, with bold eyebrows composed of the kanji for the city name. Northern Honshu is also home to Nyango Star, a cat-apple hybrid known for – what else? – heavy metal drumming. *Ultimate Guitar* even voted Nyango Star (whose name is a combination of *nyan*, or "meow", and Ringo Starr) 2021's most underrated drummer in the world.

Whether you make plans to see a mascot or just wait for a serendipitous encounter, Japan's beloved and often bizarre mascots are sure to add a playful touch to your time in Japan – and some unique souvenirs for your suitcase.

— MAKE IT HAPPEN —

Kumamon's home Kumamoto is a prefecture in central Kyushu, with the Ariake Sea to its west and Miyazaki and Oita prefectures to its east.

Kumamon's scheduled appearances, including at Kumamon Square (in Tsuruya department store, Kumamoto city), are listed at *kumamon-land.jp/kyonokumamon*. There are now so many *yuru-kyara*, created by so many different groups, that a comprehensive directory would be hard to make. Fan-run sites like *yurukyara.fandom.com* are a good starting point to learn about them, though. Tourist offices will also have information on any major (official) local mascots.

Kumamoto city is a stop on the Kyushu *shinkansen* line between Fukuoka (Hakata) to the north and Kagoshima to the south. It also has an airport with flights to Okinawa and Honshu, and a ferry port with links to Shimabara.

POPULAR JAPAN

The adorable Kumamon performing

"Meet Kumamon, the bear-like mascot of Kumamoto and a Japanese obsession."

A pop culture pilgrimage

SUGGESTED DURATION 10 days **START** Osaka; fly into Itami or Kansai airport **GETTING AROUND** This itinerary relies on bullet and regular trains, though you'll take a bus to Towada **END** Sapporo; the city has an airport with links to Tokyo, Osaka and global destinations

Area of map

Part of the joy of a trip to Japan is the chance to indulge your inner *otaku* (geek), but it's not just anime and manga that have fans obsessing. In Japan, pop culture spans a huge array of interests – sport, music, modern art, experimental fashion – and this itinerary shows you many facets of the pop culture scene. Heading from the Kansai region up to Sapporo, the capital of Hokkaido, you'll get fanatical about comic books, meet a beloved mascot, do some drain-spotting and even learn about an Indigenous culture that inspired a hit anime series. Spending time exploring Japan's entertainment scene is part of the joy of visiting this pop culture powerhouse, so lean in and get ready to embrace your *otaku* side.

3. KYOTO
From Osaka, it's a quick *shinkansen* to another pop culture paradise: Kyoto. Take a look at Nintendo HQ; stay the night in Marufukuro, a hotel in Nintendo's original 1930s headquarters; and drop into the Manga Museum. Then catch another *shinkansen* to Tokyo.

2. KOBE
On the hunt for more *otaku* shops? Take a day trip to Kobe, just 15-minute *shinkansen* ride away from Osaka. Here you'll find Kobe San Center Plaza, with its comic book stores and anime cafés.

1. OSAKA
This vibrant city is sure to get you in the pop culture spirit. Visit Den Den Town (*p162*) for video game, anime and manga shops, then catch a baseball game at Koshien (*p207*).

START

9. SAPPORO
Finish your trip in the modern city of Sapporo, reachable in an hour by JR train. It's the "hometown" of vocaloid singer Hatsune Miku, a beloved ambassador for the Hokkaido prefecture.

END

8. SHIRAOI
The living culture and ancient myths of Hokkaido's Indigenous Ainu people inspired the smash-hit *Golden Kamuy* manga and anime series. Learn about the Ainu people at Upopoy *(p58)*, then head to Sapporo by JR train.

7. HAKODATE
From Hachinohe, take a 1.5-hour *shinkansen* to the laid-back port city of Hakodate *(p175)*. Head straight to Hakodate Park, where you'll find a Pokéfuta (Pokémon-themed manhole cover). Spend the rest of your day seeking out other manhole covers and visiting the excellent Museum of Northern Peoples, then head to Shiraoi via a three-hour JR train.

6. TOWADA
It's an easy 40-minute bus from Hachinohe to Towada Art Center *(p208)*, so take a day trip to see a city revitalized by contemporary art. Look out for installations like a giant flower-covered horse and Yayoi Kusama's polka-dotted creations enlivening the streets, then head back to Hachinohe for the night.

5. HACHINOHE
Head up to the historic city of Hachinohe via *shinkansen* (just under three hours) to see the ultimate *kimokawaii* (cute but creepy) mascot, Ikadon *(p218)*, at the Hachinohe morning market.

4. TOKYO
Tokyo takes the crown for the ultimate *otaku* city, where subcultures reign. Anime fan? Check out shopping hubs like Akihabara *(p198)* and Ikebukuro, or head to the suburbs to the Ghibli Museum. Want to see the latest fashion trends? Visit Shibuya and Harajuku *(p203)*.

SEASONAL

JAPAN

Japan is incredible at any time of year – think cherry blossoms in the spring and red leaves in the autumn, as well as joyful festivals in the summer and snow adventures in the winter. Which season will capture your heart?

ON THE MAP
SEASONAL JAPAN

- 89 See fire meet snow in Nozawa Onsen
- 90 Slice through powder snow in Hokkaido
- 91 Warm up in a wintertime hot spring
- 92 Step onto the drift ice of Shiretoko
- 93 Join the seasonal sakura celebration
- 94 Enjoy the delicate plum blossoms at Kairaku-en
- 95 Feel the joy at an Awa Odori festival
- 96 Spot fireflies at Nigami's early-summer festival
- 97 Admire the hydrangeas at Unsho-ji
- 98 Immerse yourself in the colours of autumn
- 99 Share the harvest's bounty with the gods
- 100 Celebrate the beauty of autumn in Kyoto

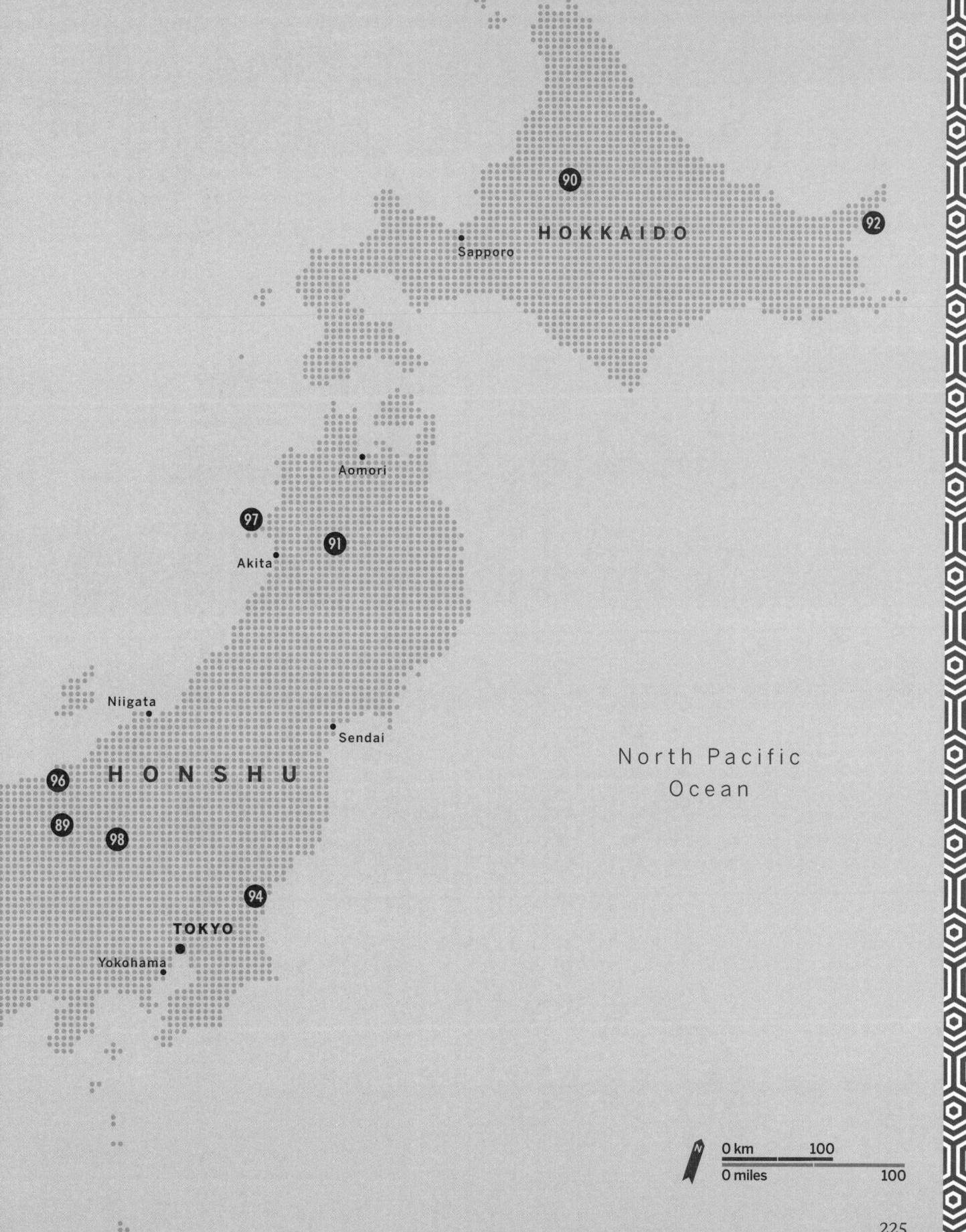

89

See fire meet snow in Nozawa Onsen

The fiery torches of Dosojin Matsuri light up the cold night at this riotous festival

In the snow-bound depths of winter, the hot-spring town of Nozawa Onsen sets the night alight – and not just in a metaphorical sense. Over a few days, the villagers erect a temporary shrine in the square, dedicated to the protective Dosojin deities, whose statues you'll see around town. Once it's completed, a crowd gathers, buzzing with excitement, as two groups of men assemble. One is made up of 42-year-olds, the other 25-year-olds; both ages are said to bring bad luck, and participating in the festival is meant to offset that.

The older men climb to the top of the shrine and begin chanting "*hi motte koi*" – "bring on the fire!" – kick-starting the chaotic, thrilling evening. The younger men guard the shrine, fending off the villagers who try to set the whole thing alight with torches. The 42-year-olds sing, dance and egg on the crowd, even throwing down kindling, and *nihonshu* (sake) flows freely. Whether the villagers break through the lines or not, the shrine is set alight around 10pm (after the men have climbed down). Everyone keeps on celebrating as the huge fire spits and crackles, toasting the men's hard work and warming themselves by the flames. Stick around until morning if you can, when the villagers roast rice cakes over the smouldering remains of the shrine. Apparently, doing so will protect you from illness for the coming year – and frankly, you might be very much in need of carbohydrates after the sake-fuelled excesses of the night.

MAKE IT HAPPEN

 Nozawa Onsen is on the northern edge of Joshin'etsu Kogen National Park, in the mountainous central Honshu prefecture of Nagano.

 Dosojin Matsuri is held annually on 15 January. Wear warm clothes that you don't mind getting slightly singed by a few stray sparks.

 The easiest access to Nozawa Onsen is by bus from Iiyama station, which is on both the Hokuriku *shinkansen* line and the JR Iiyama line.

The burning of the shrine at the Nozawa Onsen Dosojin fire festival

SEASONAL JAPAN

More excellent winter festivals

.... 1 ....

Sapporo Snow Festival
Visit Hokkaido's capital in February to see this famous festival, where huge, intricate snow and ice sculptures are displayed for a week. Sparkling white in the day and illuminated at night, they're a beautiful sight.

.... 2 ....

Takeuchi Festival
In February, the village of Rokugo in Akita becomes a battleground. Two teams meet in the village square and charge at each other with sharpened bamboo in an age-old ritual to predict the harvest. To raise the stakes for the last round, a huge bonfire is lit between them.

.... 3 ....

Aoshima Hadaka Mairi
Under the clear January skies of Miyazaki in Kyushu, over 400 people gather for the Aoshima Hadaka Mairi. Dressed in white loincloths (or simple white clothes for women), participants perform misogi, or water purification, by running straight into the cold sea.

Slice through powder snow in Hokkaido

The northern island's legendary skiing and snowboarding scene makes it a must-visit for winter sports enthusiasts

Japan is well known for its deep winters, with top-tier ski resorts scattered across the country. In fact, Japan's powder snow – the dry, fluffy, freshly fallen sort – is so legendary that it has its own nickname: Japow. And if there's one place you're guaranteed luscious layers of Japow, it's Hokkaido, a ski destination that can make any winter sports fan misty-eyed.

Head to Hokkaido in the winter, and you're spoiled for choice. The region's calling card is undoubtedly Niseko, a mega-resort often called "the powder capital of the world" and conveniently accessible from Sapporo (Hokkaido's capital city). Then there's nearby Rusutsu, equally as popular and known for its pristine back-country and tree skiing, as well as its heli-skiing. But if you fancy being spontaneous, base yourself in a city and explore its nearby resorts and ski areas, with the flexibility of deciding the day's destination based on the weather.

The laid-back city of Asahikawa is an ideal option for this approach. Its strategic location means you can explore the resorts in both central and northern Hokkaido, which are often blessed with especially dry powder you can't find nearer the coasts. Kamui Ski Links is one of the closest, just half an hour west of the city centre, and it's the perfect place to get acquainted with central Hokkaido powder. Most of the slopes are groomed, and cater to a good range of ability levels, and lift passes are very reasonably priced.

At the other end of the scale are the ski areas in Daisetsuzan National Park's wild, mountainous landscapes, also accessible from Asahikawa. Kurodake is blissfully untouched, its steep slopes and challenging terrain putting off all but the most hardcore back-country skiers, and it's often the first natural snow resort to open each year. Asahidake is on the southwest face of the tallest mountain in Hokkaido – also an active volcano – and has some gloriously varied terrain, plus the longest season in Japan (often December to May).

For all-rounder resorts, head a little further afield to the well-developed resorts of Furano and Tomamu, perfect for an overnight excursion from Asahikawa. The miles of groomed slopes, availability of lessons and cosy après-ski options are ideal for both families and learners, while the epic back country and side country are tempting for advanced skiers and snowboarders.

The added bonus of staying in a city like Asakihawa is the opportunity to experience its culture and daily life, rather than the enclosed world of a resort. Stroll along its snowy streets, which glitter in the winter illuminations; refuel after a day on the slopes with the rich, oily soy-based broth of Asahikawa ramen; and join the fun at February's winter festival, when snow sculptures are displayed around town.

— MAKE IT HAPPEN —

Asahikawa is a city in central Hokkaido, the most northerly of Japan's four main islands. Daisetsuzan National Park is just to its east, and Sapporo around 140 km (86 miles) southwest on the Ishikari plain, straddling the Toyohira River.

For more detailed information on powder snow in Japan, including Hokkaido's resorts and ski areas, check out *powderhounds.com*. The winter sports season tends to last roughly December to March, though it depends on the year and the location.

Fly to Asahikawa from Tokyo, then take a scheduled ski bus transfer to many of the area's ski resorts (book your bus a week in advance; bookings open in late September). If travelling from Sapporo, take limited express or local trains, or a highway bus. Some Asahikawa hotels offer shuttle services to certain resorts and ski areas; otherwise there is a good network of public buses.

Snowboarding on fresh powder at Niseko

SEASONAL JAPAN

"If you fancy being spontaneous, base yourself in a city and explore its nearby resorts."

SEASONAL JAPAN

91

Warm up in a wintertime hot spring

Japan's steaming natural *onsen* feel even cosier in the snowy months

One benefit of Japan's geothermally active land is its abundance of natural hot springs, out of which has developed a rich bathing culture. The Snow Country – Honshu's mountainous spine, which sees very cold winters – is known for an especially enchanting version of *onsen* bathing: *yukimiburo*, or "snow-viewing baths".

It's easy to experience it at any Snow Country hot-spring resort, but rustic Nyuto Onsen is particularly lovely. Set in the mountains above Tazawa-ko, Japan's deepest lake, the resort is made up of seven scattered *ryokan*, each with its own baths (which non-staying guests can access). There's no hustle and bustle, just the feeling of being surrounded by nature as you relax your muscles in the geothermally heated water. The indoor baths are soothing, but it's those outdoors *(rotemburo)* that steal the show. A path leads through the beech forest to a milky-white pool (the result of the high concentration of volcanic minerals, said to be beautifying and good for your health) where you'll undress and slip into the silky smooth waters. As the water warms your skin and the steam rises, the snow will melt in the air above. There's nothing quite like the feeling of soaking in a hot bath surrounded by a silent, snowy landscape – the only problem is that you have to get out eventually.

— MAKE IT HAPPEN —

Nyuto Onsen is in Akita's Towada-Hachimantai National Park in northern Honshu.

Some of Nyuto Onsen's ryokan allow tattoos in the baths if they're covered with skin-coloured patches.

Take the bus from Tazawako station (on JR Tazawako and JR Akita *shinkansen* lines).

Combine with KINOSAKI ONSEN

Onsen convert? Take a hot spring pilgrimage around Japan and stop by a venerable onsen *town like Kinosaki (p68) to see more of Japan's unique bathing culture (and enjoy a soak).*

Bathing in Nyuto hot springs

A sea eagle perched on the drift ice

92

Step onto the drift ice of Shiretoko

This national park in northeast Hokkaido is the only place in the country where you can walk on drift ice

— MAKE IT HAPPEN —

Trips usually start from Utoro in Hokkaido's far northeast.

Trips run February through March, depending on the ice conditions. Book with tour operator Picchio (shiretoko-picchio.com).

Utoro is linked to Shiretoko-Shari station (JR Senmo main line) by bus.

In the Ainu language, spoken by northern Japan's Indigenous Ainu people, *sir etok* means "the end of the earth". Shiretoko peninsula, protruding from northeastern Hokkaido, certainly feels remote – and even more so in the depths of winter, when drift ice (*ryuhyo*) clusters around the shore.

The best way to experience this winter wonderland is by walking across it – an unforgettable adventure undertaken with an expert tour guide. Most trips meet in Utoro, one of the last stops before the true wilds of Shiretoko (the peninsula's northern half is covered in dense forests, home to deer, foxes, brown bears and even the elusive Blakiston's fish owl).

And it's an entirely safe experience; once you reach the shore, you'll put on a dry-suit before stepping out onto the ice, led by one of the guides.

The view from the shore is incredible: the seascape is a study in grey, white and blue, with either vast chunks of ice bobbing in the steely waters or an almost endless expanse of white. On the ice, your sense of perspective shifts, and even the soundscape is unfamiliar. The wind flits across the ice, which creaks beneath your feet, and the air is split by the piercing calls of white-tailed eagles, and immense Steller's sea eagles. It truly feels like you've stepped off the end of the earth, into some mythical frozen land.

93

Join the seasonal sakura celebration

Nothing draws Japanese people outside like the blooming of cherry blossoms during springtime

Of all Japan's seasonal events, none is more famous – and more popular – than the cherry blossoms bursting into bloom each spring. For centuries, locals have celebrated the occasion with *hanami* (blossom viewing) events and lovingly recorded the moment in art and poetry, the flowers' brief but abundant beauty making them a rich subject. The late 18th-century haiku master Kobayashi Issa captured the reflective mood *hanami* can bring on, writing: "Without you – / the cherry blossoms / just blossoms" (translation by David G Lanoue). But he also noted the shared joy that still defines *hanami* today, as people track the blossom forecast and gather for picnics at the trees' efflorescent peak, saying: "Under the cherry blossoms / strangers are not / really strangers" (translation by Zoria P K).

The cherry blossom (or *sakura*) season usually occurs between mid-March and mid-April. Most trees are of the *Somei-Yoshino* variety, with delicate, pale-pink flowers that bloom around mid-March. Others emerge at different times: the fluffy flowers of *Shidare-zakura* begin to appear in late March, while the unusual *Shiki-zakura* blooms again in November, so you can see autumn colours and *sakura* together in places like Obara (Aichi prefecture). The main blossom season sweeps from south to north, starting with Okinawa's deep pink *Kanhi-zakura* in January, and ending with Hokkaido's blooms in May.

While you can see the blossoms nearly anywhere in Japan, there are some spots that are particularly famous for their display. Tokyo's sprawling Yoyogi Park is a go-to for *hanami* parties, with groups bagging their picnic spots hours, or even days, in advance. Meanwhile in Kyoto, the iconic Philosopher's Path is always crammed with people watching the dusty pink petals flutter to the ground.

Yet for the best *hanami* experience, it's best to seek somewhere popular enough to feel festive, but not so crowded that your view of the flowers is obscured by people's phones. Shiga prefecture strikes this balance well, with several spectacular sakura spots dotted around scenic Lake Biwa. Two sites make the official list of Japan's 100 Famous Cherry Blossom Spots. First is Ho-koen, a park in Nagahama where you can admire Nagahama Castle emerging from the frothy blooms of 600 *Somei-Yoshino* trees. Second is Kaizu-Osaki, a peninsula lined with 800 blossom trees beside Lake Biwa (it's especially breathtaking from the water). Towards the end of April, you can also see late-blooming *Oshima-zakura* and *Yae-zakura* trees by tranquil Lake Yogo (not far from Lake Biwa). The peaceful, contemplative scene is the perfect end to the season – and who knows, it might even inspire a poem or two.

— MAKE IT HAPPEN —

Shiga prefecture is northeast of Kyoto and Osaka, and west of Nagoya. It centres on Japan's largest lake, Biwa-ko. Nagahama, Maibara and Hikone are on Biwa-ko's northeast shore; the small lake of Yogo is to its north.

Follow the cherry blossom forecast online with sites like *japan-guide.com*, which provides daily updates in English. The cherry blossom season is one of the busiest times to travel in Japan. Book accommodation and transport well ahead, and expect higher hotel rates. Late blooms also often coincide with Golden Week (late April to early May), increasing domestic travel.

Maibara is on the JR Tokaido *shinkansen* line, making it a convenient base for exploring Shiga's *hanami* spots. From Maibara, the JR Tokaido main line heads south towards Kyoto, via Hikone. The JR Hokuriku main line goes north to Tsuruga (the terminus of the JR Hokuriku *shinkansen* line), via Nagahama and Yogo.

SEASONAL JAPAN

Left Blossoms framing Nagahama Castle, Shiga
Right *Shidare-zakura* blossom
Below An abundance of petals in Kaizu-Osaki, by Lake Biwa

"The cherry blossom (or sakura) season usually occurs between mid-March and mid-April."

Cherry blossom trees at Tokyo's Chidorigafuchi Park

94

Enjoy the delicate plum blossoms at Kairaku-en

At their peak in late February, plum blossoms announce the arrival of spring

Dainty little pink, white and red blossoms cling to gnarled branches, some of which are propped up on wooden crutches. People stroll by the flowers, pausing to admire them and snap photos. Stalls sell themed snacks and goods to passersby. This may sound like Japan in sakura season, but it's actually a full month earlier, when the equally beautiful plum blossoms herald the coming of spring.

Among the best places to see them is Kairaku-en in Mito. One of Japan's *sanmeien* (Three Great Gardens; *p131*), Kairaku-en was laid out by the local lord in 1841, its open, landscaped grounds designed to facilitate social gatherings and shared appreciation of the scenery. It has many lovely sections, from a bamboo grove to a cedar forest, but the biggest draw is its plum trees. There are some 3,000, encompassing over a hundred varieties, which burst into bloom each February. They're celebrated at the Plum Blossom Festival, where you can join tours of the garden and see the trees in a new light during evening illuminations.

The trees, though beautiful, were planted for a practical reason: to ensure a store of *umeboshi* (dried, pickled plums) in lean times. So be sure to try the lip-puckeringly sour snack and delicious *umeshu* (plum liqueur) while you're here.

MAKE IT HAPPEN

 Mito is the prefectural capital of Ibaraki, just northeast of Tokyo. Kairaku-en is west of the city centre, near Lake Senda and the Sakura River.

 Kairaku-en (*ibaraki-kairakuen.jp*) is open daily. The Plum Blossom Festival (*mitokoumon.com/ume*) is held mid-February to March.

 Mito is on the JR Joban line from Tokyo. There are buses from the station to Kairaku-en, plus trains to Kairaku-en station in plum blossom season.

Subtle plum blossoms taking over Kairaku-en

SEASONAL JAPAN

Feel the joy at an Awa Odori festival

Welcome ancestral spirits to the land of the living at Shikoku's most famous celebration

"It's a fool who watches, and a fool who dances. If both are fools, you might as well dance!" So sing the performers at Awa Odori, Tokushima's thrilling traditional dance festival. For a few days each summer, the laid-back coastal city bursts into joyful life, as dancers and spectators fill its streets with noise and colour. Raucous though it is, the Awa Odori is actually part of a Buddhist festival honouring ancestors, Obon. One of Japan's three major holiday seasons, Obon sees huge numbers of people return to their family home in mid-August to greet the spirits of their departed relatives, visiting their graves and making offerings at family altars. At the start of Obon, lanterns are lit to lead the spirits to the living world; they're lit again at the end, too, and floated down rivers to guide ancestors back to the spirit realm. While ancestors visit our world, families want to welcome them – hence the colourful Bon Odori dances, of which the Awa Odori is undoubtedly the most famous.

Things kick off with a "pre-festival" evening Zenyasai, a two-hour stage show where *ren* – dance troupes that are a main feature of the festival – give a glimpse of what's to come. There are hundreds of these troupes, some of which have travelled from overseas specially, but only the area's top 30 *ren* perform at Zenyasai. The next morning, the festival officially starts with the Nagashi parade, a small procession that meanders through town with people playing instruments like the three-stringed *shamisen*, the high-toned *fue* (flute) and various *taiko* (drums). Some 200 food stalls start to open, serving up yakisoba (fried noodles) and cold, sugary *kakigori* (shaved ice with flavoured syrups) to those watching the procession.

When evening arrives, it's time for the main event: performances by professional *ren*, either in the street (closed to traffic at night) or on stages around the city. People take their seats in *enbujo* (stands) as hundreds of *ren* start to dance, sing, chant and play music, complete with cheeky facial expressions, gestures to the audience and incredible styling. The members of each *ren* wear matching outfits, chosen to suit their dance and to express their unique spirit. The most iconic style is worn by the women-only *onna-odori* groups, and includes colourful *yukata* (summer kimono); paper fans with the name of the *ren*, tucked into their *obi* (belts); wooden *geta* (sandals with two vertical blocks on the base – the dancers often lean forward onto their toes); and *amigasa* (straw hats folded into a fan shape, held in place over a bun).

As you watch the rhythmic dances, you might start tapping your toes and joining in on the call-and-response chants. If you've caught the dance bug, head to City Hall before the festival ends, where the Nikawa-ren (instant *ren*) gathers and can give you a few lessons. After all, you're a fool even if you just watch – so why not join in the fun?

MAKE IT HAPPEN

Coastal Tokushima city is the capital of Tokushima prefecture, in the east of Shikoku island. The festival takes place throughout the prefecture, but mostly in the centre of Tokushima city.

The Awa Odori is held 12–15 August. Tickets for paid seating areas go on sale in early July *(awaodorimirai.com)*; it's best to book early. There are plenty of free viewing areas, too, but they won't guarantee a sight of the top *ren*. Hotels in Tokushima fill up fast, and prices rise, so consider staying in nearby Naruto or Takamatsu. Obon is a major domestic travel period, so reserve seats on transport whenever possible.

Tokushima station is on the JR Kotoku line to Takamatsu. Takamatsu connects with the nearest bullet train station, Okayama, on Honshu island, which has links to destinations including Kyoto, Osaka, Tokyo and Fukuoka (Hakata). Tokushima airport has regular flights to Tokyo and Fukuoka.

SEASONAL JAPAN

"For a few days each summer, the laid-back coastal city bursts into joyful life."

Top One of many *ren* groups
Below left A joyful Awa performance
Above *Ren* dancing down the street

SEASONAL JAPAN

Firefly viewing spots in Japan

1
Osawa no Sato
If you don't have time for a long detour from the capital, head for this leafy Mitaka district, west of central Tokyo. Its rice paddies are the perfect habitat for fireflies, so stroll the boardwalks on a June evening for a serene light show.

2
Yokohoma-machi
Firefly season drifts later as you head north. In this Aomori town, the Firefly and Spring Water Festival is held in early July. Visit to see Genji and Heike fireflies in the wild, and enjoy refreshing nagashi somen (chilled thin noodles in a bamboo flume).

3
Kushiro Shitsugen National Park
With minimal light pollution, the marshlands of Hokkaido's Kushiro Shitsugen National Park are ideal for viewing fireflies. Follow the boardwalk near Onnenai Visitor Centre to see Heike and Oba varieties in July and early August.

96

Spot fireflies at Nigami's early-summer festival

The bioluminescent insects put on one of Japan's loveliest seasonal displays

From cooling down with *kakigori* (shaved ice) to watching hundreds of *hanabi* (fireworks) displays, summer in Japan is full of sweet traditions. The most magical, however, has got to be firefly viewing. For centuries, locals have gathered in early summer to honour Japan's 26th micro-season: *kusaretaru kusa hotaru to naru*, 11–15 June. Translating to "rotten grass becomes fireflies", it refers to the fireflies that emerge from beds of wet grass in areas with just the right conditions: long grasses, clear flowing water and low light pollution so you can easily see the bioluminescent bugs.

Witnessing these critters glow at night is mesmerizing, so much so that many regions with these perfect conditions host firefly-watching festivals. One of the loveliest, the Nigami Firefly Festival, is held in the tiny town of Oshimaku Nigami from mid-June to mid-July (despite the micro-season's short timeframe, fireflies are actually visible for longer depending on where you are). During the festival, people follow a 7-km (4-mile) road, known as the Firefly Line, alongside the Hokura River. After parking, you can proceed on foot to the viewing area to watch the display unfold, with pinpricks of light glowing and fading around the rice paddies and pure mountain streams.

Fireflies glowing at night

MAKE IT HAPPEN

 Oshimaku Nigami is in Niigata prefecture. The Firefly Line road follows the course of the Hokura River, with the viewing platform just north of town.

 Oshimaku Nigami's fireflies are visible mid-June to mid-July, and the festival is held over this period. Firefly Line can get busy on weekends.

 The nearest station is Hokuhoku Oshima, a ten-minute taxi ride from Nigami. Joetsu city has the closest *shinkansen* stop, on the Hokuriku line.

97

Admire the hydrangeas at Unsho-ji

These bright, beautiful flowers are one of the most celebrated sights in the rainy season

In the heart of Japan's rainy season, hydrangeas burst into bloom. Their dense, pompom-like flower heads pop up in clusters in parks and gardens, adding pools of vibrant colour to the lush, rain-fed greens. There are some 100 varieties of *ajisai* (hydrangea) in the country, ranging from blues and whites to pinks and purples. The colour often reflects the soil's pH, so you can see a lovely gradation between pink (alkaline) and blue (acidic) from one flowerhead to the next.

Temples are among the most popular spots to view *ajisai*, and people pour into the best-known ones in June and July to see the eye-catching blooms against scenic backdrops like wooden halls and bamboo groves, or placed delicately into *chozubachi* (stone basins). Unsho-ji, in Akita's Oga region, is among the most enchanting – and its location is just remote enough to keep crowds minimal. Across the grounds here, over 1,500 hydrangeas form a beautiful carpet of blue, some with the Sea of Japan as a peaceful backdrop. The spectacular sight is the vision of one man: Deputy Head Priest Konaka Shuun. Captivated by the bloom's beauty, he dedicated years to propagating them, creating the "blue heaven" you see today. Pick up an elegant white and blue *omamori* (amulet) or *goshuin* (temple stamp) to commemorate your visit and his glorious vision.

MAKE IT HAPPEN

Unsho-ji is located near the north coast of the Oga peninsula, a charming and quite remote corner of northwest Honshu's Akita prefecture.

The temple is open 9am–5pm, with last entry at 4:30pm. Stay in Oga overnight if you can, to enjoy the area and allow more transport flexibility.

From Akita station (an Akita *shinkansen*-line stop), take the JR Oga line to Hadachi or Oga, then an Oga Kita bus to Kitaura, a stop near Unsho-ji (or a taxi).

Blue hygrangeas at Unsho-ji

SEASONAL JAPAN

Combine with KAMAKURA

Among Kamakura's historic capital's many famous temples (p28) is Meigetsu-in, also known as Ajisai-dera for its hundreds of blue hydrangeas that bloom each June. It's the perfect place to travel to after Unsho-ji.

Fiery red and orange trees, Mount Tanigawa

98

Immerse yourself in the colours of autumn

Admire the red and gold leaves covering Mount Tanigawa from a scenic ropeway

— MAKE IT HAPPEN —

Mount Tanigawa straddles the border of Niigata and Gunma prefectures in central Japan.

The leaves are usually best in mid-October; check the autumn colour forecast.

Take a bus from Joetsu *shinkansen* or Tanigawa station, or walk from Doai station.

Just as the spreading blush of the cherry blossom flowers is tracked each year, so are the autumn leaves. People check autumn colour (*koyo*) forecasts online and watch them on the news, planning picnics in the park and trips to the countryside purely to take in the trees in their finery.

The mountains are among the best places to admire the leaves turning, offering the chance to see panoramic views of slopes covered in deep red maples, bright yellow ginkgos and larches, and orange-red rowans. While hiking immerses you in the woods, giving you a close-up view of the leaves, its downside is that (quite literally) you can't see the forest for the trees. To get a sense of scale, you'll need to go higher.

On Mount Tanigawa, one of Japan's 100 Famous Mountains, you'll rise above the trees on the ropeway chairlift. In 15 minutes it surges above valleys and ridges, the reds, browns and golds below growing deeper as you approach the station at 1,319 m (4,327 ft). The mountain rises still higher beyond that, to 1,977 m (6,486 ft), the craggy, austere rock face above the treeline dusted with snow in October. Head back down on the ropeway, or make the most of the final month of climbing season by hitting the trails, ending with a restorative soak in the natural hot springs of Minakami after.

SEASONAL JAPAN

Share the harvest's bounty with the gods

In the myth-steeped town of Takachiho, locals celebrate the harvest with ancient dances and warming meals

In a cuisine that prizes seasonality, one time of year stands out: autumn. The lush green rice paddies of summer turn gold, and the rice is harvested and dried in sheaves in each region's own way – hung from a rack or on a pole, or rested in conical piles. And in a culture where the grain is an essential food staple, harvest time is cause for celebration.

You'll get plenty of enjoyment simply from savouring autumnal delicacies, from persimmons to chestnuts, and from the first snow crabs to the first sake (*akiagari*, or spring-brewed *nihonshu*, now aged enough to drink). But to understand the spirit of the season, attend a harvest festival, like the Yokagura of Takachiho. This beautiful town in the mountains of Kyushu is infused with mythology, and its harvest celebrations are appropriately ancient and mysterious. The townsfolk dress in ornate costumes, don masks and perform *kagura* dances depicting Shinto tales. Between dances, nourishing autumn foods are served as *naorai*, a meal shared with the gods. Warm your body and spirit with delicious dishes like *kappo-dori* (well-seasoned chicken and mushrooms steamed in bamboo), *kappo-zake* (*shochu* or *nihonshu* gently warmed in bamboo) and *shoke-mori* (simmered dishes and rice in bamboo baskets) – and don't forget to thank the capricious gods for such a rich harvest.

— MAKE IT HAPPEN —

Takachiho is in Miyazaki prefecture, in eastern Kyushu.

The Yokagura festival is held in late November over two nights. Shortened versions are performed every day of the year at Takachiho Shrine.

Takachiho is accessible by bus from Miyazaki, Kumamoto city and airport and Fukuoka.

Combine with NIIGATA

There are more sake breweries in Niigata (p102) than any other Japanese prefecture, so it's the perfect place to try akiagari *– directly from a brewery, or at a specialist bar.*

A *kagura* dance in Takachiho

SEASONAL JAPAN

"You'll see fierce samurai, courtly princesses and people in the clothing of all social classes."

Above left and right Costumes on display in the Jidai Matsuri parade
Left The fiery festival of Kurama Hi no Matsuri

Celebrate the beauty of autumn in Kyoto

On one October day, this ancient city holds two radically different – but equally enticing – traditional festivals

Japan's traditional culture is often seen as elegant, elevated and complex. It's the ritual and focus of a tea ceremony; the contemplative calm of a rock garden; the restrained grace of the geisha's dance. But while all this is true, there is another side to it, too: the hedonism of the "floating world" shown in woodblock prints; the colour and noise of *kabuki* theatre; the raucous festivals where spirits run high and sake flows freely. In Kyoto, you can celebrate both of these sides of Japanese culture with two very different events, which, coincidentally, take place on the same day: 22 October, the city's foundation date.

The first is the Jidai Matsuri procession, a stately parade established in 1895 to honour Kyoto's long and illustrious history. The parade features 2,000 people (and around 70 animals) and stretches for 2 km (1.2 miles) as it makes its way through the city from the grand Imperial Palace to Heian-jingu, a shrine east of the Kamo River.

Jidai means "eras", and the festival showcases key events and figures from each era that Kyoto was the capital, covering over 1,000 years (794–1868) in all. It starts with the horse-drawn carriages of the 19th century, growing ever more captivating as it unspools the centuries in reverse chronological order. You'll see fierce samurai, courtly princesses and people in the clothing of all social classes, everyone walking ahead of two *mikoshi* (portable shrines) that house the spirits of emperors Kammu and Komei, the first and last emperors to reign from Kyoto. The historically accurate clothing is unquestionably the highlight, showcasing the incomparable talent of Kyoto's artisans, who have painstakingly preserved ancient weaving, dyeing and dressmaking techniques for generations.

After the spectacle of the parade, it's time for something a little more spirited. Take the train to Kurama in the mountains, enjoying the "maple tunnel" on the way, a gorgeous section of the track surrounded by leaves that are just starting to turn red. In the year 940, when the Yuki-jinja shrine was moved to Kurama, locals helped the shrine deity find its new home by lighting the way with torches. Since then, the night has been marked with the Kurama Hi no Matsuri. In this electrifying fire festival, the residents of Kurama – many in traditional loincloths and *hachimaki* fabric headbands – light up the streets with fiery torches. At dusk, households put lanterns by their doors, lighting a path for children with small torches. Next, the adults come crashing through the streets, carrying 4-m (13-ft) torches that can weigh up to 100 kg (220 lb). Finally, the torches are thrown onto a bonfire at the shrine, in a spectacular blaze. Everyone gathers to celebrate into the small hours, the scent of woodsmoke and sound of laughter providing a lively backdrop as they pay tribute to Kyoto's remarkable heritage.

— MAKE IT HAPPEN —

The Jidai Matsuri takes place in the centre of Kyoto, the ancient capital in western Honshu's Kansai region. Kurama Hi no Matsuri is held in Kurama, a small town in the mountains north of the city.

People stake out the best spots early along the Jidai Matsuri route. To guarantee a good view, reserve a seat in the paid stands; they're sold on Ticket Pia *(t.pia.jp)* from 10 September. Many people try to see both festivals, so allow as much time as possible to travel between them, and to find a good viewpoint. Note that events in Kurama begin around dusk.

The Jidai Matsuri route is easily accessible by subway, bus or taxi from Kyoto station (a Tokaido *shinkansen*-line stop). Kurama is on the Eizan Kurama train line, which starts at Demachiyanagi station (a half-hour walk from Heian-jingu, less from the Imperial Palace). It's best to board here, as the train quickly fills with festival-goers.

A week of summer festivals in Tohoku

SUGGESTED DURATION 7 days **START** Hachinohe; the city is a stop on the Tohoku *shinkansen* line between Tokyo and Aomori **GETTING AROUND** All the stops on this itinerary are connected by regular or bullet trains **END** Sendai; the city is halfway along the Tohoku *shinkansen* line between Tokyo and Aomori

Area of map

Festivals punctuate the year in Japan, marking the turning of the seasons, historical moments and religious events. Summer is peak festival season, when no amount of heat and humidity can put people off having a party. Want to join in the summer festivities? Simply plan your trip for the first week of August, follow this tour and let Japan show you a good time.

Focusing on Tohoku (northern Honshu), where three famous festivals take place in one week (Akita, Aomori and Sendai's Tohoku Sandai Matsuri, 2–8 August), this itinerary shows you the best of the beautiful region's summer celebrations. Start in Hachinohe on 2 August and you'll enjoy a festival every day, moving daily across the region to see floats and dancers take over Morioka, Akita, Hirosaki and Aomori before heading down to Yamagata and ending on 8 August in Sendai. It may be a tiring week, but it'll certainly be one to remember.

3. AKITA
A 1.5-hour *shinkansen* brings you to Akita, where the Akita Kanto Matsuri takes place 3–6 August. Held to ward off evil and pray for a good harvest, it features night parades where teams show off acrobatic feats, balancing 12-m (40-ft) bamboo poles laden with paper lanterns on their hands, heads and hips.

6. YAMAGATA
After a nearly four-hour journey (*shinkansen* to Sendai, then JR train) you'll be rewarded with Yamagata Hanagasa Matsuri (5–7 August). To celebrate the region's traditional music and dance, over 10,000 dancers bring the streets to life with colourful costumes – notably straw hats decorated with orange safflowers – and upbeat music.

4. HIROSAKI
Take a JR train to reach this city, where the Hirosaki Neputa Matsuri is held 1–7 August. For this festival, huge, illuminated paper floats (hand-made and painted by locals) are paraded through town every night, accompanied by energetic flute and *taiko* (drums).

5. AOMORI
A 45-minute JR train takes you to Aomori, where the Nebuta Matsuri takes place 2–7 August. Every night of the festival, spectacular handmade floats featuring gods, mythical figures and dramatic scenes parade through the city, alongside hundreds of dancers.

1. HACHINOHE
Start off with Hachinohe's Sansha Taisai, a festival celebrating three Shinto shrines between 31 July and 4 August. Watch *mikoshi* (portable shrines) and colourful floats paraded through town. Next up is Morioka, a 30-minute *shinkansen* ride away.

2. MORIOKA
For the first four days of August, watch amazing synchronized dancers, drummers, flautists and singers parade through town for Morioka's Sansa Odori. It's all in honour of a local deity ridding the town of a demon centuries ago.

7. SENDAI
See out your week of celebrations at Sendai, reached by JR train in an hour and a half. Here, the Tanabata Festival – the most famous of Japan's *tanabata* festivals – celebrates the reunion of celestial lovers Orihime and Hikoboshi (6–8 Aug).

Index

A

Accommodation
   ryokan (traditional inns) 74–7
   staying in temples 73, 75
   see also Hotels
Adachi Museum of Art 130
Adachi Zenko 130
Ainu people 58, 231
Airports 15
Akasaka sleep lab 144
Akihabara 49, 198–9
Akita 249
Ancestors: Awa Odori festival 238–9
Ando, Tadao 200, 208
Animation 204, 220
Aomori 212, 249
Aoshima Hadaka Mairi 227
Apps 16
Archaeological sites
   Sannai-Maruyama 64–5
Architecture
   Azabudai Hills (Tokyo) 142–3
   a contemporary architecture odyssey 164–5
   Yokohama Bay 146–7
   Yusuhara 145
Arita porcelain 72–3
Art
   Art Islands 200–201
   Arts Towada 208–11
   manhole cover art 212–13
   Seto Art Islands 150
   teamLab Forest (Kyushu) 150–51
   ukiyo-e prints 80–81
   see also Museums and galleries
Asahidake 228
Asahikawa 228
Atami 212
ATMs 15
Autumn colours 244
Awa Odori festival 238–9
Awazu Onsen 144
Azabudai Hills (Tokyo) 142–3

B

Bamboo groves 135
Bandai-Azuma Skyline 176–7
Baseball 206–7
Basho, Matsuo 78–9, 82
Baths, public 17, 19
Beef, wagyu 106
Beppu 110, 188
Biwa, Lake 232–3
Blossom see Flowers
Boats
   to Beppu 188
   ferries 16
Breweries, sake 245
Buddhism
   Awa Odori festival 238–9
   Great Buddha, Kamakura 28–9
   Shingon school 191
   shojin-ryori cuisine 89
   staying in temples 73, 75
   see also Temples
Budget travel 14–15
Bullet trains 16, 40–41
Buses 16

C

Cable cars 182
Capsule hotels 144
Castle, Crow (Matsumoto) 43
Ceramics 72–3
Cherry blossom 31, 232–3
Children 17
Chopsticks 18
Christianity 61
Chubu 13
Chugoku 13
Cosplay 202
Crafts Gallery (Tokyo) 31
Crow Castle (Matsumoto) 43
Culinary Japan 84–111
Customs and etiquette 18–19
Cycling
   Kibi Plain 178, 189
   Shimanami Kaido 178

D

Daikanbo 182
Daisetsuzan National Park 228
Deer 127
Den Den Town (Osaka) 163
Depachika food halls 92
Department store food halls 92
Dewa-Sanzan 128–9
Diving
   Ogasawara Islands 132
   Yaeyama Islands 122–3
Doctors 17
Drift ice 231
Drinks see Food and drink
Driving 16
Dyeing, indigo 60

E

Earthquakes 181
Eihei-ji 75
Emergency services 15, 17
Enka 214
Etiquette 18–19
   onsen (hot springs) 69
   shrines 36
   tea ceremony 57
Exiles, Sadogashima 172

F

Fabrics, indigo dyeing 60
Farm-to-table eating 90–91
Fashion 203
Ferries 16
Festivals
   Awa Odori festival 238–9
   harvest festivals 245
   Kyoto autumn festival 246–7
   Nigami Firefly Festival 240
   a week of summer festivals in Tohoku 248–9
   winter festivals 226–7
Fire
   Kyoto autumn festival 247
   Nozawa Onsen 226–7
Fireflies 240–41
Flowers
   cherry blossom 31, 232–3
   hydrangeas 242–3
   plum blossom 236–7
   Rishiri-Rebun-Sarobetsu National Park 118

INDEX

Food and drink 85, 86–7
   budget travel 14
   department store food halls 92
   a food lover's tour of Japan 110–11
   izakaya 108–9
   kaiseki meals 104–5
   Nishiki Market (Kyoto) 107
   noodles 100–101
   Okinawan cuisine 98–9
   ramen 30
   rice harvest 245
   sake 102–3, 245
   shojin-ryori cuisine 89
   street food 94–5
   sushi and sashimi 44–5
   Tono Valley 90–91
   wagashi-making classes 93
   wagyu beef 106
Forests and trees
   autumn colours 244
   forest bathing 120
   Fushimi Inari Taisha 135
   Sagano Bamboo Forest 135
   Yakushima 116–17
Fukuoka 61, 72, 94, 110
Fukuoka Softback Hawks 206
Fukushima 176
Funiculars 182
Furano 228
Fushimi Inari Taisha 135
Futuristic Japan 138–165

G

Gardens *see* Parks and gardens
Geisha 26–7
Ghibli Park (Nagoya) 204–5
Goto Islands 61, 137
Government 15
Great Buddha, Kamakura 28–9
Great Kanto Earthquake (1923) 142

H

Hachinohe 218, 221, 249
Haiku 79
Hakodate 59, 221
Hamamatsu 83
Hanami (blossom viewing) 232
Health care 17
Hiking 16
   Michinoku Coastal Trail 181
   Mount Daisen 179
   Rishiri-Rebun-Sarobetsu National Park 118
   Yakushima 116–17
Hiraizumi 83
Hirosaki 249
Hiroshige, Utagawa 25, 80, 81
Hiroshima 50, 110
   Peace Memorial Park 32–3
Historic buildings
   Crow Castle (Matsumoto) 43

Historic buildings (cont.)
   Imperial Palace, Tokyo 31
   see also Shrines; Temples
Hokkaido 12, 175
   winter sports 228–9
Hokusai 25, 81
Hospitality 18, 74–5
Hospitals 17
Hotels
   budget travel 14
   capsule hotels 144
Hot springs
   Awazu Onsen 144
   Bandai-Azuma Skyline 177
   Beppu 188
   Kinosaki Onsen 68–9, 82, 230
   Nozawa Onsen 226–7
   Nyuto Onsen 230
Hydrangeas 242–3

I

Ice, drift 231
Ichiro, Suzuki 207
Iconic Japan 20–51
Iga-Ueno 79
Iizaka Onsen 177
Imabari 192
Immersive experiences 155
Imperial Palace, Tokyo 31
Indigenous peoples 58
Indigo dyeing 60
Industry, Nagoya 158–9
Inns, traditional 74–7
Iriomote 136
Iseji trail 170
Ishigaki 136
Issa, Kobayashi 232
Itineraries
   a classic tour of Japan 50–51
   a contemporary architecture odyssey 164–5
   a food lover's tour of Japan 110–11
   island hopping in the south 136–7
   a journey through traditional Japan 82–3
   a pop culture pilgrimage 220–21
   a scenic journey through Japan 192–3
   a week of summer festivals in Tohoku 248–9
Itsukushima 50
Izakaya restaurants 108–9
Izumo 186, 192
Izu Peninsula 83

J

Japan Alps 182–3
Jazz 215
Jomon civilization 64–5
Journeys in Japan 166–93
J-pop 214
J-rock 214
Juntoku, Emperor 172

K

Kabuki 62–3
Kaga Onsen 218
Kagoshima 137
Kairaku-en 131, 236–7
Kaiseki meals 104–5
Kaizu-Osaki 232–3
Kamakura 83, 243
   Great Buddha 28–9
Kanazawa 93, 165, 217
Kanazawa Kenrokuen 131
Kansai 13
Kanto 12
Karaoke 216
Karuizawa 165
Kibi Plain 178, 189
Kii Peninsula 170
Kinosaki Onsen 68–9, 82, 230
Kitakata 30, 51
Kitayama River 133
Kobe 106, 110, 220
   jazz 215
Kobo Daishi 191
Kohechi trail 170
Koraku-en 131
Koshien Stadium, 207
Kuma, Kengo 145, 149, 208
Kumamon 218–19
Kumamoto 218–19
Kumano Kodo pilgrimage route 133, 170–71
Kunio, Yanagita 90
Kurama 247
Kurashiki 189, 193
Kurobe Dam 182
Kurobe Gorge Railway 182
Kurobe-Unazuki Canyon Route 182
Kurodake 228
Kusama, Yayoi 43, 200, 208
Kushiro Shitsugen National Park 240
Kyoto 47, 50, 82, 134
   autumn festival 246–7
   bamboo groves 135
   cherry blossom season 232–3
   a contemporary architecture odyssey 164
   gardens 126
   geisha and *maiko* culture 26–7
   Nishiki Market 92, 107
   popular culture 220
   temples and shrines 37
Kyushu 13, 151

L

Lakes
   Biwa 232–3
   Yogo 232
Language 15, 19
LGBTQ+ community 17
   Kanazawa 217
Log rafting, Kitayama River 133

M

Magnetic levitation trains 153
Maiko (geishas in training) 26
Mama-chari ("mum's bike") 189
Manhole cover art 212-13
Maps
    culinary Japan 86-7
    futuristic Japan 140-41
    iconic Japan 22-3
    journeys in Japan 168-9
    outdoor Japan 114-15
    popular Japan 196-7
    seasonal Japan 223-5
    timeless Japan 54-5
    see also Itineraries
Market, Nishiki (Kyoto) 92, 107
Mascots 218-19
Matsue 192
Matsumoto 43, 51
Matsusaka beef 106
Michinoku Coastal Trail 109, 181
Minamoto no Yoritomo 28
Miraikan (Tokyo) 155
Miyazaki 110
Miyazaki, Hayao 116
Money 15
Monks, Dewa-Sanzan 128-9
Morioka 30, 100-101, 111, 249
Motonosumi Inari Taisha (Nagato) 70-71
Mountains
    Dewa-Sanzan 128-9
    Northern Japan Alps 182-3
    Mount Aso 218
    Mount Daisen 179
    Mount Fuji 25
    Mount Misen 179
    Mount Obako 170
    Mount Rishiri 118
    Mount Tanigawa 244
Murakami, Haruki 215
Murodo 182
Museums and galleries
    Adachi Museum of Art 130
    Crafts Gallery (Tokyo) 31
    National Museum of Modern Art (Tokyo) 31
    Ryukyu-mura 66
    Sannai-Maruyama 64-5
    Science Square TSUKUBA (Tokyo) 160
    Upopoy National Ainu Museum 58
Music 214-15, 216

N

Nagahama 232-3
Nagasaki 32, 61, 137
Nagato 70-71
Nagoya 158-9, 165
Nakahechi trail 170
Nakanoshima (Osaka) 162
Naoshima 193
Nara 127, 218
National Museum of Modern Art (Tokyo) 31
National parks
    Daisetsuzan 228
    Kushiro Shitsugen 240
    Rishiri-Rebun-Sarobetsu 118-19
    Sanriku Fukko 181
    Shiretoko 231
Nichiren 172
Nigami Firefly Festival 240
Niigata 102, 245
Nikko 46-7, 51
Niseko 228
Nishiki Market (Kyoto) 92, 107
Noh theatre 172
Noodles 100-101
Northern Japan Alps 182-3
Nozawa Onsen 226-7
Nyuto Onsen 230

O

Obara 232
Ogasawara Islands 132
Ohechi trail 170
Ohenro-san 191
Okayama 193
Okinawa 13, 66-7, 98-9, 232
Okinawa Honto 137
Omi beef 106
Omotenashi (hospitality) 18, 74-5
Onomichi 192
Onsen (hot springs) 69
    Awazu Onsen 144
    Bandai-Azuma Skyline 177
    Beppu 188
    Kinosaki Onsen 82, 230
    Nozawa Onsen 226-7
    Nyuto Onsen 230
    Kinosaki Onsen 68-9
Osaka 50, 164, 220
    architecture 162-3, 164-5
    manhole cover art 212, 221
Osawa no Sato 240
Oshimaku Nigami 240
Otaku 198-9
Outdoor Japan 112-37

P

Parks and gardens
    Adachi Museum of Art 130
    Kairaku-en 131, 236-7
    Kanazawa Kenrokuen 131
    Koraku-en 131
    Kyoto 126
    Peace Memorial Park (Hiroshima) 32-3
    Tokyo 31
    see also Flowers
Passports 17
Peace Memorial Park, Hiroshima 32-3
Pharmacies 17
Phones 15
Pilgrimages
    Mount Fuji 25
    sacred trails of the Kumano Kodo 133, 170-71
    Shikoku Henro 120, 190-91
Planning the ultimate trip 14-15
Plum blossom 236-7
Poetry 79
Police 17
Popular culture 195-221
Popular Japan 194-221
Porcelain, Arita 72-3
Prints, woodblock 80-81
Public transport 16, 19

R

Rafting
    Kitayama River 133
Railways *see* Trains
Ramen 30
Rat Sunrise (Sagamihara) 152
RED° Tokyo Tower 154-5, 160
Religion *see* Buddhism; Christianity; Pilgrimages; Shinto; Shrines
Restaurants 18-19
    Izakaya 108-9
    ramen in Kitakata 30
Rice harvest 245
Rishiri-Rebun-Sarobetsu National Park 118-19
Roads
    Bandai-Azuma Skyline 176-7
    Shimanami Kaido 178
Robots 160-61
Rusutsu 228
Ryokan (traditional inns) 74-7
Ryukyuan people 66-7

S

Sadogashima 172
Sagamihara 29, 152
Sagano Bamboo Forest 135
Sake (rice wine) 102-3, 245
Sakura 212
Sakura (cherry blossom season) 232-3
Sakurajima 121, 137
Samurai 25, 28, 31, 43, 46
Sannai-Maruyama 64-5
Sanriku Fukko National Park 181
Sapporo 221
Sapporo Snow Festival 227
Sashimi 45
Sayama Hills 120
Science Square TSUKUBA (Tokyo) 160
Seasonal Japan 223-5
Seikan Tunnel 174-5
Sendai 111, 249
Seto Art Islands 150
Seto Inland Sea 178, 200-201
Shibuya Crossing (Tokyo) 34-5

INDEX

Shiga prefecture 232
Shikoku 13, 120
Shikoku Henro 190–91
Shimanami Kaido 33, 178
Shimane 218
Shinkansen (bullet trains) 16, 40–41
Shinrin-yoku (forest bathing) 120
Shinsekai (Osaka) 163
Shinto 36
    Kumano Kodo pilgrimage route 170–71
    see also Shrines
Shiogama 45, 51
Shiraoi 221
Shiretoko National Park 231
Shizuoka 81, 83
Shoes, removing 19
Shohei, Ohtani 207
shojin-ryori cuisine 89
Shopping 19
    Nishiki Market (Kyoto) 92, 107
Shrines 36
    Kyoto 37
    Motonosumi Inari Taisha (Nagato) 70–71
    Nikko Toshu-gu 46–7
    visiting 19
Shugendo 128, 179
Skiing *see* Winter sports
Skyscrapers 42, 146–7, 162–3
Skytree (Tokyo) 42, 143
Soja 193
Soundscapes 135
Specific requirements, travellers with 17
Sport
    baseball 206–7
    sumo 48–9
Street food 94–5
Street style, Tokyo 203
Studio Ghibli (Nagoya) 204–5
Sumo 48–9
Sunrise Izumo sleeper train 186–7
Sushi 44–5

T

Takachiho 245
Takamatsu 164, 193
Takashi, Kuribayashi 208
Takayama 89
Takayu Onsen 177
Takemikazuchi 127
Taketomi 136
Takeuchi Festival 227
Tateyama-Kurobe Alpine Route 182
Tatsuhiko, Kawasaki 215
Tattoos 19
Taxis 17
Tea ceremony 56–7
teamLab 155
teamLab Forest (Kyushu) 150–51
Temples
    hydrangeas 242–3
    Kyoto 37

Temples (cont.)
    Shikoku Henro 190–91
    staying in 73, 75
    visiting 19
Tendo 111
Teshima 193
Theatre
    kabuki 62–3
    Noh theatre 172
Theme parks
    Ghibli Park (Nagoya) 204–5
    Tokyo Tower 154–5
Time zone 15
Timeless Japan 52–83
Tipping 18
Toba 111
Tohoku 12, 248–9
Toilets 17
    Tokyo 148–9
Tokugawa Ieyasu 46
Tokushima 238–9
Tokyo 12, 51, 83
    Akihabara 198–9
    Azabudai Hills 142–3
    cherry blossom season 232–3
    a contemporary architecture odyssey 165
    a food lover's tour of Japan 111
    Imperial Palace 31
    popular culture 221
    robots 160–61
    a scenic journey through Japan 193
    Shibuya Crossing 34–5
    street style 203
    Sunrise Izumo sleeper train 186–7
    toilets 148–9
Tokyo Skytree 42, 143
Tokyo Tower 42, 154–5
Tomamu 228
Tono Valley 83, 90–91
Torii (gates) 70–71
Totoro's Forest 120
Tour operators 14, 15
Towada 65, 208–11, 221
Toyama 51, 165
Toyota Group 159
Trains 16, 19, 40–41
    Kurobe Gorge Railway 182
    magnetic levitation trains 153
    Seikan Tunnel 174–5
    Sunrise Izumo sleeper train 186–7
Trams 16
Travel 16
    budget travel 14–15
    etiquette 19
Trees *see* Forests and trees
Tsuchiyu Onsen 177
Tunnel, Seikan 174–5

U

Uji 56, 82
Ukiyo-e prints 80–81

Umeda (Osaka) 163
UNESCO
    Aino 58
    Kumano Kodo pilgrimage route 170–71
    Kyoto 37, 47
    Ogasawara Islands 132
    Sannai-Maruyama 64
    shrines and temples of Nikko 46–7
Universal Studios Japan 155
Unsho-ji 242–3
Upopoy National Ainu Museum 58

V

Vending machines 152
Volcanoes
    Mount Fuji 25
    Sakurajima 121

W

Wagashi-making classes 93
Wagyu beef 106
Walks *see* Hiking
Websites 16
Wenders, Wim 149
Wildlife
    fireflies 240–41
    Ogasawara Islands 132
    sacred deer 127
    Yaeyama Islands 122–3
Winter festivals 226–7
Winter sports
    Hokkaido 228–9
    Rishiri-Rebun-Sarobetsu National Park 118
Woodblock prints 80–81
World Cosplay Summit 202
World War II 32, 159

Y

Yaeyama Islands 122–5
Yakult Swallows 206
Yakushima 116–17, 137
Yamabushi (mountain monks) 128–9
Yamagata 248
Yatai (street food stalls) 94–5
Yogo, Lake 232
Yokohama Bay 146–7
Yokohama-machi 240
Yomiuri Giants 206
Yonaguni 136
Yoshinori, Andoh 215
Yusuhara 145

Z

Zeami Motokiyo 172
Zen Buddhism 28
    shojin-ryori cuisine 89
    staying in temples 73, 75

Acknowledgments

The publisher would like to thank the following for their kind permission to reproduce their photographs:

(Key: a-above; b-below/bottom; c-centre; f-far; l-left; r-right; t-top)

4Corners: Susanne Kremer 34–35.

Adobe Stock: blackrabbit3 70–71; eyeblink 44bl; Hick 145; nathume 186–187; piyaset 99tr; Shiawasesamurai 30.

Alamy Stock Photo: amana images inc. 36b, 69b, 96–97, 183l, 230, 233tr, 233b; Mark Bassett 216; Patrick Batchelder 187t; Vicki Beaver 99cr; Blue Planet Archive LLC 132; J. Borruel 73; Anthony Brown 229; dpa picture alliance 111b; JESÚS MARIA ERDOZAIN GÓMES 171tr; David Fleetham 122cl; Jose Fuste Raga mauritius images GmbH 162–163; Robert Gilhooly 64–65, 65tr; GIUGLIO Gil / hemis.fr 60; Nataliya Hora 107; ICP incamerastock 50; Miho Ikeya / The Yomiuri Shimbun via AP Images 161l; Suzuki Kaku 117bl; David Kleyn 75b; Julian Krakowiak 130–131; ERIC LAFFORGUE 193b; John Lander 61; Little valleys 109tr; Trevor Mogg 80bl; Yasushi Nagao / The Yomiuri Shimbun via AP Images 164; Lars Nicolaysen / dpa picture alliance 129br; Yusuke Okada / a. collectionRF / amana images inc. 136l; Janelle Orth 122bl; Sean Pavone 31, 127, 188; Solveig Placier / Photononstop 180–181; Navapon Plodprong 183br; Norbert Probst / imageBROKER.com GmbH & Co. KG 122tl; Pongphan Ruengchai 38–39; Toshikazu Sato / The Yomiuri Shimbun via AP Images 202; SOURCENEXT MIXA 236–237; Nanako Sudo / The Yomiuri Shimbun via AP Images 144; Nikoru Suzanne 110; Ryuzo Suzuki / The Yomiuri Shimbun via AP Images 65br; Takehiko Suzuki / The Yomiuri Shimbun via AP Images 206bl; Ulana Switucha 129l; Chiharu Taoka / AFLO 93; Norikazu Tateishi / The Yomiuri Shimbun via AP Images 101; Yoshio Tsunoda / AFLO 161tr; Steve Vidler / mauritius images GmbH 83l; Noboru Tsubaki aTTA 2008; Towada Art Center photo: Edmund Sumner–VIEW 209b; BJ Warnick / Kyodo Photo via Newscom 133, 206tl, 206cl, 219, 249t; WBC ART 80br; Chris Willson 66–67; Masayuki Yamashita 120; ZUMA Press; Inc. 59.

AWL Images: Amana Images 47t, 47b; Jan Christopher Becke 41; Christian Kober 118.

Basho–o Kenshokai: 78–79.

Benesse Art Site Naoshima: Daici Ano 201tl; Rei Naito: Matrix; 2010; Teshima Art Museum; photo: Noboru Morikawa 201b; Ken'ichi Suzuki 201tr.

Getty Images: ODD ANDERSEN / AFP 203; The Asahi Shimbun 48–49, 221l, 239tr; B.S.P.I. 129tr; bonchan 104; Carl Court 173br; 226–227; DoctorEgg 24; Philip FONG AFP 154–155, 206–207; Noriko Hayashi / Bloomberg 152, 153; huayang 244; Francesco Riccardo Iacomino 2–3, 8–9; Ivan 106; JAPAN POOL JIJI PRESS AFP 62–63; Taro Karibe 192; Katsumi KASAHARA / Gamma–Rapho 245; Stanislav Kogiku / SOPA Images / LightRocket 28–29, 221r; Yuga Kurita 184–185; Kyodo News 161br; 239l, 239br; 246b; John S Lander LightRocket 190; LAW Ho Ming 102–103; Andrew Marriott 171tl; MIXA 98–99; Ippei Naoi 122–123, 124–125, 136r, 137, 173l; Tomohiro Ohsumi / Bloomberg 92; Sammyvision 44–45, 51r; Sam Spicer 117t, 117br; Tomohiro Ohsumi / Stringer 205; Shoko Takayasu / Bloomberg 95br; Tanatat pongphibool; thailand 174–175; tororo 51l; Leisa Tyler / LightRocket 76–77; Alison Wright 27br;

xun zhang 156–157; TORU YAMANAKA / AFP 99br.

Getty Images / iStock: ablokhin 109tl, 109b; aumphotography 246tl; bonchan 88bl; CHENG FENG CHIANG 248; DoctorEgg 146–147; Eloi_Omella 234–235; FilippoBacci 27l; Mariana Flores 212–213; GI15702993 193t; Samantha Gill 80t; gyro 83r; halbergman 56–57; hungryworks 44tl; kazoka30 111t; yunyan li 213tr; linegold 173tr; martin–dm 27tr; MrNovel 213br; oluolu3 82; Sean Pavone 33; Satoshi–K 88tl; SeanPavonePhoto 171b, 198–199; Beatrice Sirinuntananon 246tr, Takosan 249b; tororo 134–135; xxwp 44cl; Yagi–Studio 91.

Houshi: 75tr.

Japan National Tourism Organization: 179, 183tr.

Kakusho: 88–89.

Kobe Tourism Bureau: 214–215.

Patrick O'Brien: 231.

Shutterstock.com: Peter Adams Images 126; akarapong 36t; Florian Augustin 178; BlackRabbit3 240–241; Jujumin Chu 143; cowardlion 233tl; f11photo 42; Kinstory 187b; Thitinun Lerdkijsakul 95tr; MarkauMark 72; martinho Smart 220; Arthur Matsuo 217; Musashi2001 176–177; N_FUJITA 165t; Neography 95l; okimo 189; Rei Imagine 69tl; Shirakami 242–243; SIHASAKPRACHUM 43; TOMO 75tl; wdeon 121.

teamLab: teamLab, Graffiti Nature in a Beating Valley – Symbiotic Lives, A Whole Year per Year, Red List © teamLab 150.

THE TOKYO TOILET: Satoshi Nagare, Courtesy Shibuya City 148l, 148tr, 148br, 165b.

Towada Art Center: Yoko Ono Wish Tree for Towada, Riverbed, Bell of Peace, 2008, photo: Oyamada Kuniya © Yoko Ono All Rights Reserved 209t; inges idee, Ghost, Unknown Mass, 2010, photo: Oyamada Kuniya 210–211.

Toyooka City Office: 69tr.

Toyota Commemorative Museum of Industry and Technology: 158.

Cover images: *Front:* Getty Images / iStock: Sean Pavone; *Back:* Alamy Stock Photo: amana images inc. br; Getty Images / iStock: SeanPavonePhoto t; Shutterstock.com: Peter Adams Images bl.

ABOUT THE AUTHOR

Rebecca Hallett is a UK-based travel writer with a particular focus on Japan. Following a degree in Japanese Studies (with a stint living in Kyoto), Rebecca started her career in guidebook editing at DK and Rough Guides before expanding into writing, speaking and travel consulting – anything that lets her connect with people and share her love for Japan. She's passionate about conveying the complexities of the country beyond the clichés, and loves visiting the country's many underexplored corners, from snowy hot spring towns to local museums. You can find out more about her work, and how she can help you plan your ultimate trip to Japan, on her website *(rebeccahallett.com)*.

Senior Editor Zoë Rutland
Senior Designer Laura O'Brien
Editors Dawn Henderson, Alex Pathe, Lucy Sara-Kelly
Designers Cristina Antequera, Matt Cox
Proofreader Stephanie Smith
Indexer Hilary Bird
Factchecker Todd Fong
Picture Researcher Yoshimi Kanazawa
Senior Cartographic Editor James Macdonald
Publishing Assistant Simona Velikova
Jacket Designer Laura O'Brien
Image Retoucher Michelle Briers
Production Editor David Almond
Senior Production Editor Tony Phipps
Senior Production Controller Samantha Cross
Managing Art Editor Gemma Doyle
Editorial Director Hollie Teague
Art Director Maxine Pedliham
Publishing Director Georgina Dee

First published in Great Britain in 2025
by Dorling Kindersley Limited,
DK, 20 Vauxhall Bridge Road, London SW1V 2SA, UK

The authorized representative in the EEA is
Dorling Kindersley Verlag GmbH. Arnulfstr. 124,
80636 Munich, Germany

Copyright © 2025 Dorling Kindersley Limited
A Penguin Random House Company
25 26 27 28 29 10 9 8 7 6 5 4 3 2 1
001-351132-June/2025

All rights reserved.
No part of this publication may be reproduced, stored in or introduced into a retrieval system, or transmitted, in any form, or by any means (electronic, mechanical, photocopying, recording, or otherwise), without the prior written permission of the copyright owner.

A CIP catalog record for this book is available from the British Library.
A catalog record for this book is available from the Library of Congress.

ISBN: 978 0 2417 6031 4

Printed and bound in Malaysia

www.dk.com

This book was made with Forest Stewardship Council™ certified paper – one small step in DK's commitment to a sustainable future. Learn more at www.dk.com/uk/information/sustainability

> The rate at which the world is changing is constantly keeping the DK travel team on our toes. While we've worked hard to ensure this book is accurate and up-to-date, things can change in an instant. If you notice we've got something wrong, we want to hear about it. Please get in touch at travelguides@dk.com

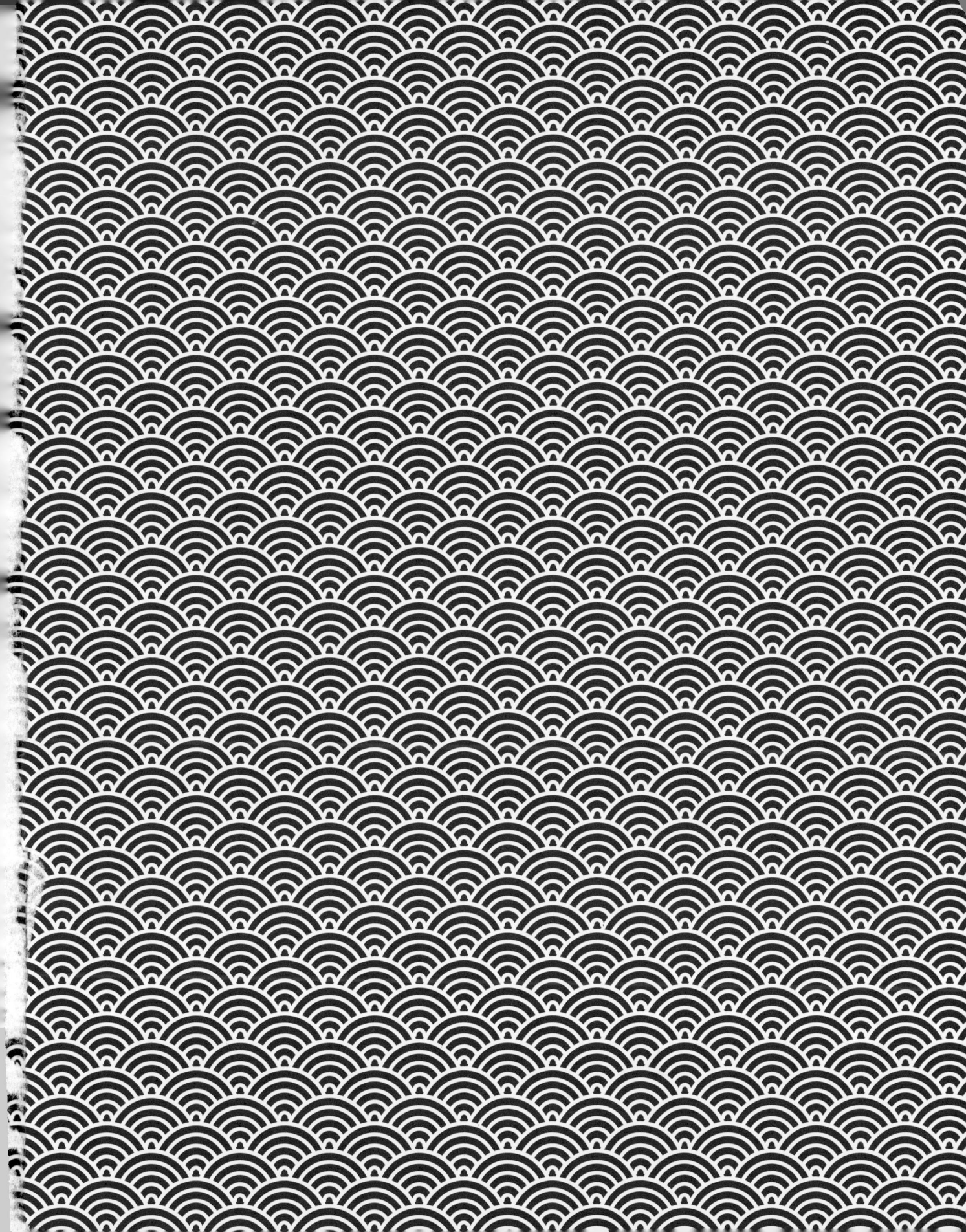